Eating Wild
JAPAN

Eating Wild
JAPAN

Tracking the Culture of Foraged Foods,
with a Guide to Plants and Recipes

Winifred Bird

illustrated by Paul Poynter

Stone Bridge Press · Berkeley, California

Published by
Stone Bridge Press
P. O. Box 8208, Berkeley, CA 94707
TEL 510-524-8732 • sbp@stonebridge.com • www.stonebridge.com

The information in this publication is accurate to the best of our knowledge. Its text is not intended to serve as a foraging guide, and the author and publisher accept no liability for negative outcomes arising from misidentifying, collecting, or consuming plants it describes.

Poem on page 97 from *Shinkokinshu: New Collection of Poems Ancient and Modern* by Laurel Rasplica Rodd, published by Brill. Used by permission.

Poem on page 132 from *A Waka Anthology*, volume 1: *The Gem-Glistening Cup*, by Edwin Cranston, ©1993 by the Board of Trustees of the Leland Stanford Jr. University. All rights reserved. Used by permission of the publisher, Stanford University Press. sup.org.

Illustration on page 144 from a photo hanging in the restaurant Tsubaki Jaya, Noto Peninsula.

Printed in the United States of America.

10 9 8 7 6 5 4 3 2 1   2024 2023 2022 2021

p-ISBN 978-1-61172-061-7
e-ISBN 978-1-61172-943-6

For John, Julian, and Rowan,

the best berry-picking companions I could ever wish for.

Contents

Introduction

君がため
春の野に出でて
若菜つむ
わが衣手に
雪はふりつつ

For you, beloved
I walk the fields in springtime
Picking wild greens
As snowflakes fall and fall on
The sleeves of my kimono

*Emperor Koko (830–87), from the
Hyakunin Isshu*

What little I know of Japan's immense and intricate culture of wild foods I owe to many people—to housewives and farmers, scientists and geographers, bureaucrats, back-to-the-landers, and countless others I met in the eight years I lived in rural Japan and the three I spent researching this book after returning to the United States. To none, however, do I owe a greater debt of gratitude than to my neighbor of three years, Sadako Ban, because it was she who first showed me that these foods are woven into Japanese culture in ways far deeper than the pages of a cookbook or field guide might suggest.

Ban-san befriended me at a funeral. My then-husband and I had just moved into a cavernous farmhouse on the outskirts of Matsumoto, that lovely old city in central Japan with its wedding-cake castle and views of the Japan Alps, and were going about our own back-to-the-land experiment in rice farming, carpentry (him), and writing (me). Ours was a traditional apple-growing neighborhood, and custom had it that whenever anyone within the community of eighty households died, a member of each household was expected to pay their respects. This time the matriarch of the local temple had passed away. Ban-san was her sister-in-law—the daughter of the temple's former priest—and after the service ended she stationed herself at the temple door to bid farewell to departing mourners. My first impression was of a tiny, bird-like, but very self-possessed woman with bobbed white hair and a gentle smile. She was already eighty-five, more than half a century older than me. Perhaps because she was curious about the new foreigner in town, or perhaps because she intuited in me a kindred spirit, she invited me to stop by her house for tea some time.

It was an early winter day when I walked the hundred yards or so up the steep road we both lived on and knocked on her door. She greeted me graciously, tucked me under the blanket of a snug *kotatsu* in the living room, and disappeared into the kitchen to get the tea ready. As I waited, I looked over her bookcases (being the offspring of a bookselling family, this is my habit in new places). There were two: a large one filled with Japanese novels and a small one for Western classics. I deciphered the names of Jean Paul Sartre and Simone de Beauvoir written in katakana on several spines before she returned. How oddly comforting it was, and how rare in that distant corner of the world, to think that she might have read those writers that I, too, admired. She set down the tray. In addition to a steaming pot of strong green tea, there were seven or eight tiny dishes piled with country delicacies: candy-like dried persimmons, paper-wrapped rectangles of pressed sugar studded with wild walnuts, enormous white beans from her garden simmered in sugar and soy sauce, and several other delicious things I have sadly forgotten. This was my introduction to the fabulous hospitality of Sadako Ban.

I returned many more times to drink tea, talk, and gradually learn the story of her life. She had grown up at the temple in the war years, the well-educated daughter of the local priest. She often told the story of how her father quietly resisted the war only to have his temple bell melted down for ammunition. Later she married a local man several years her junior. They had no children. She read and gardened and wrote lyrical essays. For me, she embodied the simple, elegant, swept-clean way of living I loved most about rural Japan. Every time I visited, she disappeared into the kitchen and returned with a tea tray that seemed to come straight from my most romantic dreams of Japan. The contents were always perfectly tuned to the turning seasons. In fall there were juicy Asian pears and salty pickled eggplants, in winter bean-cakes or cookies from her favorite confectioner, and in spring wild vegetables that she foraged at the edge of the forest—once a doll-sized plate of glowing green *nazuna* (shepherd's purse), another time a few tightly curled *kogomi* (ostrich fern) fiddleheads coated with ground sesame seeds, and another, a little pile of prehistoric-looking *tsukushi* (field horsetail) shoots.

I had grown up picking blackberries in San Francisco parks and fantasizing about living more closely to the land, but most of these foods were novel to me. Back home, I'd viewed wild foods as the province of hippies, hunters, and more recently, hipsters. They were part of my culture's periphery, not its core. (I say that as a non-Indigenous American; the reverse is true of many Native American cultures.[1]) In Japan—at least there, on the edge of the snowy mountains—the custom of picking and eating wild foods was alive and well, and it had nothing to do with either hippies or hipsters. Fiddleheads and horsetail shoots were as familiar as asparagus and peas.

When Ban-san discovered I had a taste for sansai, as the Japanese call wild mountain vegetables, she invited me to come picking with her. She owned a patch of steep meadow a five-minute walk from her house, past the temple but just before the spot where the road disappeared into dark forest. Aside from mowing a few times a year to hold back the advance of the trees, she and her husband generally left the land to its own devices. The day she took me there was in early May, and the grass was already knee high. As she led me along the concrete sluice that carried spring water through the middle of the meadow, she plucked little handfuls of this and that, instructing me on what to do with each plant. The curly *warabi* (bracken) fiddleheads would need to be soaked in hot water and ash overnight to take away their bitterness before being simmered with soy sauce and *dashi* broth. The *kogomi* fiddleheads were easier—they could simply be blanched and served with ground sesame seeds, as could the garlicky *gyoja ninniku* (alpine leeks). Tempura would transform the *tara-no-me* (Japanese angelica tree buds) into a delicacy, while the young *azami* (thistle) and *kusa-fuji* (vetch) would make good boiled greens. Who would have guessed that an overgrown meadow held such delicacies?

Soon our basket was full, and we slipped into a little wooden shack in a corner of the meadow to eat cookies and drink steaming hot tea from Ban-san's thermos. We talked for a few minutes, then headed home. That was all: a simple stroll to enjoy the afternoon and gather a few things for dinner. Yet I was captivated by the thought that she kept this little patch of land for the express purpose of escaping the rigorously human world of the farming community we lived in, where every field was utilized with strict efficiency and every wild plant was viewed as a weed. Here, she was the student rather than the master of nature, carefully tracking the seasons so as to catch every one of their fleeting gifts. She was not rich—her husband had been a caretaker at a nearby nursing home and she had carved wooden partridges to sell to tourists—so I am sure sansai brought welcome variety to their table. But I suspect she was more interested in the pleasure of picking and the incidental beauty she found along the way than in anything as practical as nutritional content. "When I have been working hard for a while, my shoulders tighten and my head begins to ache and the sadness in my heart spreads. At those times there is no greater cure than to wander in the hills behind my house," she wrote in a 1989 essay about picking sansai in the same meadow she took me to more than twenty years later.

As I learned more about sansai from Ban-san and my other neighbors, I began to wonder how these foods fit into Japan's rice-centered culture. I had heard much about the profound ways paddy agriculture shaped Japan's spirituality, foodways, social structures, and physical landscapes. As anthropologist Emiko Ohnuki-Tierney writes in her fascinating book *Rice as Self*, rice has been the main ritual food of Shinto and the staple of elite diets since it took hold in Japan over two thousand years ago—though commoners did not eat it frequently until much more recently. Each grain was thought to have a soul, and for many centuries people believed that consuming rice gave them "sacred energy and power." Because taxes were based on the assessed yields of rice in a given territory, the crop came to represent wealth and power for lords and the good life for everyone else. Rice was the most prominent symbol of the seasons and even of nature itself, while the act of growing it came to represent the quintessential Japanese lifestyle. Paddy farming dictated how water was used and what habitats were available for wildlife.

But what about wild foods? Given that they were so ubiquitous, why hadn't I read more about them in books on Japanese
history? I began to wonder how foraging had influenced culture,
cuisine, and relationships with nature. The answers I found—or
more accurately, my search for answers in the many corners of
Japan where old cultures and ways of eating still linger—became
the framework for this book.

Before agriculture, wild food was simply food. This is as true
in Japan as it is anywhere in the world. The Jomon people who
inhabited the Japanese archipelago for nearly ten millennia, from
approximately 10,000 BCE to 300 BCE, hunted, fished, and gathered
all the land had to offer. Their ancestors had migrated from the
Asian mainland to the archipelago during the preceding paleolithic era, when the two regions were intermittently connected
by land bridges. Their diets—and, we can safely assume, their
knowledge of the ecosystems from which those diets derived—
were extraordinarily diverse. Shell mounds and other archaeological evidence suggest they ate over 350 kinds of shellfish, 70 kinds
of fish, 60 different mammals, 35 birds, 30 nuts and seeds, and
several hundred wild plants, according to food historian Hisao
Nagayama. Their meals included eagles, horse chestnuts, sharks,
flying squirrels, lily bulbs, and many other foods that might raise
eyebrows today. Historian Conrad Totman describes this period
as a nearly ideal one for hunters and gatherers. The long Pleisto-
cene ice age had ended, and deciduous forests rich in nuts and
the animals that ate them spread across much of Japan, replacing
the conifers and tundra that had thrived in the previous, colder

climate. Nature was so bountiful in many places that people could survive in fixed settlements even without agriculture.

But as the Jomon period yielded to the Yayoi (approx. 300 BCE–300 CE) and then, by the eighth century, to a series of emperor-centered epochs of history, cultivated foods began to dominate Japanese cuisine. Everywhere that grains could be grown easily, wild foods faded into the role of dietary accent. The transition was less complete beyond the well-watered plains and valleys, however. Forested mountains and hills cover three quarters of Japan, and for many centuries a complete reliance on cultivated foods in these places would have meant poor eating at best and death by starvation at worst. And so, in mountain hamlets, fishing villages, and remote island outposts, people kept up the old traditions of hunting and gathering. The environmental folklorist Kan'ichi Nomoto writes in *Tochi to mochi* (Horse Chestnuts and Rice Cakes) that "the farther one moved from the cities and flat paddy land, and the closer one got to the sea and the mountains—in other words, the deeper one entered into the hinterlands—the more varied became the ways in which people attain food." Although this pattern has weakened over time, it lingers today.

Still, agriculture cast a heavy shadow over the meanings and uses of wild foods. Foraged foods became a symbol of poverty, hunger, and the failure to integrate into the dominant culture. They were the underbelly of the largely unattainable aspiration to eat rice at every meal. Land-poor farmers and those in rugged areas ate *tochi* (horse-chestnut) cakes, *warabi* starch gruel, pine-bark broth, and other wild foods in order to survive the yearly lean period before the new crop was harvested, as well as to get through the longer famines that so often devastated farming communities.

In the Edo period (1603–1868), guides were published detailing the proper use of wild plants to stave off hunger a role they were to play once again following World War Two. The association between wild foods, sorrow, and deprivation therefore remained quite strong even into the early twentieth century. Kinzaburo Henmi, who was born in 1892, wrote in his guide to edible wild plants that in the Nagano farming village where his wife grew up as well as in many other rural areas, eating such foods was considered shameful.

But it is rare today to come across such attitudes. Now that famine has been banished from Japan, wild foods are mostly viewed as a delicacy. In fact, this paradoxical image has existed since ancient times. The foods that nature provides unassisted have always served as both insurance against agricultural failure and as pleasurable, health-giving links to the land, the seasons, and pre-agricultural ways of life. A thousand years ago or more, urban aristocrats made an elegant pastime of collecting spring greens on excursions to the country and feasted on seaweed sent as tribute from coastal villages. Vegetarian Buddhist monks built a whole cuisine around wildcrafted seaweed, and Shinto priests offered up wild foods from both land and sea to their gods. In his 1704 agricultural manual *Saifu* (An Encyclopedia of Vegetables), botanist and philosopher Kaibara Ekiken suggests that sansai are naturally pure, while cultivated vegetables are extremely unclean and must be thoroughly washed before eating.[2]

Far stronger than the association of sansai with purity is that with seasonal ephemerality. Many poems in the eighth-century *Man'yoshu* and other old collections of verse—a handful of which I have borrowed to introduce the chapters of this book— evoke the seasons by referring to wild foods. Indeed, the window of palatability for a given part of a given wild plant is often vanishingly short. Bamboo shoots, for instance, are sweet and tender when they first break through the soil but can become inedibly bitter within hours. Botanical events such as this correspond less to the comically generalized seasons of the modern world (think how much nature changes over the three months of spring, summer, fall, or winter) and more to the exquisitely precise agricultural almanacs of ancient East Asia. Devised in China and adapted by the Japanese, one such almanac called the *Shichijuniko* breaks the year into seventy-two five-day-long seasons with names such as "peach flowers begin to bloom," "bamboo shoots emerge," and "rainbows begin to form after rains."[3] Similarly, each sansai bursts onto the annual culinary calendar with delicious abundance and perfection, only to vanish the next day or week as if it never existed. Nor do these delicate foods tend to hold up well after they are harvested. For this reason, a single *fuki-no-to* (butterbur bud) on an elegant *kaiseki* serving tray sings of early spring like nothing else.

Fortunately, various parts of a given plant can usually be eaten, and many different plants can be collected over time and at different elevations and locations. With *fuki*, for instance, the new buds appear only briefly on the cusp of spring, but the stalks linger through summer. In addition, when the buds have disappeared from the edges of farm fields, one can usually find them in dappled woods, and when those, too, are gone, one can climb higher into the hills for *kogomi* and *tara-no-me*. In this way, eating wild food leads naturally to a varied diet and to a deep knowledge of the landscape. This diet in turn provides a self-serving incentive to preserve a variety of wild habitats, each of which offers its own tiny increment of food security and culinary pleasure; only together do these habitats offer a comprehensive way of eating throughout the year. Perhaps this is the most fundamental difference in the way that foraging and agriculture shape attitudes toward nature.

This book is made up of three parts: a collection of essays on the culinary, cultural, and historical roles of several specific wild foods, with a recipe at the end of each; an illustrated Guide to Plants comprising important and common Japanese wild foods; and a small collection of recipes introducing classic Japanese preparation methods. I have written the book as a journalist and home cook with a long interest in the topic. My professional background in environmental reporting has influenced this project only indirectly. Climate change, habitat loss, nuclear disaster, overuse of wild resources, violence against Indigenous cultures, and changing agricultural practices are among the many factors currently devastating wild-plant populations or undermining the viability of foraging worldwide. Demographic trends, too, play a part. I wrote above that sansai are commonplace in Japanese culture, but much of the knowledge about how to pick and prepare them resides with elderly country people who lack successors to their traditions due to urbanization and changing rural lifestyles. The small mountain villages where these customs are most strongly rooted are disappearing wholesale,[4] and while wild foods remain popular, their consumption is increasingly severed from any deep connection or commitment to the land. All of these trends pose existential threats to Japan's foraging culture.

But while I care deeply about these crises and have spent much time writing about them, I have chosen not to focus on them here. I wanted to think instead about some of the reasons we might care about these problems in the first place—about the powerful strands of history, cuisine, and culture that tie us to wild places, whether a vast tract of natural forest or a patch of weeds by the garden. Most fundamentally, by eating sansai—by taking them into our bodies—these places become a part of us. It is my perhaps naïve hope that preserving and reviving ways of eating not entirely reliant on agriculture will foster more passionate defenses of these wild places. Just maybe, those of us who receive the gifts of the plant world can learn to fulfill the responsibilities those gifts entail, as Native American foragers have traditionally strived to do.[5]

I readily admit that I am neither a scholar nor a botanist nor a lifelong forager of the plants discussed in this book, and I caution readers not to base their own culinary experiments solely on the information in these pages. Some wild plants, including several that appear superficially similar to those I write about, are extremely poisonous. Specifically, *seri* (Japanese parsley) is a look-alike of *dokuseri* (northern water hemlock), one of the most toxic plants in both Japan and North America, and *nirinso* (flaccid anemone) resembles several deadly species of *torikabuto* (wolfsbane). Although these plants can be safely distinguished with experience, caution is advised. More broadly, individual bodies react differently to individual wild foods. Even plants like *warabi* and *kogomi* that are widely eaten in Japan can cause adverse reactions in some people and should be approached cautiously when trying them for the first time. Proper preparation is also very important; for instance, *warabi* and horse chestnuts must be leached to remove toxic substances. I highly recommend Samuel Thayer's series of books on foraging, not only for their detailed information on specific plants but also for his wise words about the long, slow process of truly familiarizing oneself with a new species. As Thayer points out, there is a crucial difference between "identifying" a plant using botanical descriptions and immediately, almost intuitively "recognizing" a plant one knows very well. The latter should always be the standard for collection and consumption.

In particular, the Guide to Plants that forms the second section of this book is not intended to function as a field guide; for that, devoted readers will have to turn to the many excellent Japanese sources available in both human and book form. Instead, I hope it will serve as a reference to help travelers to and foreign residents of Japan understand the wild foods they are most likely to encounter in restaurants, markets, and the homes of friends, and perhaps also as a starting point for learning how to pick and prepare them on their own. Experienced foragers in the West can use the Guide to learn what the Japanese do with wild plants whose local cousins they may be familiar with. Similarly, I hope the recipes will be useful both for residents of Japan who want to try their hand at sansai cuisine but can't read Japanese-language cookbooks and for those living in other countries who want to cook local wild foods in the Japanese style.

Finally, a few words about terminology. There is no common Japanese phrase that corresponds exactly to the English terms "wild," "foraged," or "wildcrafted" food. All of these English terms are very broad: a "wildcrafted meal" could include dandelions growing through cracks in a city sidewalk, ramps gathered in a forest, and *nori* collected from rocks along the seashore. Japanese terms tend to be more specific. The most commonly used term is *sansai*, which is made up of the characters for mountain (山) and vegetable (菜). The word literally means "vegetables that grow naturally in the mountains," but many books on sansai include a much wider range of edible wild plants, including nuts and fruits, mushrooms, vegetables that grow along the seashore, farm-field weeds, and freshwater plants (though not generally seaweed). According to the foraging field guide author Yukio Yamada, sansai is a relatively new word; in the past, people used broader terms such as "mountain cuisine" and "seaside cuisine" that encompassed both plants and animals. Additional Japanese terms for edible wild plants include *yakuso* (medicinal plants) and *yaso* ("meadow grasses," a general term for edible and non-edible plants growing in the mountains or fields). To further confuse matters, the line between cultivated and wild foods continuously shifts back and forth over time. *Myoga* escapes from gardens, and neglected groves of *mosodake* bamboo invade neighboring forests, while *warabi*, *sansho* (Japanese pepper), *mitsuba* (wild chervil), *udo* (Japanese spikenard), and many other traditional "sansai" are today widely cultivated on farms. In this book, I have alternated between using "sansai" and various English terms depending on the context.

As for naming specific plants, I have used Japanese common names in the main text followed in parentheses by the English common name at first mention, because this is how everyone aside from scientists refers to them. However, common names vary widely across time and space, a problem magnified by the fact that inconsistency exists in both Japanese and English. A single plant can have a dozen local names and nicknames, while the same name may refer to two or more entirely different plants. Scientific (Latin) names are a far clearer method of identifying and differentiating between plants. I have provided a list of common and scientific names of all edible plants mentioned in the book, should readers wish to confirm their identity (see Names of Edible Plants, page 267). For several non-edible species, the scientific name is given in the main text.

The names of people are written in the Western style, with given name preceding family name, except for some historical figures whose names are presented in Japanese style. For the sake of simplicity macrons have been omitted from Japanese names and terms, with apologies for the loss of accuracy in pronunciation. Romanized Japanese spellings are used except where alternative spellings have become common in English, such as "tempura." An "e" at the end of Japanese words is pronounced like a long "a"; for example, *take* (bamboo) is pronounced "ta-kay." Unless otherwise noted, all translations in the book are my own.

Essays on
Eating Wild

Map of Japan

with places visited
by the author

HOKKAIDO

SAPPORO

Nibutani

Mt. Moriyoshi —

— *Nishiwagamachi*

C. W. Nicol Afan
Woodland Trust

SENDAI

Tsubaki Jaya
Restaurant

NIIGATA

Matsumoto

HONSHU

Imadera
Uoka Restaurant

TOKYO

HIROSHIMA   OSAKA   KYOTO   NAGOYA

Kutsuki

MATSUYAMA

KUMAMOTO

Kitadomari

SHIKOKU

Aso Caldera

KYUSHU

OKINAWA

ONE

Common Weeds and Woodland Wonders

The First Greens of Spring

おらが世や
そこらの草も
餅になる

In this world of mine
Even humble roadside weeds
Make a pretty cake

Kobayashi Issa (b. 1763)

To borrow Shakespeare's famous metaphor, there are people for whom the natural world is a kind of enormous stage, whose trees and weeds, rabbits and rivers are the mere props against which a truer, deeper human drama plays out. But there is another kind, too, for whom the natural world itself is the most fascinating drama of all, an endlessly complex story whose every piece can be turned over and over, revealing ever more pieces and meanings.

Reiko Hanaoka belongs to this latter group. She is a tiny ball of energy, less than five feet tall and sturdy across the shoulders, exploding with stories, plant names, recipes, and other useful bits of information. She is a lover of mountains, an experimental and insatiably curious eater of wild foods, and, it seemed to me when I met her, a direct descendant of the brave souls who first dared discern edible from inedible in ancient times. She stands in my mind as a representative of those countless men and women in all corners of Japan who quietly, lovingly carry on the tradition of foraging, each amassing a mental library of flavors, seasons, and habitats that is irreplaceable by any book or website.

I had the good luck to join in one of Reiko's springtime feasts through the introduction of a mutual friend whom I happened to be visiting in April of 2016. At the time, both women lived in the bowl of an ancient volcano that rises from the approximate center of Kyushu, the large island off the southwestern tip of Honshu, Japan's main island. This volcano, called Aso, erupted and collapsed repeatedly beginning three hundred millennia ago, creating a high plateau encircled by jagged walls, today covered in grass. From above, the bowl—or caldera—looks like the rugged footprint of a massive meteor encircled by smooth, graceful slopes, which in turn are surrounded by lower, crinkled mountains that spread toward the sea. The air in the caldera is cooler and fresher than in the sticky valleys below, and the land is fertile, watered by abundant hot and cold springs. Humans have lived in Aso for over a thousand years, growing rice and grazing cows in the shadow of several smaller, active volcanos that rise from the center of the massive older one.

When I met Reiko and her husband they had inhabited the caldera for twenty years, ever since Reiko was thirty-eight and left a conventional life of jobs at supermarkets and offices in the prefectural capital of Kumamoto for life in the countryside. They were living in an old, rented farmhouse with a tiled roof and a dilapidated barn just inside the northern curve of the caldera. In the fields nearby they grew black, red, and white rice, sharing the harvest with friends and entertaining themselves by wandering up the precipitous caldera walls in search of unusual plants. Both were officially certified guides to the local ecology and geology. Every five or six years they moved to a different house, not by design but simply because that seemed to be the lifespan of the ancient places they preferred to rent: a tree grew too tall and shaded out a window, a leaky toilet became intolerable, a landlord decided to reclaim his fields. In general, the couple was on good terms with their elderly neighbors, who regarded them with amused interest. Sometimes they would deliver a can of soda as the couple harvested or planted a patch of rice by hand, like the old folks used to do half a century earlier. But Reiko and her husband did not belong to that essential rural institution, the *tonari-gumi* or neighborhood association, through which the community kept its waterways clean and its hillsides trimmed and, most importantly, its general harmony intact. They were floaters, benign outsiders, renters not tethered to their land in the way their neighbors were. Their first loyalty was not to the cultivated fields but rather to the wild, abundant nature from which those fields were carved long ago.

When I told my friend Mariko that I wanted to meet someone who knew the local sansai, she immediately thought of Reiko and arranged a lunch invitation. It was a brisk April morning when we headed for her house, the kind of temperamental spring day when gentle sun can change to the chilly verge of rain in an instant as clouds scuttle across the sky. We arrived a few minutes early, and not wanting to impose on our hostess, wandered through her quiet country neighborhood intoxicated by the spring day. The terraced paddies were still bare and brown, but the banks alongside them were lush with grass, the forests further up the caldera walls glowed with new leaves, and every garden seemed to burst with bright pink peach blossoms, yellow daffodils, white berry blossoms, and tiny purple violets.

When the precise agreed-upon time had arrived, we turned up the gravel driveway that ran along the south side of Reiko's barn before narrowing into a dirt path dividing her house from a yet-unplanted vegetable field. There she stood, waiting for us by the barn in a gray Peanuts sweatshirt and khakis, her feet planted firmly beneath her and her elven face beaming out from a frame of feathered hair. We had barely shaken hands (a thoughtful concession to my Americanness) when she turned excitedly down the narrow gap between the house and the barn to a shady cistern. At its base, a cluster of creeping rockfoil leaves sprouted between two stones. The plant's Japanese name, *yukinoshita*, means "under-the-snow" for its pretty white flowers, but its Latin name, *Saxifraga stolonifera*, seemed more fitting; *saxum* means "rock" and *frangere* means "to break." And here indeed it had made a place for itself by breaking through the toughest of conditions.

Reiko picked a handful of the plant's round, softly lobed leaves, each one covered in short hairs and striated with a lovely deep magenta and pine green. "These," she announced, "are for tempura." So that was what we would be eating. I of course had enjoyed that classic Japanese fried food countless times before in homes and restaurants. Most often, the pale, crisp batter encased a piping hot slice of some dull cultivated vegetable like sweet potato or onion. Occasionally, though, I had been served tempura made from one of the more popular sansai—especially if it happened to be spring and I found myself at a country inn that prided itself on local, seasonal cuisine. My favorite of these sansai tempura ingredients was the meaty, pungent leaf buds of *tara-no-ki* (Japanese angelica tree). Sprouting like tiny, velvety-green alien hands from last year's thorny stalks, the buds are addictive but something of a rare treat, since each stalk produces only a few harvestable buds per year.

But as Mariko and I followed Reiko into the unruly fields surrounding her house, it became clear she had something entirely different in mind. From the garden's edge, she plucked yellow *tanpopo* (dandelion) and magenta *renge* (Chinese milkvetch) flowers, spiky stems of *sugina* (field horsetail), and oval *obako* (Asiatic plantain) leaves. From a pile of discarded rice hulls—strategically mounded to ease the harvest of certain deep-rooted plants—she pulled *hakobe* (chickweed) and petite but pungent *nobiru* (Japanese wild onion). From paddy banks she picked soft purple-green *kakidoshi* (ground ivy) and silver-green *yomogi* (Japanese mugwort), its familiar spicy scent filling the air as she rubbed a piece between her fingers. From the damp corners of the paddy itself, she took *kureson* (watercress) and *seri* (Japanese parsley). Today, we would feast on weeds.

Having collected a large pile of leaves and flowers, Reiko led us inside to finish preparing the other dishes for lunch. We stepped over piles of muddy rubber boots and rain jackets in the entryway, through several nearly unfurnished tatami rooms, and into the dim, cluttered kitchen. Like the ninth-century Emperor Koko whose poem I quoted in the Introduction, our hostess had spared no effort in scouring the fields and woods for us before we arrived. One after the next she pulled small ceramic bowls from the refrigerator and put the finishing touches on sautés and stews waiting in pans on the range. There were eggs scrambled with *kureson* and *tsukushi* (the spore-bearing shoots of field horsetail); blanched young *kanzo* (daylily) leaves, sweet and clean-tasting; *seri* that she had blanched, chopped, and mixed with mayonnaise and ground sesame seeds; freshly boiled *takenoko* (bamboo shoots), thinly sliced and served with wasabi and soy sauce; blanched *nobiru*, the long green tail of each onion twisted around the bulb at its base to form a neat packet for dipping into a bowl of bitter *fuki* (butterbur) miso; steaming bowls of soup made from the same *fuki* miso, with bits of the yellow flowers floating in the broth; and an olive-green "medicinal curry" made from eleven wild herbs that Reiko had picked in the fields the previous day, puréed in the blender, sautéed, and mixed with ordinary curry paste before simmering with potatoes and carrots (it tasted like standard Japanese curry with a couple of shots of wheat grass mixed in).

Alongside her fascination with wild cuisine, Reiko is deeply interested in medicinal plants. The two categories frequently overlap. As she filled yet more serving dishes, she told us that in ancient times the Japanese ate wild herbs to cleanse their bodies at the edge of spring. Among the oldest references to this custom is an eighth-century poem by Yamabe no Akahito that tells of his plans to pick wild greens from the meadows although it has been snowing for two days. Around the same time, members of the Imperial Court adopted a folk custom from southern China of eating a soup containing seven wild herbs on the seventh day of the New Year to dispel evil spirits and bring good health in the coming year. By the Heian period (794–1185), palace cooks were offering up this soup of seven greens to the emperor in an annual ceremony, which also served as an internal cleansing after rich New Year's feasts (the custom spread to commoners only much later, in the Edo period).[6]

No one knows exactly which plants went into the ceremonial soup or how they were prepared in those ancient times, but because the New Year fell in February by the old lunar calendar, and the climate of the region around the Heian capital (present-day Kyoto in south-central Honshu) is relatively mild, it was presumably possible to find enough wild greens even at that time of year to add a bit of color and the promise of spring to the emperor's bowl. Later, in the mid-fourteenth century, the court noble, poet, and scholar Yotsutsuji Yoshinari wrote a poem specifying the seven plants to be used in the dish, which had come to be called *nanakusagayu* (*nana* meaning seven, *kusa* meaning herbs, grass, or weeds, and *kayu* meaning rice porridge—because by this point, the soup had morphed into gruel). According to Yoshinari, these were *seri, nazuna, gogyo, hakobera, hotokenoza, suzuna,* and *suzushiro.* The first five correspond in English to Japanese parsley, shepherd's purse, cudweed, chickweed, and Japanese nipplewort, all of which commonly grow around rice paddies. There is some debate as to what the last two terms referred to in the fourteenth century (perhaps wild chives and a type of aster), but they are now typically interpreted as turnip and daikon radish. Today, sad-looking packages of these seven herbs appear on urban supermarket shelves around the New Year, to be taken home by assiduous holiday-observing housewives and cooked into bowls of rice porridge that I suspect lack all but the most symbolic echo of their original cleansing and revitalizing properties. Nevertheless, Reiko told us that she saw in this ancient custom the roots of modern medicinal cuisine.

The centerpiece of today's lunch, however, was a large amount of decidedly un-medicinal tempura, a delicacy dating to the sixteenth century, when the Portuguese first arrived in Japan with their custom of deep-frying fish. After Reiko had plied us with several small glasses of wild "cider"—potent homemade ferments of *tanpopo* (vinegary and smoky), *akamatsu* (red pine) needles (what I imagine Pine-Sol floor cleaner would taste like), and *dokudami* (fishwort—pale golden, very slightly fizzy, and deliciously herby)—we migrated outside to a patch of weedy dirt under the eaves of the barn. Reiko had set up a folding camp table for eating and another, smaller one for cooking the tempura. On this second table, she set a kerosene burner and, on top of that, a wok partially filled with olive oil. As we ferried dishes out from the kitchen, Reiko's husband wandered over from behind the house where he had been plowing an uneven rice field (a rare instance in which he used a machine). Of the two, she is the driving force in mountaineering and wild-food consumption; he, a freelance accountant in addition to a farmer, comes along largely at her urging. "Last year I mostly ate plantain leaves," he joked as he settled into one of the folding chairs.

In truth, Reiko does not prepare wild foods every day, nor is she fanatically committed to eradicating cultivated foods from her diet. Like me, she is simply curious about what the plants of the fields and forest taste like and cannot resist sampling anything she has heard or read is edible. And so her husband has become the willing guinea pig for all the odd recipes in her library of edible-plant books—the medicinal curries and tonics, fritters, sautés, and salts that leap far beyond the standard sansai fare served up in most homes and restaurants today.

As we began sipping our bitter butterbur soup and nibbling on daylily leaves, Reiko prepared the tempura. One by one she dredged leaves and flowers in batter, dragged them on the side of the bowl to remove the excess, and fried them until crispy in the hot oil. When leaf supplies ran low, she hopped across the driveway to pluck a few more dandelion flowers or a cluster of juicy chickweed growing vigorously from a pile of rice husks. The whole procedure had none of the fussiness one might associate with this classic Japanese dish, yet it resulted in a far more interesting assortment of flavors and textures. She delivered the fried leaves and flowers to our plates straight from the hot oil, sprinkled with a pale green salt that set the back of my throat on fire (she had made it by boiling down chickweed juice and salt). I found the dandelion flowers addictive and vaguely reminiscent of artichoke hearts, and the ground ivy pleasantly minty. The watercress had a sharp kick and the mugwort an intriguing, cinnamony flavor, but some of the others were either so mild or so thin as to be hardly noticeable in their crisp shells of batter. The plantain could have been a piece of paper for all I knew, and the saxifrage leaves, while pretty, were equally bland. All, however, were at the very least tolerable. Tempura, it turns out, is a magical cooking method: It renders nearly any weed edible, and in most cases delicious.

After lunch, Reiko led us up the caldera wall, passing first through the terraced rice fields that climb its lower flanks. Even-

Cooking tempura.

tually cultivated land ceded to forest, and she began to point out a constant procession of plants, each of which she classified either as edible or not. The forest was alive with interest to her, luring her frequently off the main path to scramble under branches and through thickets of bamboo in search of a plant she expected to have sprouted by now. Finally, we climbed a near-vertical mud and rock slope above the village cistern, grabbing onto scrubby bushes to keep from sliding back down. Reiko wanted to take us to the absolute peak of the caldera wall, where golden grass bent silver in the wind. The path was blocked by a boulder, however, forcing us to stop several dozen meters from the top. And there we stood, looking out across the wide bowl of the volcano sparkling under the late-afternoon sun.

The second time I ate a proper meal of wild tempura was a few weeks later, in a beautiful patch of forest high in the mountains of northern Nagano Prefecture called the C. W. Nicol Afan

Woodland Trust. As its name suggests, this remote little forest has an unusual provenance. Over the course of three decades it was lovingly restored by the Welsh-born Japanese citizen Clive William Nicol. Nicol, who put down roots in Japan after stints in the Arctic Circle and Ethiopia, was a national celebrity in Japan until his death in 2020 (three years after my visit), famous both for the numerous volumes of fiction and nonfiction he has penned on topics ranging from whaling to karate and for his outspoken environmentalism and swashbuckling, story-telling, whisky-swigging personality. He poured much of the monetary residue of this fame into eighty-four acres of degraded land that he bought beginning in 1986 and transformed, with the help of his foresters, into a healthy, diverse woodland ecosystem (the trust also manages an additional sixty-seven acres of national forest).

Nicol and I happen to have shared an editor at the *Japan Times* newspaper for a number of years, and it was on the recommendation of this editor—who insisted I absolutely must visit his good friend Old Nic if I intended to learn anything at all about sansai—that I came to Afan Woodland. It was not Nicol who led me out into the forest that late April morning, however, but Kazuhiro Koriki, a fifty-eight-year-old nature guide at the trust. Nicol introduced us, and before disappearing into the depths of the majestically high-ceilinged wooden building that serves as base for the trust's administrative and educational activities, assured me that Koriki knew as much about the foods of the forest as anyone in those mountains.

I believe he was right, but it wasn't Koriki's work at Afan or the various certifications in nature education listed on his resume that convinced me. It was something Koriki mentioned offhand as we walked the dappled paths between oak, birch, elm, and alder trees. He told me that he ran a guesthouse nearby with his wife and brother and that they served sansai tempura to their guests continuously from early spring through October. Going out to the woods to collect these foods was the way he expressed his regard for his guests, he said. What he did not say—and did not need to say—was that this represented a nearly unheard-of feat of hospitality. To throw a few wild vegetables onto a lacquered dinner tray as a symbol of spring is practically a cliché of the Japanese country inn; to serve them without fail from spring through fall is evidence of immense foraging skill. To do so, the chef-gatherer must know how to follow varieties both common and obscure across the seasons and also where to find them and how they might be affected by variations in temperature or rainfall.

Koriki did know these things, and in learning them he had come to know many other interesting things about the forest, which he dropped into our conversation like fragments of some long-lost Paul Bunyan tale. There was the time he was gathering bracken ferns and a rabbit jumped out of the bushes. This was no ordinary bunny, but rather a kind of super rabbit that flew a full twenty-three feet through the air. After it landed, Koriki took the opportunity to look at its hind legs; they were, as one might expect, as muscle-bound as a barbell lifter's. Then there was the time he was driving with his wife in the mountains and spotted a patch of *yama-udo* (Japanese spikenard). He told her to stop and got out to pick some, only to realize that a snake, black and thick as a half-gallon jar of sake, had beaten him to it. The section he could see was sixteen feet long, but with head included it could easily have been twenty-five, he said (perhaps borrowing a bit of his employer's story-telling flair). These encounters were not limited to sansai harvesting, of course. Once he was driving down a narrow country road and a golden eagle happened to swoop down in front of the car. Unable to escape either to the left or the right due to the dense woods on either side, the bird was forced to soar along directly in front of the car as Koriki gripped the wheel in stunned awe. Nevertheless, picking sansai brought him out to the less-frequented woods with a regularity that greatly tipped his luck in favor of wildlife sightings.

I followed Koriki further into the forest. The Afan Woodland is akin to what the Japanese call *satoyama*: neither wilderness nor tree farm, but instead a natural forest shaped by human use. The land was originally covered in mixed deciduous forest, but by the time Nicol established the Trust, those trees had long since been cleared and replaced with a conifer plantation, which in turn was eventually abandoned. Nicol restored it to a mixture of mostly deciduous trees. His forester regularly cleared brush and dead wood and selectively harvested trunks for use as firewood, charcoal, and mushroom logs, creating a much brighter and more open woodland than would exist were it left untouched. Especially in spring, before leaves bud out in the canopy, the forest floor flourishes with sun-loving spring flowers and herbs, including many edible ones.

Similar *satoyama* woodlands once encircled most Japanese villages. Villagers relied on them for leaves and young branches to fertilize and mulch their fields as well as for firewood, wild foods, craft materials, and other essential elements of daily life. The constant and intense use of these areas in effect held back their natural succession toward denser, darker climax forest; in many places where evergreen broadleaf forests would eventually have grown, open deciduous woodlands instead remained, "frozen" by human intervention as relics of Japan's cooler climate during the last Ice

Age.[7] Beyond this ring of woodlands lay wilder forests where hunters stalked bears and boars leery of stepping into the garden-like
satoyama. In a sense, *satoyama* landscapes were similar to the vast
tracts of land in North America that Native people once managed
through controlled burning and other methods to increase populations of edible plants and animals. For the most part, these distinctive half-wild, half-managed ecosystems declined in Japan in
the decades of modernization after World War II.

During the period around the 2010 United Nations conference on biodiversity in Nagoya, Japan's Ministry of the Environment aggressively promoted the concept of *satoyama* as a global
model for sustainable forest management. It was a rather ironic
strategy, given the government's past role in the demise of *satoyama*
via the subsidized clearing of village woodlands and planting of
timber plantations. I wrote a number of lengthy articles on the
subject, and in doing the interviews for these articles I found
that many older country people talked about *satoyama* woodlands
with a particular nostalgia and pining emphasis on their loss that
I never fully understood. Walking through the forest with Koriki
that April day, I finally did. The Afan Woodland was bright and
open, even the slightest bit empty-feeling. Its floor was a carpet
of fallen leaves and flowering edible things growing between large
white and gray-brown trunks. Here and there, a stream brightened
by wasabi leaves or marsh marigolds trickled along. This pleasant
woodland room was easy to walk in and see through to a distance.
It was the kind of place one wanted to stay in, to lie down among
the flowers and nibble on wild leaves. Yes—to lose this would feel
like a tragedy, especially if one lost it to the dark, morose stands of
overcrowded timber trees that now cover so much of rural Japan.

As for edible plants, they were abundant to the point of

extravagance. *Fuki* (butterbur) were everywhere, hundreds or maybe thousands of them, their soft, round leaves carpeting huge sections of the forest floor. Most were just past the tasty stage, their flowers already open and beginning to shoot up on leafy stems. Koriki bent over to show me the powdery pollen on the flower buds, noting that it was crucial in terms of flavor to catch them before this stage. Provided the timing was right, however, one could pick as many as desired without concern for decimating the future supply; the flowers are connected by a network of strong roots ready to send up more no matter how many are taken. By contrast, the sprawling patch of *kogomi* fiddleheads that we found beside a stream, tender and vibrating with new life, are more vulnerable to overharvest. In each clump where the brilliant green curlicues pushed up from the ground, Koriki instructed me to leave three shoots—and hope no one followed behind to harvest these. This would allow the patch to produce even more the following year. As we wandered along, we also picked tender, garlicky *gyoja ninniku* (alpine leeks) and a few sprigs of *yomogi* (mugwort) and handfuls of young *kanzo* (daylily) leaves.

Even more than Reiko, Koriki was interested in the health-giving qualities of sansai. As we walked through the woods, he noted that the impulse to eat these often bitter or pungent plants is not limited to humans. Bears, for instance, spend the long winter hibernating with their waste built up inside them, and when they come out in spring, they purposely seek out poisonous plants such as skunk cabbage to purify and cleanse their system. In the same way, he said, humans instinctively eat bitter wild plants in spring to detoxify their bodies after a long winter. Botanist Thomas J. Elpel writes, along the same lines, that in the West "dandelion leaves (*Taraxacum*) are known as a 'spring tonic,' used to cleanse the liver after a long winter of eating hard-to-digest foods." When I lived in Japan, I often noticed this marked preference among country people for bitter spring plants. I used to love the mild, spinach-like leaves of *nazuna* that covered the farm fields around my house in early spring, but most of my neighbors showed little interest in these. Instead they sought out *fuki* buds, which to me were almost inedibly bitter, or the marginally more palatable *yama-udo*. (This fondness for bitter foods is not limited to sansai; my Japanese ex-husband used to chastise me for refusing to eat the pungent innards of whole grilled fish, noting that I hadn't yet developed an appreciation for what in Japan are called "adult flavors.")

Of course, Koriki said, these potent, cleansing herbs are best eaten in small quantities and thought of as medicines rather than foods to fill the stomach in times of poverty or famine. Other, milder sansai are better suited to that latter purpose. In addition, to reap the full health-giving benefits of medicinal sansai, they should be eaten locally and seasonally. That belief, he told me, reflects the Buddhist concept of *shindo-fuji* (身土不二), whose characters mean "body and earth, one and the same." The phrase was taken up by early-twentieth-century pioneers of the macrobiotic diet to express their belief that the greatest health comes from eating local foods harvested seasonally.

After our walk through the woods, we returned to the commercial kitchen of the education building and dumped our haul of *kogomi*, *gyoja ninniku*, *yomogi*, and *kanzo* onto the stainless-steel counter. Like Reiko, Koriki had arranged to make tempura for me, but his approach could not have been more different from hers. After all, he was a professional chef, or at least an assistant to his brother in the kitchen of their guesthouse. His litany of rules for the dish began with strict instructions regarding the batter: The water should be icy cold, mixed lightly with either Hanakoromo-brand tempura flour (a mixture of cake flour and baking powder) or, if that was unavailable, a half-and-half mixture of rice flour and cake flour. Contrary to the advice of many cookbooks, eggs must never be added. If the wild vegetables are picked carefully, there is no need to wash them, but if one does wash them, they need not be dried thoroughly. The frying oil should be hot enough that a drop of batter floats slowly to the top. If it stays on the bottom of the pan, it is too cool. If it breaks apart, it is too hot. Begin with the *gyoja ninniku* to scent the oil (or save them for last if you don't love their garlicky fragrance). Make sure to cut a slit in each leaf to prevent explosions, and batter lightly; wild tempura is more attractive if the green shows through. Drain the oil from each leaf as you lift it from the frying pot. Fry all leaves first, leeks or otherwise, because the oil will be slightly cooler and less liable to burn them, then move on to meatier items like fiddleheads. For improved substance and texture, dip fiddleheads and day-lily leaves in the batter in clumps of two or three. Most importantly, serve hot. Ideally, the host should cook while the guests eat.

We did not obey this last rule, but our tower of leaves and buds was still warm by the time Koriki carried it out to a table beside the education office and invited his colleagues to join the meal. As he promised, it was excellent: crisp, not very oily (at least for a massive heap of deep-fried food), and fabulously fragrant—especially the *gyoja ninniku*, which I had not had a chance to try in very un-alpine Kyushu. I was not sure whether I preferred Koriki's technically superb product or Reiko's free-spirited, experimental one, but I left the Afan Woodland knowing one thing: I did not ever want to return to the dull world of string bean and sweet potato tempura.

As delicious as weed tempura may be, there are times when one craves something closer to the old *nanakusagayu* porridge—something as clean and bracing as spring itself. At times like this there is no better food than Myong Hee Kim's *fuki* rice packets. Myong Hee lives with her husband Robert Kowalczyk in the mountains above the city of Takahama, about two hours north of Kyoto. She is an artist and he is a photographer. Together with their daughter Kya, they run the Peace Mask Project, which brings together groups of people to create pure white moldings of one another's faces from handmade paper. The hauntingly serene masks are then assembled into large murals intended to communicate a message of diversity, peace, and cooperation. In one iteration of the project, they made masks with four generations of hibakusha, the survivors of the Hiroshima and Nagasaki nuclear bombings.

It is somewhat ironic, then, that they have settled in Takahama, home to part of Japan's largest cluster of nuclear reactors. For years they had lived in an old, atmospheric house in Kyoto, from which Bob commuted to a job at a university in Osaka and Myong Hee to a studio in a hamlet close to their current home. In 2011, after the Fukushima nuclear disaster, a friend offered them a plot of his land in Takahama to build a house on. At first they resisted. To relocate near Japan's largest nuclear installation in the wake of the catastrophic triple meltdown seemed insane, especially given the family's long and deep involvement with hibakusha. But somehow, with the passage of time, the idea began to seem reasonable. Nowhere in Japan—or perhaps the world—was entirely safe, and embarking on a new path in their private life felt right.

Myong Hee had always loved the country. Like me, she grew

up in the city dreaming of leaving it (San Francisco in my case; Pusan in hers). When we met, she told me that her childhood best friend had lived in the country, and she had gone to visit this friend at every chance. She loved the plants and the quiet temples of Korea's rural villages even though her family was Christian. Later, as an adult, she traveled to the Findhorn community in Scotland to become certified in permaculture, and read books like Helen and Scott Nearing's *The Good Life* and E. F. Schumacher's *Small Is Beautiful.* "I am drawn to the simple, small things," she told me.

Eventually, she and Bob decided to accept their friend's offer. They built a modest two-story house with a large wood deck facing a cascade of fields and village roofs and mountains. In the old farm fields, they set railroad ties and flat stones, planted cherry trees, a juneberry bush (whose sweet red berries the monkeys devour), a Japanese maple, narcissus, *fuki*, and peonies. Just looking out the window, Myong Hee said, made her happy. There were ten houses in the hamlet and theirs was the highest; the only thing past it on the narrow forest-edged road was a water tank. It had been recently installed, bringing with it the municipal snow-shoveling service—a godsend, Myong Hee admitted, because the village was entirely buried in winter. In the opposite direction from the water tank, just where this small road met a slightly larger one, a set of stone steps led beneath two Shinto *torii* gates to a tiny, unpainted wooden shrine with a large round bell hanging from its pitched roof. The district was called Imadera—the Temple of Now.

I visited Myong Hee and Bob at their home on a mid-April afternoon. Although I had known their daughter Kya for several years through our mutual involvement in journalism, I had never met her mother. Her elegance awed me. She was tall and slender, with skin like waxed paper stretched over a delicate frame of bones. Thick-framed black glasses and graying hair cut in a bob and bangs set off her features, which she further highlighted with magenta

Shrine in Imadera.

lipstick and black eyeliner. To cook lunch, she donned a sheer black apron quite a bit sexier than any piece of lingerie I own. This she tied over a blue button-down shirt with white polka-dots and blue pantaloons made of heavy, soft fabric. She spoke openly, as if accustomed to telling about her life and thoughts. She and Bob, Kya had told me, were involved with a million things and con- stantly meeting with people both known and unknown; still, Myong Hee insisted they were loners, not group-joiners, and liked their quiet mountain retreat.

After Bob and I sat for a while on the sunny deck talking about the depressing state of American politics, Myong Hee—who prefers not to talk about politics and despite having founded the Peace Mask Project said she does not consider herself an activist— announced that she was going to start making lunch. She planned to prepare her famous *fuki* packets, an invention based loosely on Korean cuisine that uses the plant's leaves instead of its buds.. She began by picking a pile from her garden (although *fuki* is among Japan's most ubiquitous wild foods, it is also frequently grown in gardens and farm fields). They looked like small, slightly furry lily pads that I half expected were sheltering frogs and salamanders;

in northern Japan, they grow so large that folk songs tell of people using them as umbrellas.

I followed her into the kitchen, where a pot of water was already heating on the stove. She washed the leaves and plunged them into the boiling water. The instant they lost their dullness and turned dark green and limp, she drained the pot and cooled the leaves in running water. She then carefully plucked them out one by one, laid them flat in a stack on her hand, and firmly squeezed out the excess water. Next she prepared the filling, scooping out freshly cooked white rice from a large cooker on the floor and folding in a drizzle of sesame oil, a large pinch of sea salt, and a sprinkling of ground sesame seeds. When everything was ready, we sat at the dining table scooping a spoonful of rice onto each blanched leaf and gently folding up the edges. "Like wrapping a baby in a blanket," she said, leaving the small white face poking out from the top. We nestled the packets on an old blue-and-white serving platter with a scalloped brown edge, which she decorated with a sprig of wild blackberry blossoms. In Korea, she told me, the leaves are picked and blanched in the same way, but instead of being stuffed with rice they are used to wrap grilled meat with miso. She also likes them stuffed with tuna salad. This can be done at any time of year, although the flavor becomes harsher as summer progresses. In Japan, it is not the leaves but the flower stalks and flower buds that are typically eaten, the stalks often simmered with soy sauce and sugar to a glistening candy-like state and the buds minced, sautéed, and mixed with miso.

Myong Hee urged me to try a packet. When I did, it filled my mouth not so much with flavor as fragrance—a green, slightly medicinal aroma that hovered at the back of my throat. The flavor, which came after, was bitter, but not so bitter as to be difficult or unpleasant to eat. To go with the *fuki* packets, she prepared a salad

Myong Hee Kim's butterbur packets

Fuki leaves are ideal for this recipe, thanks to their distinctive flavor and shape. Other greens can be substituted, however, as long as they are large enough to wrap around a spoonful of rice. Try garlic mustard leaves before the stalks have emerged—they are smaller than *fuki* but similarly potent tasting. Serves 4.

INGREDIENTS

1 cup white short-grain rice
1¼ cups water
About 20 small *fuki* leaves, stems removed
¼ tsp salt
1½ TBS coarsely ground roasted sesame seeds
1 tsp sesame oil

sprinkled with sour *gishigishi* (dock) leaves and wild chives also plucked from the garden. She mixed yogurt, garlic, salt, pepper, oil, vinegar, and honey to make a gently sweet dressing that was also tasty spooned into the rice bundles. Despite all her years in Japan, she had never come to like the cloying, sweet-salty seasoning of much homestyle Japanese cooking; instead she preferred these light, bitter, and sour flavors. She said she found them cleansing and energy-giving.

Bob joined us for our simple lunch, which seemed to perfectly encapsulate the fresh spring day outside. For dessert Myong Hee sautéed bananas in butter and dark brown sugar and served them with strawberries, ice cream, and tea. Afterward, she gave me a little bell to warn off bears and pointed me in the direction of the local temple. The morning rain had lifted and the sun had

1. Wash and drain the rice and place in a medium pot with the water. Bring to a simmer and reduce heat to low. Cover and cook for 10 to 15 minutes, until the water is absorbed. Remove from heat and let steam with the lid on for another 5 to 10 minutes.

2. Meanwhile, bring a large pot of water to a boil. Add the *fuki* leaves and cook only until they become limp and dark green. Drain and cool under running water. Remove the leaves one by one, lay flat in a stack on your palm, and gently squeeze to remove excess water.

3. Sprinkle the salt, sesame seeds, and sesame oil over the rice and gently fold in, taking care not to smash the rice. Adjust seasoning to taste.

4. Place a leaf on your palm with the stem side pointing down; put a heaping tablespoon of seasoned rice in the middle of the leaf, leaving a narrow margin around the edge. Fold up the bottom of the leaf (where the stem was attached) and then the sides, leaving the top open to reveal the rice. Repeat with remaining leaves and rice.

broken through the clouds, warming the road that wound in and out around the waist of the mountain, the woods on either side dotted here and there with tiny orchids and pale-purple wild irises. The temple, twenty minutes or so down the road, was surprisingly crowded with photo-snapping tourists. I wandered for a few minutes around the big old wooden building, its time-worn walls and roof busily ornate with carvings. A magnolia tree in the courtyard had just passed its peak, and its meaty brown-edged petals were beginning to tumble onto the smiling statue of a horse below. On the way back, I noticed that someone had emptied a few boxes of daikon radish, taro root, and half-collapsed sprouting onions into a dark corner of the forest. It was a sure sign of spring. Last year's wilted vegetables had no more use beyond nurturing the earth they came from: new green life had already taken their place.

TWO

Tree of Life

The Rise and Fall of the Japanese Horse Chestnut

栃を伐る馬鹿、植える馬鹿

It's a fool who cuts down a
horse-chestnut tree, and a fool who
plants one.

Saying in Misakubo, Shizuoka Prefecture[8]

It seems a sad tendency of the American mindset to blithely over-look the role of certain ordinary objects in shaping our collective path. We fill our history books with benevolent kings and heroic generals, forgetting that the plough and the mosquito explain much more. So it was for me and horse chestnuts. In all the years I lived in Japan, I never recall paying any attention to *tochi-no-ki* (Japanese horse chestnut trees, *Aesculus turbinata*) or their pun-gent yellow nuts (*tochi-no-mi*), although their role in the country's history is monumental. As a child, I remember gathering similar nuts with my mother at a park near our house in San Francisco, having mistaken them for the sweet, mild nuts of the chestnut tree. How disappointed we were, after carefully poking each one with a knife and roasting them in the oven, to find them so revolt-ingly bitter we couldn't swallow a single bite. They must have been either buckeyes or European horse chestnuts, both of which are close relatives of Japanese horse chestnuts. All three belong to an entirely different botanical order from true chestnuts, and without proper processing are toxic enough to cause vomiting, diarrhea, twitching, paralysis, and very occasionally, death. Fortunately, their awful taste usually prevents anyone from getting that far.

In Japan, too, I am sure I must have eaten *tochi-no-mi* more than once (properly processed ones, of course). My former hus-band and I spent many an afternoon driving through the moun-tains in search of large old trees we'd heard or read about. This odd hobby took us to exactly the sorts of remote villages where people still made *tochi mochi*, an ancient variation on pounded rice cakes that incorporates the nuts after they have been thoroughly leached to remove toxins. We even lived for several years near the city of Owase, one of the places known for its *tochi mochi*. But I never gave the speckled tan mounds any thought. After all, shops were full of *yomogi* (mugwort) mochi, strawberry-and-cream mochi, matcha mochi, classic bean-paste mochi, and countless other spinoffs. *Tochi mochi* hardly stood out.

As I began the research for this book, however, I realized that the horse chestnut is among the *ur*-foods of Japan. Not only were the calorie-rich nuts a key source of energy during the height of the Jomon period—that long expanse of time, far longer than the agricultural age, when hunters and gatherers inhabited the archipelago—but even after those inhabitants learned to farm, *tochi-no-mi* remained an essential safety net against famine. For thousands, perhaps even millions of people, they were the sole barrier between life and death. In some regions this continued into the 1960s. The great twentieth-century folklorist Tsune-ichi Miyamoto, who walked the length and breadth of Japan recording the stories of its rural people, talked about being served freshly pounded *tochi mochi* in the mountain villages of Gifu Prefecture (it is traditionally pounded in a large wooden mortar called an *usu* using a mallet called a *kine*). In one of these villages, he was told that it was thanks to the horse chestnut

Usu *and* kine.

that the local people had never experienced starvation. Whenever a woman married, the villagers said, she was given a horse chestnut tree by her family—or more accurately, she was given the right to collect the nuts from a tree in her village. Each fall she would walk to the tree, gather the nuts, and bring them back to her new home, storing them in the attic to be preserved by the smoke drifting up from the hearth. Sometimes even now, when an old farmhouse is torn down, the attic will spill forth a cache of dusty horse chestnuts. In lean years, the woman and her husband and children would supplement their staple diet of grains with the nuts. When Miyamoto asked how common this practice was, he was told that people across quite a wide area shared the tradition, and that "this was a great source of strength in surviving the harsh mountain life." Interestingly, *tochi mochi* was also a celebratory food eaten at festivals. Although by the time he recounted this tale in 1980 it had become a novelty produced mostly for tourists, he noted that "the horse chestnut was once an important food that allowed us to survive."[9]

Miyamoto was not the only scholar to describe the horse chestnut in such dramatic terms. Ryozo Wada, the author of a book on the tree published in 2007, wrote: "To study the culture surrounding the consumption of horse chestnuts is to investigate the foundational culture of Japan, the culture of its mountain villages, and the ways that relationships between the natural environment and human activities have developed through history." When I later spoke by telephone to his coauthor, the forestry scientist Shingo Taniguchi, he described the horse chestnut as a kind of miracle tree. The larger specimens will reach thirty meters tall and over two meters in diameter, with branching trunks and huge, three-to-nine-fingered leaves. In a bountiful year these trees will bear two or three thousand nuts, which can easily be stored for a decade and provide more calories by weight than white rice (369 to rice's 352 per 100 grams). The riparian trees hold riverbanks in place with their sprawling roots, send up fragrant towers of creamy white flowers that feed bees and other pollinators, house bears and birds in their cavernous hollows, and provide medicine from their bark, dye from their nuts, and all manner of furniture, tools, utensils, and musical instruments when and if they are ever cut down (the wood is especially well suited to forming the backs of violins).

But Taniguchi's interest in the tree was by no means purely practical. "Your call reminded me that I haven't eaten *tochi mochi* yet this year," he noted longingly; he was currently living on the southern island of Okinawa, one of the few areas of Japan where the trees do not grow. When I asked if he wanted to say anything else before finishing the interview, he thought for a moment, then replied, "The bitterness of *tochi* lingers in your memory. Our ancestors survived by eating the nuts of these trees, and so we are here today. I believe a fondness for their flavor is in our genes, imprinted from the Jomon period when eating them was a means of survival."

By this time, I was very curious to try the nuts myself, as well as to learn what magic cooking techniques were used to transform them from nuggets of potent poison into a life-giving substitute for rice. Through acquaintances I learned of a town called Kutsuki in Shiga Prefecture, about an hour and a half north of Kyoto, where *tochi mochi* was still produced and a movement was underway to protect some of the local trees. It happened that the main group behind this movement, called the Association to Protect Large Trees and Water Sources, was holding a lecture during the time I planned to be in the general area and that several geographers studying the trees would be attending. They invited me to join them, and I jumped at the chance. I also arranged to visit several villages the following day so that I might see some of the trees and observe how *tochi mochi* was made.

This was how I ended up in a rental car with the geographers Yuichiro Fujioka and Koki Teshirogi on a beautiful Sunday morning in late March, heading north from the wide basin of urban Kyoto toward the mountains. Fujioka was a lecturer at Kyushu University and Teshirogi at Setsunan University; both were youngish, neatly dressed, and extremely polite, handing over their business cards the moment we met and eagerly offering to help me with my luggage. As Fujioka threaded through a snarled Kyoto traffic jam, we talked about their joint research in Kutsuki; their latest project involved mapping groves of large *tochi-no-ki* and trying to figure out why they had remained standing in those particular places.[10] They were equally interested in other edible wild plants. Fujioka in particular had an omnivorous interest in foraging culture and questioned me avidly about my recent research into *warabi* (bracken) roots and *oubayuri* (Japanese cardiocrinum) bulbs. For my part, I was eager to confirm some of the peculiar stories I had been reading about horse chestnuts.

"Do people in Kutsuki pray to horse chestnut trees?" I asked.

"Yes, there is a large old tree that people pray to because they believe it is inhabited by the god of the mountains," Fujioka replied. "Of course, when you think about how magnificent they are, it's not so strange that they would be associated with deities."

"And what about *narikizeme*, is that practiced too?" I asked.

A week or two earlier I had come across an odd passage in Kan'ichi Nomoto's book *Horse Chestnuts and Rice Cakes*—so odd, in fact, that I doubted my reading of the Japanese. In it, Nomoto recounted a story told to him by a man from Shizuoka born in 1922.

Each year on the morning of the fifteenth of January (Little New Year, when farmers traditionally pray for a bountiful harvest), the man, then a child, would walk two kilometers with his mother and father to a large horse chestnut tree. His father would strike the tree with a cleaver while reciting the lines, "Will you bear, or will you not? If you don't, I'll cut you down!" In response, his mother, playing the role of the persecuted tree, would chant, "I'll bear, I'll bear!" while rubbing its wounded trunk with rice-and-adzuki-bean porridge. This "curse-like rite," Nomoto wrote, was a type of *narikizeme*. The term is made up of the characters for *naru*, meaning to bear fruit or nuts, *ki*, meaning tree, and *semeru*, meaning to urge, press, or torment someone into doing something.

Fujioka said he had not heard of Kutsuki's residents doing anything similar.

"But this prayer, have I misread it? Do people really try to threaten trees into giving a bountiful harvest?" I asked.

"Oh yes," said Teshirogi. "*Narikizeme* is quite common. It's usually done to persimmons or Japanese plum trees, and at the end of the prayer, people sometimes cut off branches or scar the trunk."

Now I was even more surprised. Some prayer, I thought, as the geographer cheerfully shredded my romantic notions of nature-worshiping mountain people. But his next words reversed my line of thinking once again.

"Actually, there's a scientific basis for it. Applying stress can induce a plant to bear more," he said. Modern orchardists sometimes "girdle" a tree by cutting off a shallow ring of bark around the trunk or branches. This temporarily damages the tree's circulatory system so that carbohydrates produced by the leaves become concentrated in the branches rather than flowing to the roots. The result is fruits that become larger or more abundant. Ancient Japanese were apparently not the only ones to intuit this effect long before science proved it; over a century ago, Scottish anthropologist James George Frazer described ceremonies nearly identical to *narikizeme* in Malaysia, Croatia, and Bulgaria.

By this time, we were well into the mountains, speeding through a narrow river valley as we approached Kutsuki. We had taken a road called the Saba Kaido, or "mackerel highway," so named because it was historically used to transport fish south from the Japan Sea coast to the Kyoto metropolis. Before long the valley widened, and we emerged into central Kutsuki. The town is part of Takashima, a much larger municipality on the northwestern coast of Lake Biwa, Japan's great freshwater lake. Kutsuki is made up mostly of densely forested mountains dotted with hamlets. The "downtown" where the lecture was to be held consisted of a few residential neighborhoods on either side of the Adogawa river and a handful of shops. No trace remained of the deep winter snow that had melted just a week earlier. Plum trees were blooming, streams were sparkling aqua with snow melt, and roadsides were lush with new sprouts of *yomogi* (mugwort), *fuki* (butterbur), *kanzo* (daylily), and *hakobe* (chickweed).

We had some time before the afternoon lecture, so we met up for lunch with Yoshihiko Iida, another geographer involved in researching the *tochi* trees. Together we walked to the event venue, an old department store turned community center. "How about some *tochi mochi*?" Fujioka asked as he led us to a table in the cozy post-and-beam café occupying the building's first floor. I excitedly agreed, and he ordered four bowls of *tochi zenzai* from the ancient, amiable waitress leaning on the kitchen counter.

It arrived in a lacquer bowl, a golden-brown, golf-ball-sized lump dissolving softly into a bath of warm, sweet adzuki-bean soup. I took a bite. The texture was dense and sticky, like regular mochi, but slightly nubbier. The flavor was oddly familiar. What could it be? I took another nibble. It tasted like . . . a pancake made with too much baking soda? I mentioned this to my companions. They told me I was probably tasting the ash used to leach toxins from *tochi-no-mi* and render them edible; baking soda and ash are both alkalis and share a similar unpleasant taste. I took a third bite. Below the baking-soda flavor was a distinct, unfamiliar pungency. This, I realized, must be the flavor of the *tochi*. It balanced the cloying sweetness of the adzuki beans perfectly.

That evening, at an elegantly rustic restaurant tucked into a wooded hillside, I ate *tochi mochi* again. This time, the sticky golden cakes were deep fried and immersed in a bowl of savory broth spiked with grated daikon radish and sliced scallions. They were crisply oily on the outside and meltingly soft inside, their slight astringency countering the heaviness of the fried mochi just as it had the sweetness of the adzuki beans. I thought about the weed tempura that Reiko Hanaoka had served me in Kyushu and of how much better it was than tempura made from cultivated vegetables. Once again, these bitter, intense wild foods were drawing me in. Later, Misato Shimizu—a member of the Association to Protect Large Trees and Water Sources with whom I would spend the following day—told me she had heard the allure of *tochi mochi* compared to that of tobacco. No one would call it delicious in the conventional sense of the word, but there was something irresistibly attractive about it. *Tochi-no-mi*, she said, are nostalgic rather than tasty. They represent the flavor of the mountains, of a past so old it might well be woven into Japanese genes, as the forestry scientist Shingo Taniguchi had also suggested.

Although the first written record of *tochi* nuts being eaten in
Kutsuki dates to 1733, people in the region have likely been eating them in some form or other for much longer. Not far away,
at the southern tip of Lake Biwa in what is now the city of Otsu,
archaeologists have discovered several submerged shell middens
from the Jomon period that reveal much about ancient diets. One
of these ancient underwater trash heaps, called Shell Midden No.
3, dates to the Middle Jomon period, from approximately 2,500 to
1,500 BCE. Midden No. 3 is made up of alternating layers of shells
(mostly freshwater clams) and nutshells (acorns, water chestnuts, and *tochi-no-mi*), along with a generous sprinkling of catfish,
soft-shell turtle, boar, and deer remains. The neat layers formed
because people gathered shellfish in spring and summer and nuts
in the fall. Initially, the midden was located on the shore of the
lake, where the nutshells would have decomposed, but later the
water rose, fortuitously submerging and preserving them. Altogether the pile represents over twenty million calories worth of
food. Horse chestnuts make up nearly a third of the nutshells, from
which fact archaeologists surmise that they accounted for a stun-
ning thirty-nine percent of the overall diet. Clearly, these ancient
people did not eat *tochi* merely in times of famine but rather as a
staple—perhaps even as their most important single food. Clearly,
too, they had mastered the process of removing toxins from the
nuts.

But why go to the trouble of leaching out toxins (and risking
sickness if you failed) when milder and easier-to-prepare foods
like chestnuts and acorns also grew in the area? When I posed
that question to Taniguchi, he gave me two answers. First, horse

chestnuts are the largest nut native to Japan, which meant a high caloric return on time spent gathering. Second, the production of wild nut trees varies by year, so that a sparse acorn year might be a bountiful one for horse chestnuts, and vice versa. A diverse diet was therefore a safer one, even if it required bothersome labor.

Similar evidence of horse-chestnut consumption by the Jomon people has been discovered throughout Japan. Wada lists 164 archaeological sites spread across nearly every prefecture (including two others in Otsu) at which such evidence has been found. A few date back as far as ten thousand years, but starting around four thousand years ago, the sites become much more common. The Japanese horse chestnut itself is thought to have evolved during the early Miocene Epoch some twenty-three million years ago; fossilized remnants of the species from around this period are abundant in Japan. At that time the Japanese archipelago was much colder than it is now; today, too, the trees thrive best in places with cold, snowy winters, such as the side of Honshu facing the Sea of Japan and more mountainous areas elsewhere. Taniguchi told me he suspects they achieved their current broad distribution in warmer areas in part thanks to human activity. Although there are no records of them being planted, people likely spread the seeds by using them, or by selectively cutting other trees while leaving horse chestnuts untouched because of their dietary value.

Toward the end of the Jomon period, a series of changes occurred that dramatically transformed the way people ate. The islands cooled, and the conifers that had dominated ice-age landscapes resurged in some areas. This brought a decline in edible plants and animals and a consequent dip in human population. When settlers from the Korean Peninsula crossed to the southern island of Kyushu with revolutionary technology for growing rice, historian Conrad Totman suggests that the hunters and gatherers they encountered may well have been primed by climate-induced hardship to adopt a new lifestyle. And indeed, starting around 400 BCE, rice farms spread steadily northward throughout the wetlands and river valleys of the archipelago. By the time Japan's first centralized government was established a millennium or so later, rice had ascended to the starring role it would occupy from then on in the nation's mythical histories, religious ceremonies, and elite food culture.

Yet for those who lived in mountain hamlets and cold, northern realms less suited to cultivation, agriculture did not replace hunting and gathering practices so much as ease alongside them, forming a way of life dependent on both wild and domesticated foods. *Tochi-no-mi* remained particularly important in many places. Villages developed rules governing when and how the nuts in commonly held forests could be harvested and strictly punished those who cut down the trees without permission. Within living memory, preparing and eating horse chestnuts was a matter of course in places like Kutsuki. The elderly residents whom Fujioka and his colleagues interviewed for their research confirmed that until the 1950s these skills were as common as those for growing rice or radishes. It was only with the rapid modernization following World War II that *tochi* at last became unnecessary. Loggers lumped them together with other *zoki*, or "miscellaneous trees," and cut them down by the grove to make way for stick-straight timber species like Japanese cedar and cypress. In the 1960s alone, government-funded projects converted more than 850,000 acres of such natural forest to plantations every year nationwide.

Taniguchi was born in 1965 in Hyogo Prefecture, west of Shiga, smack in the middle of this era of mass "afforestation."

During our phone conversation he recalled witnessing a number of large old horse chestnut trees being cut down near his home and thinking, as a child, that it was a strange and wrong thing to do. "These were trees that had lived two or three hundred years, many times a human life," he told me. Yet the moment their utility in supporting human life disappeared, the motivation for protecting them did as well. Evidence of what was lost lingers in the many place names that incorporate the word *tochi* despite lacking any actual horse chestnut trees. Unfortunately, no data exist on how many of the trees were cut down after the war, because bureaucrats did not pause to distinguish them from all the other trees in the mixed forests.

Things were no different in Kutsuki. By the 1960s people had stopped eating *tochi mochi*, and forest conversion projects were proceeding with cruel efficiency. In the 1980s, a group of residents successfully revived production of the mochi as a tourist product, but even this was not enough to safeguard the stately old trees indefinitely. Soon, mochi makers began buying their nuts from other towns because they were too old and weak to haul them from the mountain groves themselves anymore. In this way the food was severed from local ecology.

"Around 2008, people in the backwoods hamlets started seeing helicopters carrying away the trees one by one," Misato Shimizu, the young Association to Protect Large Trees and Water Sources member, told me. At the time, she was living near the shore of Lake Biwa, but she has since moved to one of those backwoods hamlets herself. "They'd say, oh, that's probably the horse chestnut from so-and-so's land." It turned out that a timber dealer had gotten wind of the valuable trees that still remained along property lines and river bottoms and had started making visits to the homes of their elderly owners (in Kutsuki, most forested land is privately held, which distinguishes it from other communities). The dealer offered around ¥50,000 ($450 at the time) per tree, Shimizu said, which was far below market value: a single slab measuring around two meters long by one across can sell today for six times that or more. The wood is typically used to make dramatic tabletops whose unfinished edges evoke a sense of "nature" for their wealthy buyers, or for flooring.

Still, the dealer's offer sounded good to many of the old folks, because the trees had become worthless to them in a practical sense. They didn't need the nuts to survive. *Tochi* were no longer a miraculous source of life but just another tree; their many valuable services to other forest creatures and to the preservation of clean mountain streams were less obvious and therefore less valued. And so they signed the contracts. Other villagers, however, objected furiously. They understood the value of the trees, both as living links to past ways of life and as protectors of Kutsuki's waterways. Someone reported the sales to the prefecture's Environmental Protection Division, and staff began poking around. As the gears of government slowly started to turn, concerned residents of Takashima and neighboring areas formed the Association to Protect Large Trees and Water Sources. The group petitioned the governor, renowned scientist and environmentalist Yukiko Kada, to take action.

By then, sixty large horse chestnut trees had already been cut; the largest was so stout it would have taken five people to wrap their arms around its base. There was still time, however, to save another fifty-three trees for which contracts had been signed and money handed over but the fatal chainsaw blow not yet delivered. A lawsuit was launched to render the contracts invalid on grounds of deceptive buying practices; eventually, a settlement was reached. The not-for-profit Japan Bear & Forest Society stepped in to repay the lumber dealer the equivalent of nearly $90,000 in exchange for ownership rights to forty-eight of the standing trees, while the original tree owners kept the money the dealers had paid them as well as the rights to the land beneath the trees (the remaining five trees were bought back directly by their owners).

This arrangement, which resembled a tree-specific version of a land trust, was favorable for two reasons. First, the conservation organization could protect important trees without the burden of managing large tracts of land mostly covered in plantation forest. Second, the owners would part only with the right to cut or resell certain trees in the future, not with land that had been in their families for generations. In order to prevent the same situation from arising again, the prefecture signed agreements with the owners of 140 more trees in Takashima, as well as some in Nagahama, which hugs the northeastern edge of Lake Biwa adjacent to Takashima. By law, the government could not actually buy the trees, so it arranged instead for payments equal to about $500 per tree as a sign of "appreciation" for each owner's promise not to cut or sell in perpetuity.

By the time the geographers and I attended the afternoon lecture at the old department store in Kutsuki, the Association was focused mostly on cataloging the remaining *tochi* trees and planting more, as well as educating the public through festivals and events. The lecture consisted of a brief update on these activities, followed by a slideshow by an organic farmer in one of the downstream communities[11] that depends on the clean, abundant water flowing from Kutsuki's forest streams. Governor Kada (whose second term had ended in 2014) was among the crowd, and at the end she stood up to say a few words about the value of reviving traditional forestry and farming techniques. Her cheerful, can-do message was appealing, but as she spoke, I wondered silently whether practices swept aside by broader social and economic developments could be revived on a scale large enough to matter. Still, Iida and Shimizu both told me her support had been essential in rescuing Kutsuki's remaining *tochi* trees.

That night, I stayed at a guesthouse on the Adogawa river run by a Japanese photographer and his wife, a translator originally from the United States. In the morning, I sat by the picture windows and watched kites wrestle for territory against a hillside so sheer it looked like a wall of trees. Around ten o'clock, the Association's president Akemi Komatsu arrived to pick me up. A small woman in her late sixties, she wore blue jeans, a dark-green fleece, and a brown felt cap lined in mustard yellow that made her head look like a fuzzy *tochi* nut. She greeted me brusquely, but when she smiled her face became a beaming heart, her sharp eyes nearly disappearing above her round cheeks. It was another beautifully blue-skied day.

We drove north through the little downtown, then turned onto a side road winding into the mountains. The hamlets nestled against the roadside every few kilometers looked to me as picturesque as a postcard of rural Japan, with clusters of steep-roofed farmhouses looming over little vegetable and rice fields. Here and there, an old woman scraped at the bare spring soil with a hoe. But even from the road I could tell that many of the houses were abandoned, and most of the land between them was taken up by dark, monotonous groves of Japanese cedar. Komatsu, who had been an environmental activist for most of her adult life, scowled out the car window at them.

"These are the trees they should be cutting down!" she muttered scornfully. Instead, the plantations for whose sake mixed forests had been razed now went uncut because timber prices were too low to make proper management profitable. Meanwhile, dealers targeted the few remaining *tochi* trees for tabletops. I asked Komatsu if she could countenance the cutting down of a *tochi* tree under any circumstances. "Definitely not," she replied. "Especially not by these companies that ignore the impact on nature for the sake of profit. People used to use every part of the tree. Now they toss what they don't want in the valleys and carry away the trunks! That, I cannot forgive."

After driving for about twenty minutes, she pulled off the road and parked in the sun-drenched courtyard of a post-and-beam farmhouse. Shimizu—a friendly woman around my age with blunt bangs and a hippyish outfit of skirt over jeans—came bounding out to greet us, followed by Tsuyuko Yamashita, the more subdued owner of the house. Yamashita placed her hands on her knees and bowed gracefully. Recently retired from an office job in town, she had taken over her late father-in-law's task of making several hundred cakes of *tochi mochi* each week to sell at the local tourist market. Her father-in-law was among those who originally revived their production in the 1980s. She had agreed to take a break from the morning's work to show me the process.

Rendering horse chestnuts edible takes about two weeks,

most of which is spent extracting the tannins and saponins that make them so bitter. Tannins are water-soluble compounds present in many types of edible plants. In small quantities they are innocuous or even desirable; they give wine its dry complexity and over-steeped black tea its tongue-puckering astringency. In larger amounts, they render foods inedible. This is why, for instance, most types of acorns must be leached in water before eating. Saponins are also bitter and toxic in large quantities; native peoples in various countries traditionally used them to poison fish. Unlike tannins, however, saponins are not fully soluble in water and must be removed with wood ash.

In Japanese, the process of removing undesirable substances such as these is called *aku-nuki*. The word *aku* is written using the characters for ash (灰) and liquid (汁). Originally, it referred to lye used for washing and dyeing cloth, made by mixing water and ash, letting the solids settle out, and skimming off the liquid. Eventually, *aku* also came to refer to the substances in plants that cause unpleasant bitterness or acridity and can be removed using a similar mixture of ash and water. Today the term is used very broadly to indicate everything from the saponins in *tochi-no-mi*, to the gray scum that rises to the top of a soup pot during cooking, to an overly strong, pushy personality. *Aku-nuki* means the removal of *aku*—a process to which much of Yamashita's life was now devoted.

She led me to the edge of the courtyard, where a large tub full of nuts was soaking in cool, clear spring water. The water ran from the mouth of a pipe that receded across a field next to her house and disappeared into the forest beyond; it was free and abundant, giving rural *tochi mochi* makers a key advantage over any potential urban competitors. The nearby forest also contained horse chestnut trees, but Yamashita said she no longer collected them there. The work was too heavy, and the season overlapped with the rice harvest. Instead, she bought them from another part of the prefecture.

These particular nuts, gathered and dried two falls earlier, had already been in the constantly running water for about a week. They would stay there another three days, until they were rehydrated and had begun to give up some of their water-soluble toxins. Yamashita scooped out a few cups of nuts in a metal colander and carried them over to a small charcoal hibachi set up in front of a shed, where a pot of water was warming. She tipped them in, touched the water, and decided it was too warm. Water temperature at all stages of processing is essential: too cold and the nuts will remain bitter; too hot and they will dissolve. Shimizu rushed to fetch a saucepan of spring water to cool it slightly.

Next, Yamashita pulled out a nut, set it on top of a rock, and squatted to whack it firmly with a hammer. The warmth of the sun on our backs mingled with the warm smoke of the charcoal. For a moment I felt as if I had slipped back in time, or rather as if time had ceased to move forward but instead formed an endless circle that enclosed us all within it. When a split appeared in the damp brown shell, Yamashita nimbly peeled it off to reveal the vibrant yellow nutmeat within. Her father-in-law had used a different tool, called a *tochi heshi*, to remove the shells. She showed me one. It looked like an oversized wooden clothespin with hatch marks carved on the inner surfaces. It was used by placing it on the ground, sandwiching a nut between the two paddles, stepping on the bottom one, and gently rocking the top one to loosen the shell. Yamashita said she preferred the rock and hammer.

Shimizu handed me a fragment of peeled nut to taste. I placed a tiny sliver in my mouth and immediately felt a powerful but just barely tolerable bitterness spread over my tongue. A moment later, the back of my mouth filled with a more clinging acridity. I thought back to a story Taniguchi had told me. As a young research student, he had wondered if the raw nuts were really as awful as every-

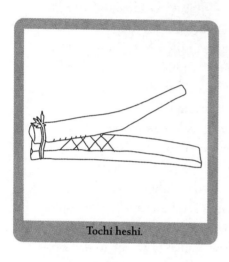

Tochi heshi.

one said; after all, they looked so delicious in their lustrous brown skins. One day when he was out in the forest, he picked one up from the ground, peeled it, and took a bite. He had chewed for no more than a few seconds when its pungent-bitter flavor overwhelmed him and he vomited uncontrollably. He was sick for the next two days. It had been like eating soap, he said. This is how the trees protect their potential offspring from predation.

After Yamashita shelled all the nuts she would soak them again in flowing spring water for three to four days. The runoff, she said, foamed constantly from the saponins beginning to leach out. She would then boil them outside for half a day in a large iron pot, mix them with wood ash, and leave them soaking overnight in this thick sludge. Quite a lot of ash was required, which was a problem now that so few people heated their homes with wood stoves. (Mochi makers, she said, were known to cruise the countryside in search of stovepipes, knocking on the doors of promising houses to plead for ash.) The final step was to rinse the nuts, shave off their thin inner skins, and steam them for several hours. They were then ready to be pounded with steamed sticky rice— at a ratio of about one-part nuts to three-parts rice—and formed into cakes. In the past, land-poor families used a much higher ratio of nuts in order to stretch their scant stocks of rice, making strongly flavored *tochi mochi* a symbol of poverty. Today, the reverse is true: Because preparing the nuts requires so much labor, a high proportion of nuts is considered extravagant rather than stigmatizing.

Yamashita had stored a bag of unsteamed but otherwise fully processed nuts in the freezer of a small free-standing kitchen across from the main house. She pulled one out for me to try. This time it was no longer exactly bitter, but instead almost sour, with a kick that made the tip of my tongue tingle. In fact, it was so pungent I could hardly imagine eating the nuts in their pure form as a staple food, as the Jomon people had done. My modern taste buds much preferred the diluted flavors of the agricultural age, when the nuts were mixed with grains to mellow them. But Komatsu informed me that the spicy tongue tingle was the signature of a well-prepared nut. "You don't want to remove so much of the *aku* there's no flavor left," she said authoritatively.

Afterward, we sat on stools in the sun and talked for a while about wood ash and water temperatures and the economics of making mochi. Yamashita said that she scarcely turned a profit once her time was taken into account. I asked why she continued all the same. "I want to pass on the tradition, because most people my age don't know how to do it anymore," she said. "And I like that moment at the end, when you've gone through this whole long process, and you end up with something delicious. I like that it comes out a little different each time I make it."

Shimizu, Komatsu, and I said goodbye and continued down the road away from town. The hamlets grew sparser and the dark stretches of conifers longer, until only a few abandoned houses

Deep-fried mochi in savory broth

This recipe was inspired by a dish I ate at Hasegawa Restaurant in Kutsuki (described on page 57). Their version uses fresh *tochi mochi*, but since that is nearly impossible to find outside Japan, I have substituted homemade chestnut mochi here. The nubby texture and tan color resemble that of *tochi mochi*, although chestnuts lack the distinctive pungency of horse chestnuts. If you don't have time to cook and peel your own chestnuts, buy peeled, precooked chestnuts, which are sold in plastic packets at many Asian grocery stores (make sure not to use candied chestnuts in syrup). *Mochiko* (glutinous rice flour) is sold at Japanese grocery stores. The unfried chestnut mochi also makes a nice snack on its own. Serves 4.

INGREDIENTS

4 oz cooked, peeled chestnuts
½ cup plus 2 tsp water
¾ cup plus 2 TBS *mochiko* (glutinous rice flour)
Cornstarch for dusting
¼ daikon radish or 8 regular radishes
2 scallions
Vegetable oil for deep frying
2 cups strong *dashi*
1 TBS soy sauce
1 TBS mirin
1 TBS sake

remained along the road. Presently we came to a ramshackle but clearly inhabited farmhouse, with a little garden enclosed in log fencing out front and a rice paddy across the road. This

INSTRUCTIONS

1. Pulverize the chestnuts using a Japanese *suribachi* or mortar and pestle until fairly smooth. You will have about ½ cup of floury chestnut paste.

2. Place the water in a medium bowl and gradually stir in the *mochiko* to form a stiff, uniform dough. Cover and microwave for 3 minutes. Check to make sure the dough has turned translucent; if not, continue microwaving 10 seconds at a time. Let cool for a few minutes, then add the chestnut paste to the bowl and knead until evenly incorporated. Transfer the chestnut mochi to a cutting board dusted with corn starch and pat into a flat circle about ½-inch thick. Use a dough-cutter or knife to cut in four pieces, then cut each piece into three strips.

3. Grate the daikon or radish using a Japanese daikon grater (*oroshi-ki*), which will yield a fluffy mound resembling shaved ice instead of the distinct pieces you'll end up with if you use a cheese grater (a food processor also works). Finely slice the scallions. Begin heating about an inch of vegetable oil over medium heat in a deep saucepan.

4. Combine the *dashi*, soy sauce, mirin, and sake in a small pot and bring to a simmer.

5. When the oil reaches 350° F, fry the mochi, a few pieces at a time, until they are puffed and golden, about 2 minutes. Before you drop each piece into the oil, pull and stretch it slightly to increase the crispy surface area.

6. Divide the hot broth between four serving bowls. Set three strips of hot mochi in each bowl, resting them against the edge so they are only partly submerged. Top with a spoonful or two of grated radish and a sprinkling of chopped scallions. Serve immediately.

was Shimizu's house; she had rented it shortly after becoming involved in the Association to Protect Large Trees and Water Sources because she wanted to be closer to the *tochi* trees. Behind the house was a freshly poured concrete foundation where she planned to build a commercial *tochi mochi* kitchen. It struck me as an exceedingly modern thing to do. In the past, villagers loved and protected the trees because they were an important source of food, but Shimizu had come to love *tochi mochi* through her environmentally motivated desire to protect the trees. What Jomon—or even twentieth-century Showa—person would have had the same romantic impulse? "We can live just fine without *tochi-no-mi* now, but we have the water to process them, and back there are the *tochi* groves, and this is Kutsuki's culture," she told me. "If that connection with nature were to be lost, I would feel somehow lonely."

We stopped briefly at the house to eat *onigiri* (rice balls) made from rice Shimizu had grown in her fields and to feed some banana peels to a three-legged doe she had adopted, then continued on, parking near a stream that meandered through a sparse, sunny patch of cedars just below the road. A large old *tochi* tree grew from a rocky sandbar in the stream. We picked our way out to it through the shallow water. Usually the trees grow near rather than directly in the water, but this particular stream meandered back and forth across its wide, flat bed, so that some years the tree's feet were wetter than others. Several more grew along the sloping banks.

Komatsu and Shimizu had decided to take me here because it was still too snowy higher in the mountains to reach the larger groves. The large tree on the sandbar, they speculated, was perhaps two or three hundred years old. It had a chaotic shape, with twisting, still-bare branches jutting out at all angles from the short, thick main trunk. Its branches looked rough, almost scruffy. I pressed my hands into the spongy fur of moss and ferns covering the trunk. The tree made me think of a threadbare old bachelor, the luster of his skin and the whiteness of his teeth long gone but his stature still as imposing as ever. It looked out of place amidst the army of cedars surrounding it, as much a relic in its environment as *tochi mochi* is a relic in the dietary landscape of rice. Both tree and nut had a certain harshness and irregularity to them, but at the same time a character much richer than their domesticated counterparts. As I leaned against the ancient trunk, I felt certain that this was the secret behind the strange, persistent draw of the Japanese horse chestnut.

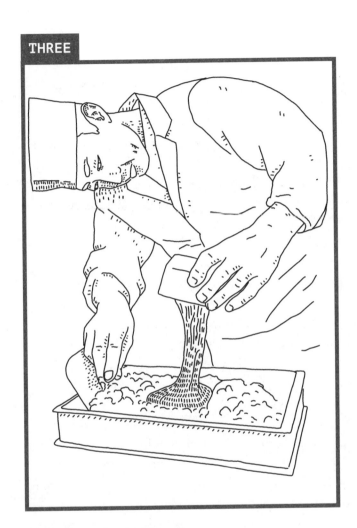

THREE

Feast and Famine

The Split Personality of a Globe-Conquering Fern

石走る
垂水の上の
さわらびの
萌え出ずる春に
なりにけるかも

Beside the falls
Racing rampant over rocks
Fiddleheads shoot up
Spring has come

Prince Shiki (d. 716), from the Man'yoshu

The town of Nishiwaga, deep in the mountains of Iwate Prefecture in northern Honshu, prides itself on bracken. Its residents boast of fiddleheads so sweet and tender they can be eaten like asparagus, its restaurants serve bracken sushi, and its hot-spring inns sell bracken pickles. Its pâtissiers use a starch made from the underground stems, or rhizomes, of the plant to craft pillow-soft sweets once enjoyed by fifteenth-century aristocrats. It wouldn't be much of an exaggeration to say this struggling community has staked its future on the humble fern the Japanese call *warabi*.

From a global perspective, it's an odd choice. *Warabi* is the cockroach of the plant world: ubiquitous, widely reviled (fiddlehead devotees aside), and, at the species level, nearly indestructible. The plants have slender, branched shoots and large, triangular fronds fringed with leathery leaves. By sending out hundreds of millions of spores from each frond and pushing their rhizomes horizontally through the soil, these quiet opportunists have expanded their dominion further than nearly any other plant on Earth. They grow from pole to pole, sea level to mountaintop, shady forest glade to sunny meadow.

Warabi have achieved this extraordinary success through a diverse arsenal of ecological strategies. More than fifty-five million years of evolution have rendered the plant resistant to most diseases and tolerant to all but the harshest extremes of cold, heat, and wind. It can grow in sand or clay and survive soil as acidic as vinegar or as alkaline as baking soda. It dispatches plant competitors by releasing growth-inhibiting chemical compounds into the soil and burying other species beneath a heavy mat of rotting fronds. It keeps most animals away with the terrible flavor of its fronds. As Nishiwaga resident Tadashi Yuzawa aptly wrote, "The ancestors of *warabi* are thought to have been a primary food of herbivorous dinosaurs. The dinosaurs went extinct, but the bracken stubbornly remained, and now grow rank across the surface of the earth."

Success from a plant's perspective, however, looks remarkably like pestilence from a human one. Scientists attending a 1985 conference on bracken held in Leeds, England, noted the plant's reputation as a "sinister" form of "biological pollution," a "slowly spreading green plague," and "one of the world's worst weeds." It invades pastures, kills cattle and sheep, and obliterates archaeological ruins. The fronds contain toxins linked to cancer and beriberi, a disease that causes nerve inflammation and heart failure in farm animals. Many suspect the plant is bad for humans, too. Researchers have suggested widespread consumption of *warabi* may be one reason rates of stomach and intestinal cancers in Japan are so high, and American foraging guides routinely recommend avoiding it. The link remains unclear, however, in part because cooking the fiddleheads in water with ash or other alkalis—as the Japanese typically do—appears to render their carcinogens less potent.

Even in Nishiwaga, *warabi*'s past is complicated. For centuries, the plant was a famine food used to survive the crop failures that haunted the community's remote hamlets. It is a symbol of pain as much as sustenance, destitution as much as rarefied luxury—a comlexity that drew me to Nishiwaga one chilly mid-March morning. I wanted to understand how a single plant could take on such contradictory roles throughout history. And, I'll admit, I wanted to taste those medieval sweets.

The first place I went in Nishiwaga was the home of Kaoru Odashima, an eighty-eight-year-old farmer and forester who helped elevate *warabi* to its current glorified position in the town. Odashima's house perches on the slope of a narrow valley not more than fifteen minutes from Nishiwaga's central train station, but as I walked up to the front door that March morning I felt like I had tumbled out of the ordinary domesticated world and into a deep, rough pocket of the mountains. Perhaps it was the dingy spring snow obliterating the view outside the car windows on the way there, or perhaps the steep, craggy hills on either side of the road, or perhaps simply my own preconceptions about Japan's remote northeast, but I couldn't help wondering as we pulled up in front of that snow-deep house why anyone would choose to live—and moreover, to farm—a patch of land so seemingly resistant to human habitation.

I had arrived in Nishiwaga that morning at the invitation of a pair of affable city hall employees both named Takahashi. The Takahashis and I had never met before; our connection was the tenuous kind journalists so often rely on to get them to out-of-the-way corners of the world—this time the result of a cold-call from me to city hall a few months earlier, after I heard about the town from a sansai aficionado in Tokyo. The telephone operator had delivered me into the hands of the hapless Naoyuki Taka-hashi, who was kind enough to arrange a tour when I explained my interest. And so I had spent the previous night in Kitakami, an industrial city on the Shinkansen line that shoots up the middle of Iwate, and headed westward on a local train that morning.

As the train swayed gently toward the mountains, I sank into the green velveteen seat and watched business hotels give way to concrete-edged rice fields, then ravines frosted with snow. With each tunnel the snow piled up higher alongside the tracks. I had come recently from the southern island of Shikoku and was mildly shocked to find that my view soon consisted of two striated white walls scrolling past like a geological record of winter. Tohoku—the Japanese name for the northern section of Honshu to which Iwate belongs—is known for its heavy snow, and Nishiwaga more than lives up to the reputation. Spread across a long, thin strip of alpine land hemmed in on three sides by the Ou Mountains, the town regularly receives over thirty feet in winter. These are the perfect conditions for a culture of foraging to thrive. Wild vegetables push through the cold ground before most domesticated ones are even sown and are met with all the more joy for the barren winter that has come before. In spring, foragers dot the roadsides and markets overflow with sansai. There is no better place to sample the wild foods of Japan.

Rocking slowly along, I closed my eyes and ran through what else I knew about northern Honshu. I had been to Iwate before, but never this part of it. The prefecture was among the three that suffered most from the earthquake and tsunami of March 11, 2011. When that disaster struck I was living in Nagano and working as a journalist, and I came to know Iwate's coast fairly well in the course of reporting on the aftermath. But I had never ventured inland. My image of Iwate beyond the disaster zone therefore consisted mostly of hazy stereotypes, starting with the often-repeated idea that Tohoku was (and to some extent still is) Japan's internal colony—a remote and impoverished realm mined ruthlessly for its hardy labor and natural resources. For quite a few centuries its native people, the Emishi, resisted incorporation into the Japanese empire and for their trouble earned a reputation as backward, bear-hunting savages. Urban snobbery aside, much of Tohoku really was more suited to hunting and gathering than agriculture.

That is the distant past, however. Today, the miracle of crop breeding has made northern Honshu the rice-basket of Japan, and an overdose of modernity has turned "backward" into a compliment rather than an insult among city dwellers. As the historian Nathan Hopson puts it, the region's image has been "nostalgified." "It's grandma's house when you go over the river and through the woods," he told me over the phone. Much as the heartland is for coastal Americans, Tohoku for the average Tokyoite is a flyover zone: the place that their food comes from and that represents the essence of the nation, but where they would never actually consider living.

Now I was seeing that flyover zone comeinto focus as an intricate and fascinating landscape. As we approached Nishiwaga's central commercial district, the mountains opened out to make room for a dam lake dyed serpent-green by the copper in the surrounding slopes. The train rolled past a smattering of small houses with red and blue roofs pitched steep to shed the snow before pulling into a rustic wooden station (later, I discovered it had hot-spring baths inside, with a traffic light to tell bathers when the next train was coming). I stepped off, scanning the waiting room for the Takahashis. It didn't take long to find the youngish pair in their glasses and parkas, smiling and waving among the sparse crowd. They introduced themselves as Naoyuki and Chikako before ushering me into their waiting van to head for Odashima's house in the hamlet of Motoyashiki.

Fifteen minutes on winding mountain roads and a knock on the door later, the three of us were sitting around a low table in Odashima's cluttered living room, enveloped by the dry, smoky warmth of a wood stove as we ate slices of strawberry-and-cream cake and listened to our host tell stories about the old days. Odashima did not look like he was eighty-eight years old. His legs were crossed in a limber pretzel, his back straight, and his receding hair curled duckling-style above a sprightly, well-tanned face. Every now and then one of the Takahashis interrupted to interpret his heavy local accent for me, but mostly, he just talked.

For centuries, Odashima said, people in his valley grew rice, millet, beans, and buckwheat. But the fields were small and the need for calories great, leaving little room for vegetables. Instead, when the snow began to melt in May, families went to the mountains to pick *warabi* and another type of fern called *zenmai* (Asian royal fern), both of which they preserved in large quantities. *Warabi* was especially suited to the grand old beech forests and long winters of these mountains. Buried beneath the snow for six months or more, its roots absorbed nutrients from deep in the soil, feeding the rhizomes that spread as the world above ground slept. When spring sun poured through the bare branches of the trees and melted the snow, the ferns emerged in astounding numbers.

And so the families of Motoyashiki would set out on late spring mornings to pick the newly emerged fiddleheads. Despite their English nickname, the shoots don't look much like the compact wooden spirals at the end of a violin neck; instead, the slender stalks split into three branches toward the top, each of which ends in a mess of curls covered with tiny red-orange hairs.

Nishiwaga wasn't the only place these fiddleheads were eaten, of course; they are as ubiquitous in Japan's culinary history as they

Digging warabi *rhizomes.*

are in its physical landscape. If we are to believe the evidence offered by the eleventh-century *Tale of Genji*, aristocrats were as fond of them as farmers. In that ancient novel, an ascetic mountain priest picks a yearly basket of the first *warabi* shoots for a prince who is his religious follower. When the prince passes away, the priest sends the same basket to his two beautiful daughters, Nakanokimi and Oigimi, as a token of remembrance. The following year, when Oigimi, too, has passed away, he sends the basket to Nakanokimi together with a touching poem recalling her father. She responds sorrowfully with one of her own, translated here by Arthur Waley: "Since with the dead I cannot share them, in the trough of remembrance shall they be left—these young shoots of the hill!"[12]

For Genji's cloistered beauties, the quintessential symbol of life's yearly renewal became a reminder of death. *Warabi* doubtless held symbolic meaning for the men and women of Motoyashiki, too, but more importantly they were sustenance. As the days warmed, Odashima's family and their neighbors moved further up the slopes to newly melted patches of ground, loading the baskets on their backs with twenty or thirty kilograms of the shoots. The plants grew in sunny openings in the woods, but also in cow pastures and patches of forest cleared in the winter by villagers who

pulled the wood out on sleds to turn into charcoal. They grew with
particular vigor from the blackened ground of meadows burnt early
each spring to renew the grasses used to thatch roofs. Watered
by snowmelt and fed by their long underground hibernation, the
warabi of Nishiwaga were so tender and mild that villagers often
ate them as a blanched vegetable, their bitter toxins mellowed with
a handful of ash thrown into the boiling water, rather than in the
salty-sweet simmered dishes more common elsewhere. Each family also put aside two or three large wooden barrels of the stalks,
layered with up to a third their weight in salt and pressed down
with heavy stones, to eat in place of field vegetables throughout
the year.

This was the practice when Odashima was a child, during
the relatively prosperous postwar years when a number of copper mines operated in town. Earlier, beyond the reach of his own
memory, the ferns were put to other uses. For much of its history,
Nishiwaga was plagued by chronic grain shortages. This was due
partly to the scarcity of arable land, partly to the vulnerability of
old grain varieties to inclement weather, and partly to an exceedingly snowy climate with brief, often cold summers. Rice was
especially vulnerable; a drop of just a few degrees below twenty
centigrade could cut yield from these heat-loving plants by one-
third to one-half.

It is no surprise, then, that in the Edo period Nishiwaga's
inhabitants often filled their stomachs with acorns, horse chestnuts, and starch extracted from those sprawling networks of
warabi rhizomes. They dug the latter in fall, after frost killed back
the tops, then washed the finger-width sections and beat them with
wooden mallets. One method of separating the starch from the
resulting fibrous mass was to mix it with water in barrels, pour the

liquid into boat-shaped troughs carved from hollowed-out logs, called *nebune*, and rock the troughs to slosh off more of the root debris. The remaining starchy sludge was then left to settle into a two-layered cake: white starch called *shiropana* on the bottom and starch mixed with plant debris called *kuropana* or *amo* on the top. The rhizome fibers were spun into a sturdy black twine that was used, among other things, to bind the hedges of Edo Castle.

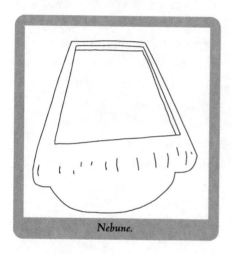

Nebune.

The pure white *shiropana* was a prized export product for the town; during the Edo period, it was sent to Kyoto where it was sold as the finest of mold- and insect-resistant glues to samurai employed in producing paper umbrellas in their slack time. In 1863, 761 gallons of this starch were carried west over the Kaya Pass (if that figure seems low, consider that *warabi* rhizomes yield only five percent their weight in starch). The low-grade top layer was kept at home for lean times, when it could be combined with water and adzuki beans or rice that had failed to mature, forming a flavorless, gluey porridge, or mixed with millet, buckwheat, or acorns to make dumplings. One benefit of the starch was that it had a similar caloric density to white rice. Land-poor farmers in particular relied on *kuropana* to get through the yearly hungry stretch when last year's grain was gone but this year's not yet ripe. But when famine struck—as it did with sickening regularity—*warabi* became a weapon against death for wealthy and poor alike.

Lest this remain at the level of abstract horror, as mention of famine so often does for those of us who live awash in high-calorie foods that appear on our tables with no apparent connection to weather or other fluctuations of nature, I would like to pause for a moment to consider an extraordinary document called the *Sawauchi nendaiki* (Chronicle of Sawauchi).[13] This yearly record of agricultural harvests and other events was kept between 1673 and 1900 by a string of anonymous community leaders in what today is the northern half of Nishiwaga. The first thing this document makes clear is the routine difficulty of farming in the region. Harvest quality is noted for the first time in 1675, when it is recorded as *daikyosaku*, meaning roughly "wretched"— a term contemporary readers of the document believe indicates essentially no harvest. This is followed by several years of middling crops and spotty recordkeeping. Then in 1689 the crop is poor, and in 1690 there is a regional famine that leads to distribution of rice by a local lord. Another poor year is 1691, and 1692 is a terrible one; the recordkeeper notes that "the people are exhausted from four years of poor harvests." In 1694 the *Chronicle* records a good harvest for the first time since recordkeeping began. This, however, is followed by a famine year in 1695, when cold weather prevented grain from forming. When rice failed to mature the next year, too, and other crops yielded only a third of normal, young men poured from the mountains into the Sendai Domain to the south in search of wage labor; many who stayed behind starved to death. In 1697 the rice harvest was half of normal, and the next year both rice and other grains were equally bad. The following year's harvest was horrible, and starting in 1701 there were three years of famine. And so it continues until the late 1800s, when finally the bad years become rarer. In several instances, the records specifically mention that people ate *warabi* rhizomes to survive.

Into this context came the great crop failures of the Edo period: the Tenmei Famine of the 1780s and the Tenpo Famine of the 1830s. The former was caused primarily by the eruption of the Mt. Asama volcano, in Nagano, whose ash blocked the sun and caused several cold summers. The latter was caused by a string of cold, wet growing seasons. It hit Tohoku particularly hard. Although historians do not know how many people died in these catastrophes, harrowing first-hand accounts of piled bones and ghost-villages suggest the number was significant, according to anthropologist Alan Macfarlane. Even today, writes Conrad Totman, these two famines "evoke images of social catastrophe and cannibalism" in Japan.

The *Chronicle of Sawauchi* is mysteriously terse regarding the Tenmei Famine—whether due to a taciturn recordkeeper or a relative lack of local impact, I do not know—but it describes the Tenpo Famine in detail. In 1832, grain did not form on the rice stalks. This in itself was commonplace, but the following spring was dry, and some farmers could not plant their paddies. Then frigid winds swept in and rain fell ceaselessly. All summer, the *Chronicle* tells us, no one had use for light clothes or fans. A somber quiet descended on the hamlets. Flies, cicadas, and other insects were strangely absent, and starting in July, not a soul had the heart to sing in the fields or on the roads. Then an August hailstorm knocked the buckwheat off the stalks, and a heavy frost devastated the other grains. Snow fell during the rice harvest. By fall people were eating through any hope of harvest the following year as they consumed their seed rice, along with the horses that should have tilled their fields and the cows that should have provided manure.

They killed and ate their cats and dogs, too, and if the records are to be believed, they threw their children into rivers or abandoned them in the mountains before fleeing somewhere, anywhere, themselves. "It was the kind of poor harvest that ends in death," the records note. In many households, every family member starved.

Those who survived did so largely by eating wild foods. In 1833 the record notes that villagers ate kudzu roots, nuts, horse chestnuts, acorns, tree leaves, plantain leaves, and lamb's quarters. In winter they dug under the snow for roots and peeled the bark from pine trees. As the snow melted, they went every day to the mountain and the river to gather wild plants. Many were so weak they could not plow the fields and instead simply scattered seeds on the hard, weedy surface. Somehow, they managed to stay alive until July, when the fields began to yield food. But the bad years continued, and in 1836 they were again forced to survive on wild plants.

The situation was similar across Tohoku. One region, however, is said to have escaped the scourge thanks to a wise ruler and a more systematic reliance on wild foods. During the Tenmei Famine of the 1780s Uesugi Harunori (Yozan) had been daimyo (lord) of Yonezawa Domain—today part of Yamagata Prefecture, southwest of Iwate—and managed to soften the disaster's impacts by purchasing grain from other regions and distributing the contents of the domain's own storehouses. His actions embodied his belief that the lord exists to serve the people, not the other way around.[14] But starving peasants were still getting sick from eating unfamiliar wild plants out of desperation, and Harunori's relief measures were so costly they threatened the progress of a broader slate of economic reforms he was attempting to implement. Something more proactive had to be done.

In 1783, at the height of the famine, Harunori ordered one of his top officials to research wild and domesticated plants that could be mixed with grains to "stretch" them—a category of food known as *katemono*. The official, Nozoki Yoshimasa, worked with domain doctors to complete a pamphlet on 127 such plants that year. He continued his work after the famine, now with a pared-down team focused solely on wild plants. In 1802 *Katemono* (Famine Plants) was published and 1,575 copies were distributed, mostly to farming villages. The book detailed 80 plants that could be eaten to stave off famine, as well as other useful information such as instructions for preserving fish and game. When crops failed again in 1832 during the Tenpo Famine, the residents of Yonezawa are said to have survived without a single starvation death by referring to its instructions (although other measures were also crucial, such as the domain's network of emergency storehouses[15]). This helped *Famine Plants* become the most famous of several so-called "famine herbals" to circulate in Japan during the Edo period; even today, Japanese field guides to edible plants include largely the same species as this nineteenth-century volume. *Famine Plants* did more than promote the safe use of sansai, however; it also locked into place their association with famine.

As I researched these official documents, I found myself wondering how the long-ago residents of Nishiwaga felt toward the plants that saved their lives. Did the first juicy *warabi* shoots spark elemental pleasure at the arrival of spring and the rolling on of life's eternal cycle? Were they grateful for the untilled soil that yielded a harvest even in the coldest summers? Or were those fronds, reaching like angry fists toward the unfeeling sky, only a reminder of the struggle to keep body and soul together when agriculture failed? I found no answer in the pages of either *Famine Plants* or the *Chronicle of Sawauchi*.

Odashima had no answer for me, either. He and his seven younger siblings never tasted *warabi*-rhizome porridge because they grew up in an era of relative prosperity when such foods were no longer needed. The land they lived on was laced with copper, and in the early 1900s a mine had opened nearby. It was among more than fifty that operated in Nishiwaga in the nineteenth and twentieth centuries, turning the sleepy region of six thousand residents spread across nearly as many square kilometers into a prosperous town of twenty thousand.

By the time Odashima was a child, worker dormitories had sprouted down the road from his home, along with shops and a school. Handsome profits flowed to big industrialists in Osaka and Tokyo, but the mines nevertheless brought economic benefits to all: a railroad line that shortened the journey to the hospital in Kitakami, electricity long before most mountain villages even dreamed of it, taxes that freed the village from reliance on government subsidies, and jobs in the mine that—however dismal, backbreaking, and dangerous—brought some of the highest salaries for miles around. Most of the mines were small or mid-sized, but at their height they produced more than ninety percent of the prefecture's copper ore.

I wondered at the positive picture my hosts were painting of this massive extractive enterprise. Elsewhere in Japan, early industrial mining caused horrific damage to human and environmental health. In fact, it was the intensive extraction of copper from the Ashio mine, south of Iwate in Tochigi Prefecture, that caused Japan's first large-scale pollution disaster and ignited the environmental movement in the late 1800s. "Ashio created civilization for some Japanese; it destroyed worlds for others," writes environmental historian Brett Walker.[16] Did Nishiwaga's mines, too, destroy worlds? Later, I learned that when a group of citizens tested water at four closed mines in 1976, they discovered levels of copper, zinc, and cadmium at one site that were respectively eighteen, fifteen, and twenty-four times higher than government safety standards allowed at the time, leading them to petition the prefecture to deal with the pollution. I turned up no direct evidence of harm to human health, however.[17]

In any case, Odashima did not want to work in the mines. His lively mind was obvious even so many decades later, as he sat beside me with eyes as clear as my own, telling stories larded with sly jabs at the two city hall workers. I can imagine the revulsion that the prospect of a lifetime spent chipping at the walls of deep dark tunnels must have evoked in his younger self. He escaped instead to Tokyo and joined the Forestry Agency. Eventually he received a transfer to the agency's local branch so that he could tend his own ancestral woods even as he oversaw the government-sanctioned clearing of ancient beech forests and their replacement with uniform stands of Japanese cedar and cypress. "Those forests will take five hundred years to return, if they return at all," he said as we sat in his living room. His voice was tinged with regret, but at the time, he said, he thought little of his actions; he had scant interest in sansai, or in the old ways and old landscapes of his village.

By the time Odashima retired at sixty, Nishiwaga had begun the downward demographic slide that eventually brought its population back to Edo-period levels. The mines closed and the young people flowed to the cities, leaving the older generation to find new ways to eke out a living from the mountains. As development ran in reverse, as it has in so many of Japan's mountain villages, a sort of involuntary rewilding claimed fields and houses. The lively company outpost in Motoyashiki became a ghost hamlet of two households.

It was at this stage that Odashima hit on an idea: Why not bring the wild vegetables Nishiwaga was so famous for into the fields and cultivate them as commercial crops? The plan made sense for two reasons. First, the government was trying to reduce the acreage of rice being grown in order to reign in overproduction, which meant that subsidies were available for alternative crops. Second, the aging population was having more and more trouble climbing the steep mountains to harvest wild plants. Not only would the government pay subsidies to those who planted novel crops in their rice fields, but the farmers would also be able to sell sansai without the trouble of gathering them wild. He began with *zenmai* and *warabi*, experimenting to find the best way to cultivate them. The mayor backed him; the idea caught on in the village, and soon *warabi* was at the center of its branding and revitalization plan. A production and marketing network that was formed to promote the plant swelled to 140 members and, according to its president at least, is currently the "liveliest organization in town." As it has many times over the centuries, the line between wild and farmed was once again shifting.

Here Odashima ended his story and led us outside to snap a few photos. As the four of us stood around his driveway chatting, he mentioned that he sometimes found interesting relics when he was digging in his fields. He ambled into his garage, retrieved a green plastic bucket, and returned to set it down on the concrete. We peered in. There were arrowheads and other stone blades, shards of singed orange pottery decorated with the snaking coils that give the Jomon period its name, and even a few serow horns. All except the last item offered proof that people had been here,

making a life in this precise spot, for millennia. Indeed, archaeological relics discovered in another part of Nishiwaga suggest people have lived in the area since the Paleolithic age.

As we bent over this unexpected bucket of treasures, I voiced
the question that had come to mind when we first arrived. Why did
those ancient people choose such a difficult place to live, deep in
the mountains where winter ends in May and starts again in October? But think, Chikako replied: For a hunter-gatherer society it
must have been a nearly ideal setting. After all, the mountains were
full of bears and small mammals to hunt, the undammed streams
thick with trout, salmon, and eels from the coast, and the woods
dense with wild vegetables and nut-bearing trees. It was only the
advent of agriculture that made this place appear unsuited to
human habitation.

Chikako's words felt immediately and intuitively true. Or
were we merely romanticizing the pre-agricultural past, as so many
discontented moderns have done? Certainly, famines occurred in
the days of hunting and gathering,[18] often in the wake of natural disasters or large-scale climatic change, and foragers needed
an enormous range of knowledge and skills to keep themselves
alive. But agriculture made hunger routine; that much was clear
in the suffering-laden pages of the *Chronicle of Sawauchi*. Not too
far north, on the snowy island of Hokkaido, the Indigenous Ainu
people chose a different path, keeping the emphasis of their diet
on wild foods for much longer than their neighbors in Tohoku. In
part, the contrasting choice of the snowbound Iwate farmers was
forced upon them: Rulers collected tax in the form of rice, and to
pay it, peasants had to till their paddies, no matter how illogical
that act must have seemed at times. Yet there were no doubt other
factors at play as well, not least among them the predictability of

a life centered on agriculture and, perhaps, a taste for cultivated grain. Which way of life was "better" or ultimately more secure? The question lingered in my mind, unanswered and perhaps unanswerable, for the rest of my travels.

From Odashima's house the Takahashis chauffeured me back down the winding mountain road, across a bridge spanning the serpent-green lake, and into the central part of town to learn about *warabi*'s alter-ego as the star ingredient in a very fancy, very old concoction called *warabi mochi*. Our destination was a sweet shop run by Shinobu Takahashi (no relation to the other two Takahashis), one of several pastry chefs in town who have recently begun using starch from locally grown *warabi* to make the classic summer confection. These days, I should mention, a product masquerading as *warabi mochi* can be purchased for a few dollars at most convenience and grocery stores in Japan. The clear, jiggly balls or cubes usually come on a Styrofoam tray accompanied by little packets of *kinako* (roasted soybean powder), *kuromitsu* (black-sugar syrup), and a plastic spear for stabbing the mochi. They're not bad, especially chilled on a hot, sweaty day, but they're a world away in spirit and substance from the item that Shinobu Takahashi makes. To start with, mass-produced *warabi mochi* isn't actually made with *warabi* starch—or much of it, at least. Consumer protection law doesn't forbid labeling sweets made with cheaper, more stable sweet-potato starch as *warabi mochi*, so that's what most manufacturers do. Real *warabi mochi*, by contrast, is a rare delicacy with a shelf life of about thirty minutes. Only a few shops in Kyoto sell the pure stuff, and they draw lines out the door of curious patrons willing to wait as their mochi is made to order. This latter market is the one that Nishiwaga's sweet shops are trying to stake a secondary claim to.

Naoyuki maneuvered the van down the narrow, crooked streets of the central shopping district and pulled up in front of a tiny storefront whose wooden sign read Okashidokoro Takahashi, or "Takahashi Sweet Shop." As we stepped inside, Shinobu greeted us with a gentle smile from behind the gleaming glass display case that took up most of the room. Dressed in an immaculate white chef's beanie, jacket, and knee-length apron tied with a bow around his slender waist, he looked as elegant as any pastry chef in Kyoto or Paris. After a quick bow, he invited us to squeeze behind the display case and follow him into his equally tiny kitchen. The moment I walked beneath the indigo *noren* curtains hanging between the two rooms, the heavenly smell of baked butter hit me in a warm wave.

"I just took a batch of financiers out of the oven," Shinobu said, handing each of us one of the miniature golden cakes to try. As I lost myself for a minute in a rich, sweet flavor infinitely more familiar and comforting than the bouncy balls whose recipe he was about to demonstrate, he explained that financiers were one of his specialties. He'd grown up in Nishiwaga in the 1960s and learned the traditional art of Japanese sweets from his parents, who opened the shop just before he was born. His formal training, however, included French techniques as well as Japanese, and since taking over the shop he'd expanded its lineup to include classics from both repertoires.

While he pulled a hammered-copper pot down from a shelf and set it on the worktable next to a portable gas burner, I took the opportunity to look around the kitchen. Every surface was polished to a mirror and stacked or hung with the tools of his trade: copper and stainless-steel bowls, piles of wooden trays for transporting sweets, a big old-fashioned mixer, scissors, sieves, wooden pastry brushes, and a petite, well-used straw hand broom for sweeping up stray flour dustings. The room gave off the pleasant, reassuring aura of a well-run operation equipped with all the essentials but not a single unneeded item.

The process of making *warabi mochi* is actually very simple and not all that different from cooking up the gluey famine porridge of old. It essentially consists of mixing bracken starch with sugar and water, heating the mixture until it thickens, and cutting or pulling it into bite-sized pieces. As he poured sugar into one bowl and water into another, Shinobu told me proudly that royalty and aristocrats were eating it in Kyoto all the way back in the Heian period a thousand or so years ago.

Technically speaking, that claim might be a slight stretch. Evidence of *warabi mochi*'s ancient royal pedigree does exist, but only in the form of a comic play named *Okadayu* first recorded in 1642, some four-and-a-half centuries after the Heian period ended. In the play, a dull-witted husband goes to meet his father-in-law for the first time and is offered a plate of *warabi mochi*, which he has never tried before. He likes it so much that he scarfs down the whole plate. His father-in-law mentions that his daughter knows the recipe and can make it for him at home. After the forgetful husband asks to be reminded of the delicacy's name about five times, the father-in-law tells him it has a nickname that should be easier to remember—Okadayu, or "Lord Oka" (*dayu* means lord and Oka is a family name that also means hills). In Don Kenny's translation of the play,[19] the origin of this nickname is explained as follows:

> Long ago, during the reign of Emperor En'yu [969–84], one
> time when that emperor was on an outing, some farmers served
> him some of these very bracken rice cakes. He found them so
> very amusing that he gave them court rank on the spot and
> named them Lord Oka. And it is for this reason that they have
> gone by the name of Lord Oka from that time forward.

Of course, on returning home, the husband is not able to
remember this little anecdote, and it is only thanks to his witty
wife's excellent ability to remember classical poetry—which he
boorishly tries to jog with a beating—that they are able to figure
out what the father-in-law served him (one of her favorite poems
mentions bracken).

A dueling explanation for the sweet's nickname has its roots
in an even older Chinese tale. As the Shang dynasty ceded to the
Zhou in 1046 BCE, legend has it that two sons of the lord (*dayu*)
of a Shang province moved to Zhou territory. They later fell out
with the Zhou ruler, however, and fled to the hills (*oka*), where—
unwilling to eat the grain of the conquerors—they subsisted on
fiddleheads. When they learned that these, too, belonged to the
Zhou, they stopped eating altogether and died of starvation. The
confection is said to be named in tribute to these righteous "lords
of the hills."

Both or neither of those old tales may be true, but by the
fifteenth century, *warabi mochi* was without a doubt being eaten in
Japan. It is mentioned in writing for the first time in 1489, and a
(sugarless) recipe is given in the 1643 cookbook *Ryori monogatari*
(Tales of Cookery). The poet-priest Soboku ate *warabi mochi* in
a Shizuoka teahouse in March of 1545, shortly before his death,
having set out from Kyoto to bathe in the Shizuoka hot springs.

He describes the journey through a country at war with itself in his travel diary, *Togoku kiko* (Account of a Journey to the Eastern Provinces),[20] and includes a poem about the mochi:

> with my years mounting
> I'd not thought to eat this food
>   again but such is
> the life I've been allotted
> *warabi mochi*

The verse plays on a twelfth-century poem by Saigyo also written on a journey through Shizuoka, translated here by Laurel Rasplica Rodd:[21]

> with my years mounting
> I'd not thought to pass this way
>   again but such is
> the life I've been allotted
> Middle Mountain of the Night

A few centuries later, Toraya Confectionery Company, purveyor of Japanese sweets to the emperor since the late sixteenth century, began making the confection for Kyoto's upper echelons; the Imperial Guard supplied the *warabi* starch.

In the little kitchen in the Tohoku mountains, Shinobu cut open a small plastic packet of that same fine white powder. Here, finally, was the hallowed *shiropana warabi* starch. He told us it cost him the equivalent of $300 per kilo when he bought it from local farmers (which he always did). It was available for about a hundred dollars less from Kyushu, where the industry is much more established, and for less than $50 if he was willing to buy it from Chinese suppliers (which he was not). He emptied the starch into the pot, poured in the water, and mixed everything together with his hand to form a thin white liquid. Next he tipped in a bowl of white granulated sugar and heated the mixture over a burner, stirring constantly with a wooden spoon. As he stirred, he explained that *warabi* starch is the most expensive type of starch used in Japanese sweets. *Kuzu* (kudzu) starch—made from the arm-width roots of the very same vine that has run rampant over much of the southern United States—is its next rival in luxury, at around $50 per kilo. Then there are the far cheaper derivations of agricultural products such as cornstarch, potato starch (used to cut kudzu starch), and sweet potato starch (used to cut *warabi* starch), which can cost as little as $4 per kilo.[22]

"So what makes *warabi* starch so special? Why is it worth that price?" I asked him.

He mulled the question for a moment.

"The flavor?" I prodded.

"No, it's definitely not the flavor, because there really is no flavor," he admitted.

"The texture, then?"

"Yes, partly the texture. Bracken roots have a very particular, tender glutinous texture," he said. He paused again.

"And something else?"

"The rarity factor, I think."

So there it was. People were willing to pay one hundred times the price of a passable alternative simply for the privilege of sampling this rarest and most ancient of starches. For Shinobu, there was also value in using a locally grown product deeply tied to the history and culture of his village.

After a minute or two of stirring, the mixture in the pot had thickened and started to take on its characteristic gluey texture. It was almost clear now, with a slightly yellow tinge (by contrast, *warabi* starch from Kyushu tends to be gray or black). It reminded me of the embryonic glop that encases aliens in B-grade sci-fi flicks. Shinobu affectionately called it "slime," and it was true— the mixture did bear an uncanny resemblance to that weird mixture of glue, borax, and liquid starch so beloved by American children.

He began to stir harder, beating air into the mixture as he heated it. By now the mass in the pot was so sticky it stretched into a thin sheet with tiny bubbles suspended in the film when he lifted the spoon chest high. He removed the pot from the burner and scraped its contents into a small ceramic dish to cool for a few minutes. Meanwhile, he sifted a large pile of light-brown *kinako* into an even larger lacquered tray. The dry, roasted scent of soybeans wafted appetizingly toward me.

"Mochi made from pure *warabi* starch can't be prepared in advance," he said as the pile of *kinako* grew into a tawny pyramid. If it sits for more than thirty minutes or so, he explained, it loses its magically airy tenderness. The handful of Kyoto shops that sell fresh *warabi mochi* prepare the dessert as their eager customers wait, dropping it into ice water to firm it up slightly and then serving it with *kinako* and *kuromitsu* syrup. But Shinobu preferred it warm and soft.

"Have you developed any variations?" I asked, thinking of the endless strawberry-matcha-coffee-guava spin-offs on mochi made from rice. A slightly horrified expression momentarily overtook his mild face.

"*Mottainai!*" he exclaimed. What a waste! He sells it only as

Nishiwaga warabi sushi

This recipe is inspired by one in *Nishiwaga no sansai ryori* (The Edible Wild Plant Cuisine of Nishiwaga), a collection of local sansai recipes published by the Nishiwaga Eco Museum. In Nishiwaga these simple, light rolls are made with unseasoned steamed rice, but I've added seasoned vinegar for more flavor. Serves 3.

INGREDIENTS

1 cup short grain rice
1¼ cups water
2 TBS rice vinegar
1 TBS sugar or honey
½ tsp salt
3 sheets *nori*
18 *warabi* stalks, prepared according to instructions in the Guide to Plants (see page 214)

it was eaten centuries ago by Kyoto aristocrats—that is, swathed in a powdery, moisture-sucking cloak of *kinako*. He does make the concession of offering it frozen to more distant customers.

He tipped the slightly cooled mochi into the pyramid of *kinako*, tossing to coat it as he deftly tore off small pieces and shaped them into round, plump disks, two of which he transferred to a scalloped maroon plate for me to sample. I took a cautious nibble.

Ah, that texture. So difficult to describe. The flavor was easy: it was the taste of diluted sugar, balanced by the dry, ever-so-faintly bitter richness of the soybean powder. But the texture . . .

INSTRUCTIONS

1. Wash and drain the rice and place in a medium pot with the water. Bring to a simmer and reduce heat to low. Cover and cook for 10 to 15 minutes, until the water has been absorbed. Remove from heat and let steam with the lid on for another 5 to 10 minutes.

2. Heat the vinegar, honey or sugar, and salt in a small saucepan until dissolved. Transfer the cooked rice to a wooden bowl (I use a large, shallow salad bowl) and pour the vinegar mixture evenly over the top. Using a wooden spoon or rice paddle, gently fold the vinegar mixture in, taking care not to smash the rice. With your other hand, fan the rice with a paper fan. Continue folding and fanning until the rice looks glossy and has cooled somewhat.

3. Cut the *nori* in half lengthwise. Remove the curly tips of the *warabi* and save for use in another recipe.

4. Place half a sheet of *nori* on a cutting board or sushi mat. Spread 1/6 of the seasoned rice (about ½ cup) onto the *nori*, distributing evenly almost to the edges. Lay three *warabi* stalks lengthwise on the center of the rice. Roll up firmly and cut into bite-sized pieces with a sharp knife. Serve with soy sauce and wasabi.

as I wracked my brain, Shinobu told me that the editor of a Japanese food magazine had recently visited for a sample and resorted to describing it as "a texture beyond description"—a phrase he allowed himself to use only two or three times a year. It was far too soft to call rubbery, yet entirely different from either American Jell-O or its firmer, seaweed-derived Japanese cousin *kanten*. The best word I could come up with was "gentle"—the gentle sweetness and warmth of the mochi matched by its gently resistant tenderness. Whatever this unnameable texture was, it was oddly appealing. I found myself wanting to eat just one more of these strange, ancient sweets I would most likely never taste again.

Or was I simply succumbing to the lure of rarity, just as I had succumbed to the romance of the hunter-gatherer lifestyle earlier at Odashima's house? And how were these two things connected? The puzzle I had come here to solve was how *warabi* had ended up as a symbol of both luxury and poverty. As I stood in Shinobu's kitchen nibbling his glorified version of gruel, the only answer I could come up with was that agriculture makes wild foods abnormal, and there are always two sides to abnormality: despicable aberrance and sought-after rarity. If eating farmed grains was "normal," then eating *warabi* could be either a privilege (for aristocrats who did so of their own free will) or a curse (for starving peasants who had no other choice). It was only when I traveled north to meet with Ainu cooks in Hokkaido that I encountered a third perspective—one that viewed wild foods not through the distorting lens of agriculture but simply as something good to eat.

FOUR

The Tallest Grass in the World

Tales of Bamboo
Wild and Tame

かがやける
緑はそよぐ
竹やぶを
おもいつつ賞つ
たけのこの味

Emerald bamboo groves
Sway and shimmer in my mind
As my tongue is charmed
By the taste of bamboo shoots

Shigeru Goto

うす味の
けふ生い出けむ
竹の子の
この味こそは
日本の味わひ

The delicate taste
Of bamboo shoots born today
Seasoned softly, yes
This is the taste of Japan

Miyoko Goto

*Written together on a visit by the couple
to Uoka restaurant*

In a quiet residential neighborhood on the southwestern edge of Kyoto, wrapped around a garden enclosed in persimmon-colored earth walls, stands a hundred-and-fifty-year-old restaurant where one can eat an eleven-course meal featuring bamboo shoots in every course. Yes, the green *noren* curtains hanging at the gate are faintly edged in grime, the red carpet lining the dim hallway is faded, and the face of the kimono-clad waitress who leads you down that hallway to your private dining room is forbiddingly solemn, but I know of no other restaurant in Japan that so deeply reveres *takenoko*, as the Japanese call bamboo's tender new sprouts. The high priest of this shrine to bamboo is Yoshinobu Komatsu, fifth-generation scion of Uoka restaurant. Komatsu is a man obsessed, perhaps even possessed, by bamboo. From morning to night, spring to winter, he mulls its cultivation, harvest, preparation, potential for transforming the world, and general excellence. Over the several days I spent with him, I found his level of interest alternately appealing and mystifying. After all, who could imagine a similar cult of carrots or cabbage? Yet like so many people I met during my research for this book, Komatsu seemed to have found a secret door to layers of meaning in the plant world that elude most of us, and he was eager to open that door for all who would follow him through. This was fortunate, since as soon as I discovered that his restaurant existed, I desperately wanted to eat there. When I called asking not only for a reservation several months down the line but also to spend a day in his kitchen bothering his chefs and getting in the way of his waitresses, he did not object. To the contrary, he seemed thrilled.

Takenoko occupies a special place in my forager's heart because it was the first wild food I harvested after moving to Japan—or at least, I thought at the time it was wild. I was living back then on the hot, humid coast of southern Mie Prefecture, where stands of yellow-green bamboo stripe the darker cedar and evergreen broadleaf forests covering the hills. To my unaccustomed eyes, they gave the landscape an exotic atmosphere entirely different from that of the northern California coast where I had grown up. I soon learned that the beautiful arching stalks with their plumes of delicate leaves were called *mosodake* (moso bamboo, also called *mosochiku*) and that they were the source of the delicious shoots I had enjoyed a few times during the first spring I spent in Japan. As spring approached once again, I was curious to try digging some myself.

One day on a walk, I discovered a grove of the stalks growing in a shallow, unkempt ravine not ten minutes from the little house by the sea where I lived. Perfect! Assuming somewhat rashly that the neglected state of the ravine meant either that it had no owner or that its owner did not care very much what happened there, I patiently waited for winter to end. When it did, I took a plastic bag and a hoe-like garden implement called a *kuwa*, tromped out to the

ravine, and boldly hacked a few fat new shoots out of the ground
(fortunately, not a soul was present to witness my crime). Back
home, I boiled them with rice bran to remove their astringency and
happily ate them simmered, sliced, stewed, and sautéed until the
sight of them made me sick to my stomach. Only years later did
it dawn on me that the land where I dug those shoots was almost
certainly private property, the bamboo was most likely planted on
it at some point in the past, and the shoots were undoubtedly an
eagerly awaited (and sorely missed) yearly treat for the landowner.
In other words, I was a bamboo thief.

Sordid origins of my bamboo love affair aside, I have been
hooked on *takenoko* ever since. Eleven courses of it in the name
of research sounded like a dream come true. Still, I wasn't sure
it counted as a wild food. At least 1,400 species of bamboo grow
around the world, from the frigid Kuril Islands to the southern
Andes. Of these, over 100 are native to Japan, and 7 or 8 are eaten
there with some regularity. Several are harvested only in the wild,
most notably a bushy, snow-hardy variety called *chishimazasa*. But
at Uoka I would probably be eating *mosodake*, which is by far the
most commonly consumed species in Japan. *Mosodake* was introduced from China in the eighteenth century and has been cultivated as an agricultural product ever since. In Japan at least, it is
no more a wild food than apples or oranges.

Under certain circumstances, however, apples and bamboo
alike can go feral. In Japan this is happening because bamboo baskets, rice spoons, fishing poles, and all the other products once
made with this terrifically sustainable resource are being rapidly
and heartbreakingly replaced by plastic. This, together with a rise
in cheap imported *takenoko* from China and the aging of Japan's
farmer population overall has led farmers to abandon a great many

mosodake groves. In Kyoto Prefecture, nearly all groves north of the city of Kyoto had been abandoned by the early 2000s, and satellite data suggest that at least two-thirds of groves nationwide are similarly untended. Often, too, *mosodake* spreads to neighboring woods and, if farmers are not vigilant in uprooting it, soon dominates the forest ecosystem. A resourceful (or perhaps I should say criminal) forager can easily find an untended grove to dig around in. Well, what was it then—tame or half-wild? Did *mosodake* belong in a book about sansai? After agonizing over the question for a while, I decided that a visit to Uoka was justified because even if Komatsu served me cultivated *takenoko*, the recipes and information I gathered at his restaurant would apply to their wilder relatives. I soothed what remained of my guilty writer's conscience by promising myself I would investigate more genuinely wild species in the near future.

I arrived at Uoka at 10 a.m. on a Friday afternoon in late March. Komatsu greeted me in the garden of his restaurant looking exactly like the photo he had emailed to me along with various other background information: white chef's coat and trousers; short, round cap; and square, freshly shaven face glowing with earnest enthusiasm. Although he was only a dozen years older than me, the formality of his bow combined with the genteel dilapidation of his restaurant seemed to come from a different era. He ushered me right away through the large main kitchen, down a corridor where his gracious kimono-clad wife oversaw the hospitality end of the business, and into a small prep kitchen where a short, sinewy man with grizzled salt-and-pepper hair, a big nose, and wire-framed glasses stood in front of the sink. The guy looked like he could be frying eggs at a greasy spoon in New York City. In fact, he was Shoji Onoue, the sixty-nine-year-old master of the whole refined operation. To say that ingredients reign supreme in Japanese cooking is a cliché, but a true one, and in this case the one ingredient to which all others played a supporting role was the bamboo shoot. The sorting and initial cooking that took place in this room were therefore of the greatest importance.

When I arrived, a pile of silky yellow shoots already lay sprawled across a steel sink counter. Onoue told me these were the cleaned and boiled remnants of Thursday's haul. A few minutes later, Komatsu announced that a dealer had turned up with today's batch. I rushed outside on Onoue's heels. The dealer had parked his van outside the kitchen door, and as we stepped into the bright morning light he pulled six or seven cardboard boxes from the back and set them on the sidewalk for inspection. Onoue squatted, cigarette in one hand, and pawed through the boxes with the other. Each contained shoots of a different size.

"Pretty hard, eh?" he grumbled, his face set in a critical scowl.

"It hasn't rained for a week," the middle-aged dealer replied with a mixture of sheepish apology and righteous self-justification. When the spring rains stall, *takenoko* grow slowly, giving them more time to develop tough fibers as they push through the hard, dry soil. This is the bane of Kyoto's bamboo farmers, whose sole aim is to ease the birth of their "children" (the *ko* in *takenoko*) in order to ensure minimum acridity and maximum tenderness. Toward this end, they labor through the winter layering fluffy rice straw and dirt onto their terraced fields; if they do not, the roots grow year after year into the same shallow layer of soil, rendering it an increasingly matted and hostile environment for the children to push through on their way toward sunlight. As for flavor, they strive for something between asparagus and corn. But nature has many ways of undoing the farmer's work, and the shoots delivered that morning were harder than Onoue would have preferred. He took them anyway, since most of Uoka's suppliers are located in the neighborhood and therefore share the same climatic challenges.

The kitchen door slid open behind us, emitting a delicious gust of rich, fishy steam from the vats of *dashi* boiling on the stove, and a teenage boy emerged to carry the boxes back to the prep kitchen. This was Onoue's assistant Ueda-kun, who was finishing up high school via correspondence classes as he decided whether or not he liked the chef's life (as for bamboo, he had little opinion in favor or against; he told me he'd hardly tasted the elaborate dishes served at the restaurant). Onoue himself began cooking at nineteen. He grew up in Kutsuki, the same mountain village I visited to research horse chestnuts, and got his start at a river-fish restaurant before landing at Uoka thirty-three years ago. In this way, the most and least experienced cooks in the kitchen worked side by side on the most crucial yet simplest of all tasks.

Back in the prep kitchen, Ueda had dumped the *takenoko* into a large industrial sink, where they bobbed like the horns of some rarely glimpsed forest animal, their outer leaves covered in soft brown fuzz and their bottoms a fresh, unsullied cream color. As Ueda plunged his arms elbow-deep into the cold water and began to scrub with a *tawashi* brush, Onoue continued to grumble. "No good, no good," he muttered, picking up a steel scrubbing pad to help Ueda. "Tough, eh?" He lifted one into the air and gestured to its sheath of outer leaves. "See how dark these are? In good *takenoko*, they're pale all the way up. And here at the bottom, the nubs"—he pointed again, this time to a circlet of crimson bumps around the base— "these should be white." The flavor and texture would probably still be far better than any *takenoko* I'd ever eaten— better, at least, than the semi-feral shoots of neglected country groves, which must do without the loving ministries of Kyoto farmers, and better still than the insipid, fibrous rectangles I had grown up eating at American Chinese restaurants.

Ueda tossed the scrubbed shoots onto a counter, where Onoue swiftly lopped off the tips and bases and cut a slit in the sides with a firm whack of his knife. When the pile had become a mountain, he transferred it to four huge pots siting on a row of gas burners on the concrete floor. As a garden hose filled the pots with water, he dropped four or five dried chilies and a saucepan full of rice bran into each one to leach away any bitterness they might have. It would take an hour for the water to come to a boil and another for the shoots to become tender, at which point they would be divvied up for use in various dishes.

At this moment Komatsu returned to fetch me. It was time for his morning round of the local farms. He gets his shoots from a range of sources including dealers, individual farmers, and central markets. This serves as insurance of sorts, since he is so dependent on a single local item that varies dramatically in quality and quantity each year. For the same reason, he is careful to cultivate relationships with a large number of local farmers. "My role is to be a diplomat," he said as he maneuvered his little truck down a road just wide enough for it to fit. This morning, for instance, he would purchase *takenoko* from three small farms within several kilometers of the restaurant.

Komatsu grew up in the Rakusai neighborhood where Uoka is located, a historic center of bamboo production in Kyoto, and knows its human and agricultural landscape well. Before I met him, he sent me a beautifully evocative description of his childhood there, part of which read as follows:

> From the time I was young, I grew up surrounded by bamboo groves. The thickets were my playground, in which my friends and I often pretended to be explorers. I remember testing our bravery by walking through the dark thickets when the sun went down. I remember, too, falling into a pond while running around a thicket at the age of three or four, and nearly drowning.
>
> In spring, I watched as the *takenoko* were dug and prepared. The world was enveloped in the smell of cherry blossoms and the particular scent of *takenoko*, and of the rice bran that was thrown into the cooking pots in order to remove their bitterness. In summer, the mosquitoes from the thickets would bite me even inside the house, and the incense we burned to kill them became an indispensable necessity. When typhoons passed over, the bamboo stalks bent dramatically, scaring me with their resemblance to howling beasts. In fall, fertilizer was spread over the bamboo groves. The smell was quite strong, but it gave the neighborhood a pastoral mood, and I loved to be there then. In winter, sparrows and other little birds rested in the thickets, and when I passed by in the morning, they would chirp and flit about, making me feel fresh and clear. The stalks would bend from the weight of the snow on their leaves, and the groves would become white. When the temperature rose, I heard the sound of the snow falling to the ground. I couldn't take my eyes off the sight of the groves returning to their original state. Throughout the four seasons, I always sensed the presence of bamboo beside me.

After college, Komatsu moved to Tokyo for a number of years. When he visited home, the bamboo-filled landscape struck him as monotonous. But at thirty, his grandfather died, and he returned to help run the family restaurant. His grandfather was the one who had made bamboo cuisine Uoka's specialty, and Komatsu recalled that he used to dig bamboo himself every spring. He decided to do the same, learning from a neighborhood farmer. The more time he spent with the farmer, the more complexity he discovered in the plant. This was the beginning of his obsession with bamboo. He learned that acre upon acre of the groves were being abandoned, partly due to a lack of successors on the farms. Was there no way to restore the beautiful groves of his childhood, to value the wisdom of those who cultivated them, and to find more uses for these plants that had once served such diverse and essential roles in Japanese culture? "I came to feel that this was my mission in life," he wrote. He began to network with scientists and entrepreneurs exploring new uses for the plants, eventually becoming a self-appointed global emissary for the restoration of bamboo groves and the use of their various products. I suppose this role included welcoming curious American journalists to his restaurant.

The previous day, he had taken me to visit one of the farms with which his connection is strongest. It was a beautiful, warm spring morning a few weeks into the *mosodake* season, and we walked the four or five blocks from the restaurant to a patch of land farmed by thirty-nine-year-old Yasufumi Ueda. Ueda had returned to the family business after stints in advertising and nightclub management, a past that still showed in his head-to-toe outfit of crisp, dark-blue denim. His ancestors had established the fields six generations earlier, just as Komatsus were opening their restaurant as a watering hole for travelers headed to the city. This was in the last quarter of the nineteenth century, when the hills of southwestern Kyoto were being converted from mixed forest into the fields that locals call *take yabu*, or "bamboo thickets." Ueda's land, however, was far too open and airy to merit that term. Fat, widely spaced stalks—or culms, as they are properly called—soared above sun-dappled dirt terraces, their leaves rustling soft as silk skirts. I found it a deeply peaceful place. Ueda greeted us outside his small processing hut, beaming; his wife had just given birth to their first son. Unfortunately, he was too busy tending his bamboo children to stay by her side at the hospital.

The language of the bamboo farm is disarmingly human: The mature stalks are *oyadake*, "parents," who *umu*, "give birth," to *ko*, "children." A parent bears abundant children every other year for approximately six years. In order to keep track, farmers use a brush and ink to mark new stalks with a number indicating their birth year. When the sixth year is up, the farmer saws the stalk down, but only after selecting a promisingly plump replacement shoot and allowing it to sprout leaves, rendering it independent from the parent to whom it is connected by umbilical-cord-like roots. Even then, the grove remains a single interconnected organism collecting and distributing nutrients. The nodes on the roots can develop into either shoots or more roots. In summer, the plant determines how many of each to produce the following year based on the amount of nutrition available. If nutrients are plentiful, it makes preparation to birth lots of children; if not, it sends out new roots to extract nutrients from more distant soil. Sunlight is also a factor: If it is plentiful, as in the widely spaced cultivated groves, the plants send up shoots to fill in the open space and take advantage of the sun; if crowded and dark, they do not. Therefore, while Ueda's groves appeared sparse, they are in fact far more productive than the nearly impenetrable abandoned groves.

Creeping underground expansion of this sort is the primary means by which many bamboo species proliferate. According to Masatoshi Watanabe, a lifelong scholar of bamboo who lives in Kyoto, all the *mosodake* in Japan have identical DNA, which means that those original stalks brought over from China in the 1700s have spawned a national army of clones. Bamboo does have the capacity to reproduce via seed in its own strange way, however. Many species grow for years, decades, or even centuries without flowering. Then, all at once, vast swaths of a given species will flower, die back, and regrow from seed. This is called "gregarious flowering," a behavior shared by only one other type of plant, the talipot palm of India and Sri Lanka. The flowering intervals of bamboo vary by species but are often unknown due to the difficulty of studying century-long cycles. The mechanism by which their internal alarm clocks remain so curiously in sync also remains a mystery.

When widely utilized species like *chishimazasa* and *madake* (Japanese timber bamboo, *Phyllostachys bambusoides*) undergo these grand explosions of flowers, the impacts can be momentous. Entire groves turn to clacking brown graveyards that can take years for full regeneration. In the wild, bamboo flowering cycles sometimes control the growth cycles of other plants. This is true in the beech forests of northern Japan, where the dense *chishimazasa* understory dies back only once every sixty to one hundred years, opening a precious window for new beech seedlings to establish themselves and the forest to be renewed. For humans, the sudden windfall of seeds that these mass flowerings produce can be both a bless-ing and a curse, as the famous scholar of bamboo Koichiro Ueda described in his 1968 book *Take* (Bamboo). In 1833, when the vast groves of *suzudake* (*Sasa borealis*) around Takayama happened to flower during a poor rice year, residents collected over five million liters of the wheat-like seed for use in dumplings, gruel, and noo-dles. But in 1855, when the *sasa* bloomed in Yamagata Prefecture, hordes of hungry rats descended, consumed the bamboo seeds, and then moved on to other crops; 350,000 of them were eventu-ally caught. A similar infestation occurred in Ehime in 1966, this time leading to the decimation of cypress plantations by raven-ous rodents. Fortunately for both Ueda and Komatsu, *mosodake* does not undergo this type of dramatic mass flowering and die-back. Instead it regenerates itself little by little, so that the impact on growers is nearly unnoticeable. Harvest continues year in and year out, until years stretch into decades and decades into centuries.

Ueda showed us the tool Kyoto farmers use to dig bamboo, called a *horiguwa* or *horikuwa*. It consists of a smooth wooden handle about waist-high, and a blade of approximately the same length attached at a right angle at the bottom. This allows the farmer to gently pry the shoots

Horiguwa *and* takenoko.

from the underground root system without bending over. The tim-ing of this operation is essential, as the delicate, slightly sweet fla-vor of bamboo starts morphing into tongue-curdling acridity the

instant the shoots encounter sunlight and begin to photosynthe-
size. The transformation continues after harvest but can be halted
with cooking, which is why Onoue rushes his *takenoko* into pots
with such urgency. They grow with notorious rapidity as well,
shooting up like expanding telescopes at a speed that is literally
visible to the naked eye; in 1970, scientists observed one *mosodake*
plant grow nearly four feet in a single day. The *takenoko* farmer is
therefore in competition with his crop as to who can get up the
earliest. Ueda's days typically begin at 6 a.m. as he, his mother, and
his wife's father scan the soil for subtle cracking or buckling that
signals children on the verge of emergence.

As we walked through his cool groves, he explained all of
this with a healthy dose of hyperbole: He digs twenty times faster
than his father-in-law, has muscles twice as big at the end of the
season as at the start, eats *takenoko* every day without fail during
the growing season, and of course produces the most delicious
bamboo shoots in the neighborhood. Somehow, though, his boasts
did not bother me. To the contrary—I found his enthusiasm for his
odd crop as charming as Komatsu's.

On Friday, our farm visits were much more cursory. We stopped
first at a place run by a middle-aged man and his mother, who
Komatsu later confided produce shoots of average quality. Still,
he bought three boxes and offered a price slightly above the day's
market price. This was his strategy for ensuring they call him first
and give him pick of the haul—a bone of contention with his
father, who is still co-owner of the restaurant and prefers the old
model of going for the lowest price possible. The second farm,

located across the street, was run by an eighty-eight-year-old man and his eighty-four-year-old wife. This morning was their first harvest of the year and they had called Komatsu specially. He bought a small box, but later told me the quality was not very good. Our third stop was a farm run by a pair of brothers whose main line of work was construction. They were smoking cigarettes outside their office when we pulled up, dressed in matching blue coveralls. Across the street, rows of *takenoko* lined the floor of a small shed, neatly arranged by size. Komatsu only wanted the largest ones—by that point he had accumulated plenty for the restaurant—but the brothers pressed him to take them all, and he gave in, mostly to oil the relationship. On our way back to the restaurant Komatsu told me he'd have Onoue pickle the extras in soy sauce to serve at drinking parties throughout the year, noting with trepidation that the head chef was sure to tell him off for buying too much.

Back once again in the prep kitchen (where I, at least, saw no sign of a telling-off), another round of cleaning, trimming, and boiling had begun. Onoue was sorting shoots by size and tenderness. The mid-sized, slightly more fibrous ones would be sliced in half lengthwise and grilled with a sauce of mirin, soy sauce, and sake for a popular dish called *katachi-yaki*, which shows off their geometric interior chambers. The tenderest large shoots would be sliced into rounds and simmered in a subtle broth of *dashi*, light soy sauce, salt, and mirin to make the restaurant's specialty, *kagami-ni* (*kagami* means mirror, referring to the circular shape of the slices). The smallest shoots would be cut into half-circles to sandwich with shrimp paste and deep fry as a sort of bamboo-and-shrimp burger.

By this time, the lunch orders were coming fast and thick and the main kitchen was getting busy. Already as we made our rounds of farms Komatsu had been checking his watch nervously, the strained tension of the midday rush coming on; now the chefs scowled whenever Komatsu instructed them to tell me what they were doing or pose for a photo. I decided it was time to make my exit. I would be back soon enough to sample the fruits of their labor.

The following day was Saturday, and I had arranged to meet two friends for dinner at Uoka. One—the daughter of Myong Hee Kim, who prepared *fuki* for me in the mountains of Takahama— was a Kyoto native, the other a long-time expat resident. They appeared to be anticipating the every-course-*takenoko* meal with a mixture of curiosity and good-natured skepticism. After all, how good could such a single-minded menu really be? Inside the persimmon-colored walls we followed a faded wooden sign away from the kitchen, through the lush stone-paved garden to the restaurant's entrance. The solemn waitress in the green kimono greeted us and led us to our yawningly spacious private din- ing room, where we settled in around a low table on the tatami floor. Before she backed politely out between the sliding doors, she pointed out several clumps of bamboo growing in the garden outside, as well as a pair of chest-high, glaringly phallic speak- ers made from polished bamboo in the alcove. Later, the Kyoto native deemed the whole place far over the line in terms of kitsch. Come on, she said—bamboo-themed décor, bamboo-shaped serv- ing dishes, a menu entirely devoted to bamboo? Not exactly sub- tle. She was right: For the hip Kyoto crowd, I'm sure dinner here would feel like a trip back in time to a countrified outpost. Still, I

couldn't help respecting what Komatsu had done. It wasn't a gim-
mick, it was an expression of love—unabashed, earnest, maybe a
little embarrassing to those looking in from the outside, but nevertheless pure and real. This is what we ate:

- A cup of bright-green, faintly salty Uji sencha tea served with
  a small rectangle of adzuki bean jelly whose glassy surface
  crackled as I bit into it—the only course missing *takenoko*.
- The silky inner sheaths from the tip of the bamboo shoot,
  tossed in a creamy marinade and topped with salmon roe
  and finely shredded radishes, served with rapeseed blossoms
  steeped in *dashi* and *komochi konbu* (golden herring roe laid on
  sheets of kelp, forming a strange crunchy-spongy sandwich
  that expelled salty juice when chewed).
- Chilled lozenges of *takenoko* on bamboo skewers, one topped
  with intensely sweet-salty red miso, the other with a milder
  white miso. Pleasantly substantial to crunch through, but tasting more of miso than bamboo. Served with one *sazae* (turban
  shell sea snail); two cold, delicious fava beans; two oily, salty
  herrings; and one odd, sweet-sour-salty dumpling made of
  sieved yams topped with smoked salmon. The plate had gold
  and green bamboo painted on it.
- Clear broth garnished with sliced *takenoko*, *wakame*, and a
  kinome leaf. A curl of steam laden with *kinome*'s spicy aroma
  swirled up to my nose when I lifted the lacquered lid. Delicious and slightly tongue-numbing.
- Five half-moon slices of *takenoko* "sashimi" served on a
  bamboo-shaped plate, accompanied by a *shiso* flower, wasabi,
  a scattering of tiny, deep-maroon sprouts, salt, and soy sauce.
  The sashimi—which was not actually raw, as the name might

suggest, but rather boiled and chilled—was delicate, tender, and sweet, almost as if it had been simmered with a few spoonfuls of sugar. A dish that relied entirely on the quality of the bamboo and its preliminary preparation—in other words, on Onoue.

- *Takenoko kagamini*: two thick, round slices from the bottom of the shoot, simmered in seasoned broth and topped with finely shaved *katsuobushi* and *kinome* leaves. Gently warm, fishy, and rich, with the faintest bite of acridity. Reaching my natural satiation point for *takenoko*.
- Cubes of *takenoko* in a creamy, gently sweet, green sauce flavored with *kinome*. Starting to get tired of *kinome*.
- Whitefish sushi wrapped in *sasa* (dwarf running bamboo) leaves smelling of wet grass—a special gift from the chef, since I'd noticed strips of dried rush hanging in the kitchen the day before and asked what they were for. He told me they were used to bind little sweets—or in this case, sushi—bundled in damp *sasa*. Packaging aside, a respite from bamboo.
- *Takenoko katachi-yaki*, grilled with a sweet-salty glaze and topped with the ubiquitous *kinome*. Pretty, but a bit cloying. Hitting a *takenoko* wall. Still three more courses to go?
- *Kogomi* (ostrich fern), *taranome* (Japanese angelica), and *takenoko* tempura in a fabulously crispy batter studded with sesame seeds, plus one of those *takenoko*-shrimp sandwiches on the side. The sesame seeds take on a roasty flavor when fried that makes this one of my favorite courses so far. Nice trick to slip in a little more *takenoko*.
- Soothing, mild rice studded with thin slices of *takenoko* and served with a hearty red-miso soup, *takenoko* and mustard-leaf pickles, and rustic *bancha* tea. We soldier on, the end in sight.

- Cream-cheese mousse laced with pieces of *takenoko* and topped with a black bean and a mint leaf. I like it, but the Kyoto native is not impressed.

When the meal ended, we all agreed—without the slightest exaggeration—that we could not be paid to eat *takenoko* again until next year's season. Our cravings had been sated, or rather, obliterated.

A year and a month later, I found myself crouching in a beech forest near the peak of Mt. Moriyoshi in Akita Prefecture with a bear hunter and a train conductor, scanning the ground for wild *takenoko*. Specifically, we were looking for the new shoots of *chishimazasa*, also called *nemagaridake*, a slim, relatively short variety of bamboo that grows in vast thickets across snowy northern Japan. *Nemagari* means "bent-root," a reference to the fact that the shoots emerge from the ground at odd, low angles and only straighten as they mature. Thus the need to crouch; if we didn't, the shoots blended in bewilderingly with the jumble of beech saplings, old bamboo stalks, and fallen leaves and twigs on the forest floor. My head inches from the ground, I trained my eye up the steep slope, past a mossy snag and a cluster of ferns—jackpot! The thrill of discovery shot through me. I scrambled up the slope, grasped the slender shoot firmly at its base, and pulled. With a satisfying squeak that hinted at the juicy flesh inside its sheath, it snapped off in my hand, and I added it to the bundle already in my bag.

I thought back to those manicured groves of *mosodake* in Kyoto, the ground below them soft with rice hulls and the still air broken only by the silky rustling of bamboo leaves high above. Then I looked around at the beautiful, messy, gnat-and-mosquito-infested beech forest of Mt. Moriyoshi, here in the far north of Honshu, burgeoning with all the pent-up life that had been sealed underground over the long winter. Never was the difference between wild and cultivated so clear. Those *moso* groves had a quiet, hard-earned beauty to them, but the *sasa* thicket had excitement: the thrill of the hunt, and of life unfolding beyond my control, subject to the whims of rain and sun and earth. Could anything compare to those brief moments when the universe aligned to give me a perfect, vibrant, tender shoot, so easy to overlook and so elementally gratifying when I managed not to?

"We have the mountain goddess to thank," the bear hunter, Hideyuki Oriyama, had said as he drove the three of us up the mountain half an hour earlier, just after dawn. We were talking about how excellent it was that the emergence of the shoots had lined up perfectly with my arrival. His mention of the mountain goddess wasn't at all metaphorical. It is a custom of the *matagi*—as traditional hunters of northern Japan are called—to pray to the goddess before hunting on her mountain and to thank her when she permits them to catch a bear. In Oriyama's words, she is a "not very pretty" deity who becomes exceedingly jealous when beautiful women enter the forest but likes men very much and sometimes keeps them for herself when they come hunting. To appease her, the hunters offer her sake and a hideous spiny fish called *okoze* ("devil stinger" in English), which they believe makes her feel better about her own appearance.

I was staying at the guesthouse Oriyama runs with his wife in the nearby farming hamlet of Nemorida and had asked his help in arranging an outing to pick *takenoko*. This had led to the introduction of the train conductor, Takumi Sugibuchi, a weekend mountaineer who sold *chishimazasa* in addition to driving the one-car train that had carried me, my sister, and my ten-month-old son through the mountains to Oriyama's guesthouse earlier that week (my research team had grown significantly since my trip to Kyoto the previous spring). I suspect Oriyama selected Sugibuchi as a guide because at forty-four he was at least two decades younger than any other local expert on *chishimazasa*, which meant he spoke in standard Japanese that I would have a chance of understanding rather than the thick local dialect that was nearly incomprehensible to me.

Sugibuchi had arrived at the guesthouse at 4:30 that morning, his standard departure time for picking *takenoko*. He had close-cropped, wavy black hair, rectangular black-rimmed glasses, and a trim frame clad in a pair of those blue coveralls that in Japan signal one's intent to do serious work. He was very polite, but not at all cold. As soon as I met him, I detected a kind of vulnerability or openness immediately below the surface. Oriyama, too, was friendly and helpful, but his shell of manly confidence was quite a bit thicker; he lectured more than conversed. The two men had become friends several years earlier when Sugibuchi rented a field from Oriyama to grow vegetables in. Like Oriyama, Sugibuchi lives in a village with plenty of its own uncultivated fields, so I was perplexed as to why he would rent one elsewhere. When I asked, he explained that his father, with whom he lives, is an avid gardener and a tyrant with regard to weeds. Sugibuchi was sure that if he tried to grow a garden on his own ancestral land his father wouldn't be able to resist meddling. Therefore, he had taken the understandable if somewhat extreme step of renting a field half-an-hour's drive away, between the train company's office and the town where he lived. He mentioned that he had grown up in that town but left between the ages of eighteen and thirty-four to follow his passion for climbing mountains, which made him an unusually alienated local. He had no children and was not married.

It was only four or five years after moving home—that is, five or six years before I met him—that he began foraging for wild foods. An older colleague was retiring from the train company, and Sugibuchi wanted to find a way to keep up their friendship. As it turned out, the man was an expert forager, and since Sugibuchi was already a passionate alpinist, he became his apprentice. He said the old forager had an uncanny ability to walk at a steep angle up and down the slopes, a keen sense of where to find particular plants, and a complete comfort in the mountains. The relationship he described made me think of a children's novel by Mamoru Hosoda called *Okami kodomo no Ame to Yuki* (Wolf Children: Ame & Yuki) that I had translated the previous year. In the story, a pair of half-wolf, half-human children move with their mother to the countryside, where the son, Ame, begins to spend more and more time wandering the mountains. Eventually he becomes the apprentice of an old red fox, who is described as follows:

> Teacher knew everything Ame had ever wanted to know, though Ame hadn't even known what that was before they met. Afterward, the things he was searching for became extremely clear. The more he learned, the more new questions bubbled up inside him.
>
> A fox of few words, Teacher mostly let Ame observe him and the mountain.
>
> But for Ame, each observation was a revelation. Everything was so different from the "ecology of wild animals" he had read

about in books at the school library. There was an enormous gulf between "nature" as humans viewed it and wrote about it and the truth of the natural world. Ame took it in through Teacher's eyes and learned about every nook and cranny.

For example, Teacher had a different name for the beech trees, and the rhododendrons, and the gentian flowers, too. ... Some words could not even be translated into human language. When Ame explained that certain things lacked a corresponding human equivalent, Teacher was flabbergasted. He wondered aloud how one could live without such things. The shock ran through Ame like an electrical current.

An entirely new world surfaced before his eyes.[23]

In truth, this awakening is closer to Oriyama's experience of the countryside than to Sugibuchi's. Oriyama grew up in the prefectural capital, a stereotypical city kid who loved video games and disliked going to his grandparents' house in Nemorida. When the earthquake, tsunami, and nuclear disaster of March 11, 2011, hit, he was living far to the south in Tokyo, the older of his two daughters just three months old (she was eight when I visited). Suddenly he realized their vulnerability. Everything from diapers to food was brought in from elsewhere, and even the water was polluted by fallout. He felt that if his family moved to the country, they would have a certain degree of security; at least in the mountains, there would always be something to eat. Soon after, they returned north to Nemorida and turned the empty ancestral home into a guesthouse.

They were the youngest family in a village full of elderly farmers who could no longer keep all their fields mowed and fruit trees picked. The boundary between the forest and the farmland

Uoka's kagami-ni

This recipe calls for fresh *mosodake* bamboo shoots. To prepare them, remove the dirty outer leaves from freshly dug shoots, slice off the tip of the leaves at an angle (taking care not to cut off any of the tender shoot inside), and make a vertical cut into the top half of the leaves. Place in a large pot of water, bring to a boil, and add a few handfuls of rice bran (*nuka*) and two whole chili peppers. If you can't find *nuka*, which is sometimes sold in Japanese grocery stores, try adding a handful of rice. Reduce the heat to a low simmer, cover, and cook for one to two hours, until a toothpick can be easily inserted into the base. Periodically skim the foam from the top of the pot. Cool in the cooking water, drain, remove remaining fibrous outer leaves, and rinse. (The recipe below is courtesy of Uoka restaurant.) Serves 4–5.

INGREDIENTS

About 2 lbs prepared *mosodake* shoots
5 cups *dashi* (see recipe p. 232)

had begun to blur. Bears would wander into town to pick persimmons and raid the snacks set before gravestones as offerings to the dead, causing an uproar. Sadly enough, shooting them was the usual solution,[24] but only one person in the village had a gun permit: Oriyama's eighty-three-year-old neighbor. When he died, no one was left. So Oriyama became a matagi, as men of his village had done for centuries. He said he felt he had to protect his family and community, to "teach the bears that humans are frightening beings." The meat was a side benefit. When I met him, he had been a hunter for five years.

I was fascinated by how wholeheartedly he had embraced matagi culture, even though it was fairly new to him and only a small part of his livelihood (he worked full-time at the local dam). "Our culture straddles the natural and human worlds," he told me,

½ cup mirin
½ cup sake
1 TBS salt
3 TBS light soy sauce
4 small handfuls finely shaved *katsuobushi* (*itokatsuo*)
4 sprigs fresh *sansho* (see page 203)

INSTRUCTIONS

1. Slice the bottoms of the bamboo shoots into rounds about 1 inch thick. Save the upper portion (the inner leaves) for another use. Bring a large pot of water to a boil and simmer the rounds for 5 minutes. Drain.

2. Return the rounds to the pot and add the *dashi*, mirin, sake, salt, and soy sauce. Simmer for 35 minutes, remove from heat, and cool the rounds in the cooking liquid.

3. When you are ready to serve the shoots, warm them again in the liquid. Remove and divide between serving dishes (about two rounds per serving). Garnish with the *katsuobushi* and *sansho* sprigs.

spreading two fingers apart on a bear-skin rug in the guesthouse living room; the word *matagu*, from which "matagi" may be derived, means to straddle. Matagi go into the mountains not only to hunt but also to fish and forage for sansai and mushrooms. In *Horse Chestnuts and Rice Cakes* Kan'ichi Nomoto details the food-procuring activities of a matagi in Yamagata Prefecture, just south of Akita, in the 1930s. In addition to farming paddy and dryland fields (both permanent and rotating slash-and-burn types), the man hunted bears, flying squirrels, marten, rabbits, and pheasants; fished for six types of river fish; and gathered sansai, eight types of wild mushrooms, chestnuts, horse chestnuts, wild grapes, walnuts, and mountain yams. It was this way of living in the mountains that Oriyama had begun to experience, albeit in much simplified form.

One evening, he showed me a documentary about matagi

culture. It was made just thirty years earlier but depicted another world. The elderly men wore thick black-rimmed glasses and fur vests made from the pelts of their favorite hunting dogs so they would not be separated even in death (they never wore bear pelts, lest they mistake one another for an actual bear). They slid down the snowy slopes as fast as skiers and climbed them like antelopes, sleeping in remote huts for a week or more at a time. In the mountains, they spoke a special language and took on set roles to surround and flush out the bears. They never killed more than one a day, gathering round afterward to skin and butcher it, nibbling on pieces of the fat as they did. The meat was always equally divided. The bears they shot with rifles, but the rabbits were victim to an older, rawer method. First, the hunters tossed out woven grass disks that produced a sound like the wings of a crow, sending the rabbits racing for their dens. They then thrashed through the snow after them, pawed their way into the dens like rabbits themselves, and snatched the beautiful white creatures out by their hind legs to kill.

Oriyama said that in the past, a single bear generated enough money for a family of four to live on for a year, but today the value has fallen to a mere few hundred dollars. No one wants the pelts for rugs anymore, because a bear pelt makes a poor match for vinyl flooring, and the sale of various parts for medicinal purposes has been regulated (though a large black market still exists). The number of matagi in the local hunting association has dropped from a hundred to twenty-two. Although regulation is beneficial from a conservation perspective, this drop in the value of the bear struck me as a sad development. It seemed such a hard, cold reflection of how the value placed on all the mountain's gifts has withered over time.

It was around eight o'clock by the time Oriyama, Sugibuchi, and I returned from the mountain with our basketful of *takenoko* and motley assortment of other *sansai* we'd picked along the way: fiddleheads, *shiode* (wild asparagus), a couple of young *udo* stems, and some *mizu* (a kind of nettle). My heart was still pulsing with awe at the abundance of the mountain—at all it provides and also at the peculiar way in which the character of those plants so perfectly matches our own needs and wants. I was filled to the brim with that feeling, which I am too urban and unattuned to experience more than once in a great while, of being part of the whole, a small piece in the cosmic puzzle, shaped to fit it just as it is shaped to fit me.

Harvest basket.

Oriyama started a small charcoal fire for us in the *irori* of the guesthouse living room, then left for work. An *irori* is a traditional Japanese hearth, usually square and sunk into the floor, over and around which all sorts of delicious things can be cooked. Sugibuchi, my sister, my son, and I arranged ourselves on the bear-skin rugs around this hearth and began to cook a portion of our *takenoko*. This was a very simple process. Sugibuchi placed a small metal stand over the charcoal and arranged a handful of the shoots on top. Each was about six inches long and as thick as my thumb at the base, wrapped tightly in a green and pink sheath. After about ten minutes, when the sheaths lost their dullness and began to glisten with moisture, he pulled them off and handed them around to us. One by one we stripped off the thick husks to reveal the moist, glowing, yellow-green spikes inside. These we sprinkled with salt and ate steaming hot. The flavor was delicate and sweet like the end of a corn cob, with a very faint hint of astringency. Little by little the pile of discarded husks beside us grew. I was reminded of a photograph Sugibuchi had snapped on his phone earlier that morning when he ventured up a slope too steep for me to follow. It showed a similar pile left behind by a bear enjoying the same springtime treat as us humans.

Sugibuchi stayed with us until noon, blanching and peeling the rest of the shoots and preparing the handful of other sansai we had gathered. When that was done, we cooked a simple feast of rice, miso soup with *takenoko*, and tempura made from *takenoko* and the other sansai we'd gathered. The food was delicious, and the habitually over-scheduled Sugibuchi announced he was delighted to enjoy the pleasure of a leisurely meal. But of all the dishes we made and all the elaborate concoctions I had sampled at Uoka, the best by far were those fresh shoots we grilled over the hearth for breakfast: impeccably fresh, entirely uncomplicated, and above all, eaten slowly and sociably, each one unwrapped and relished like the gift it was.

FIVE

Seasons of the Sea

A Vanishing Tradition of Wildcrafted Seaweed

名寸隅の
船瀬ゆ見ゆる
淡路島
松帆の浦に朝凪に
玉藻刈りつつ
夕凪に
藻塩焼きつつ
海人娘女ありとは聞けど

From where we stay
Here in the roads of Nakizumi,
   Over in Awaji
The Bay of Matsuho lies in view:
   There, as I have heard,
When the sea lies still in the
morning calm
   The shore girls come
To take their harvest of the gemlike
weed,
   And in the evening calm
They light their fires to burn the
weed for salt.

By the poet Kasa-no-Kanamura, in the
Man'yoshu *(trans. Edwin Cranston)*

I mentioned in the Introduction to this book folklorist Kan'ichi Nomoto's observation that as one moves from the agrarian flatlands of Japan toward either the mountains or the sea, the ways in which people procure their food becomes more varied. Cultivation cedes ground to hunting, fishing, and gathering. Rice shares the table with horse chestnuts and bracken starch, trout and bear meat, fiddleheads and wild walnuts—or so it was in the days when diets were by necessity more local than they are today. I tasted the remnants of these old ways of eating in the mountains of Kyoto, Akita, Iwate, and Kumamoto, and even during the years I spent living in Mie and Nagano. Many meals and many cooks taught me that to live in the Japanese mountains is almost inevitably to be a forager. Oddly enough, I had given little thought to the seaside half of Nomoto's formula. I say oddly because seafood and seaweed are hugely important elements of Japanese cuisine, and also because oceans worldwide are humankind's last, long-suffering frontier of hunting and gathering. The Danish food scientist Ole Mouritsen estimates that while ninety percent of plant and animal species raised on land for food were domesticated at least 2,000 years ago, ninety-seven percent of those raised in oceans were domesticated only in the past 120 years. Which is to say, the transition from tending the wild garden of the sea to farming it like a plot of land is still very much a work in progress.

And so, in the early spring of 2018, I began to search for Japan's wild seaweed eaters. I happened to be spending a few weeks on the southern island of Shikoku, killing time between a conference in Tokyo and the start of the bamboo-shoot season in Kyoto; it seemed like the perfect opportunity to start poking around for ocean foragers. Without too much trouble I turned up a curator at the prefectural museum in Tokushima who studied the subject. But when I met Hironori Isomoto in the monumental marble-staired building where he works, he told me my timing was off for the *tengusa* harvest on the island of Tebajima and the *hijiki* harvest on the island of Ishima. Thankfully, *wakame* was in full swing. Isomoto said that hardly anyone harvested wild *wakame* on Shikoku anymore, but that if I was lucky, I might find a couple of old folks in the fishing hamlet of Kitadomari who still did. Before I left, he gave me the name of the fisheries-cooperative president there, Akira Okamoto.

One morning a few days later, I set out to meet him. I had no idea what to expect. Over the phone, Okamoto had been taciturn: Yes, there were still a few elderly people around who harvested wild *wakame*; no, he could not introduce me to them; and yes, I could come meet him in person if I really wanted to. Given that this was my one and only lead, I said that would be wonderful. Kitadomari is part of the city of Naruto, one of Japan's most famous *wakame* terroirs (yes, Japan has terroirs for its seaweed), known in particular for a method of sprinkling the fronds with ash before drying to better preserve their flavor, texture, and color. The city occupies the tip of a green peninsula in northeastern Shikoku, gazing across the lucid blue Naruto Strait to Awaji Island, where the poet Kasa-no-Kanamura pined for seaweed-gathering "shore girls" in the eighth century, and beyond that to Kobe, Osaka, and the rest of Honshu. The currents in this strait are said to flow faster than any in Japan, swirling into an enormous whirlpool that can reach ninety feet across at spring tide. This is what makes Naruto's *wakame* so superior: The currents stir up nutrients, keep the water clean, and buffet the seaweed, making it fleshier, firmer, and supposedly more delicious than its competitors. In the Heian period local rulers sent it as a gift to the Imperial Court.

I took the first train to Naruto from the inland guesthouse where I was staying and transferred downtown to a rattletrap bus. As the bus threaded its way through the quiet city to its rural outskirts, the streets soon became so narrow I worried we might scrape against the concrete walls of the gardens on either side. The sky was a crisp, clear blue. It had rained for a few days earlier in the week, and the wind had kept the fishermen home, but today was a gorgeous, mild day. Presently we arrived at Kitadomari. There wasn't much to see—no stores or parks or even signs, just a narrow strip of tile-roofed houses squeezed between the clear blue sea and the thickly forested hills. A concrete seawall, brown-green with age, mostly blocked the ocean from view. As we headed toward the end of the peninsula, however, I glimpsed a series of docks through the gaps in the wall. They were crowded with men and women bent over huge piles of glistening amber-olive seaweed.

I got off at the last stop and followed the seawall north around the tip of the peninsula to the fisheries-cooperative office, where

I had arranged to meet Okamoto. A few minutes later he arrived, nodded curtly, and handed me his business card. "Did you want to see some seaweed?" he asked. Well, yes, of course! Without another word, he led me across the desolate co-op parking lot to a nearby dock where a woman swathed up to her eyes in windbreakers stood by a small wooden boat piled with farmed *wakame*. At Okamoto's instruction, she pulled out a piece and proudly held one end over her head to display its length, the other end trailing down the steps that led into the water. The central stem, or stipe, was long and tapering, with flat, leaf-like blades attached at intervals along the sides and a beautiful, wavy mantle called the *mekabu* just above the anchor. Seaweeds have no need for true roots, since they can absorb nutrients directly from the water, and in fact are classified as algae rather than plants; this is why an alternative vocabulary is used for identifying their parts. On land, the *wakame* looked messy and awkward, like a seal waddling clumsily along the shore. But just as the seal turns to a sleek silver bullet underwater, I knew from botanical illustrations that this tangled mess of seaweed was once a tall, undulating amber feather, its delicate blades illuminated by sunlight filtering through the water.

The woman picked up a curved hand scythe, lopped off a huge clump, pulled a plastic bag from her pocket, and stuffed the seaweed into it. Taste it, she urged through the windbreaker covering her mouth. I took a nibble. It was powerfully pungent, pleasantly firm, and as salty as the ocean she had pulled it from. I would hardly have guessed this was the same seaweed routinely added to miso soup, where it functions mainly to break the monotony of the broth with a few insipid green shreds. As we left, she pressed the bag of wakame on me to take home.

Back in the office, Okamoto's secretary handed him a mug

of green tea and me a dainty cup of coffee as we settled in to talk. He told me he was born in Kobe and spent the first years of his life there, but when the Americans bombed the city in March 1945 he was sent back to his family's hometown of Kitadomari. He was five or six at the time. Then as now, Kitadomari had very little in the way of fields or paddies; mostly there were forested hills and a thin sliver of human settlement along the shore. Its seasons were the seasons of the sea. Like *fukinoto* and *nazuna* on land, *wakame* signaled spring underwater, flourishing when the sea was still so cold it would instantly numb an immersed hand. This was followed by wild *mozuku* in May, *tengusa* (the source of the jelly-like noodles called *tokoroten*) in June and July, and various fish throughout the summer. Okamoto grew up in this watery world, and when he reached adulthood, he went into the seaweed

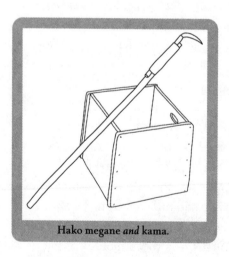

Hako megane *and* kama.

and fishing business. At the time, *wakame* was harvested wild. The men would go out in their boats early in the morning to places where the water was between nine and fifteen feet deep and slice off lengths using long bamboo poles tipped with curved blades called *kama*. In order to see below the surface, they floated wooden boxes with open tops and glass bottoms on the water to cut the glare. One can still pick out wild-harvest boats by the presence of these *hako megane*, as they are called in Japanese.

The tea must have loosened Okamoto's tongue, because he

was growing less taciturn by the minute. He told me that when he was around thirty-five, the fishermen in Kitadomari began to farm *wakame* using technology developed in northeastern Honshu in the late 1950s. Seaweed aquaculture had begun in rudimentary form in Japan some three centuries earlier, but only in the twentieth century did technologies advance enough to transform the industry. Today, the Fisheries Agency estimates that over eighty percent of seaweed produced in Japan is farmed. That figure is certainly reflected in Naruto. If the ropes used to grow *wakame* there were strung together end to end, a local food promotion company has calculated, they would reach clear around Shikoku.

The seasonal cycle of *wakame* is essentially the reverse of that for land plants. It is seeded on rope frames in November, left to mature over the winter, and harvested in February and March. Like most seaweeds, it is an annual. I commented to Okamoto that this was an amazingly fast pace of growth. No faster than rice, he answered matter-of-factly. True enough, but rice does not grow taller than a man in the span of three or four mid-winter months. Later, I learned that seaweeds are able to direct most of their energy toward growth because they do not need to support themselves with rigid structures as land plants do. This rapid growth is advantageous because all seaweeds rely on photosynthesis to fuel their existence, which of course requires exposure to sunlight. The faster they approach the surface of the water, the better they can compete with other seaweeds for that sunlight. Depending on the species, they typically grow between two and fourteen times as fast as temperate terrestrial species.[25] Giant kelp even beats out rocket-paced bamboo as the world's fastest-growing species.

In any case, the switch to cultivation increased the amount of work and technology demanded of Okamoto and his neighbors, but also greatly improved the predictability of their harvest. Wild *wakame* varies drastically in yield from year to year and is limited in overall quantity, as are many wild foods. When Okamoto was young, he and his neighbors relied on diversity to ensure their livelihood: In a poor *wakame* year, they increased their harvest of *mozuku* or *tengusa* or any number of fish species. Switching to aquaculture meant a steady harvest year in and year out, which allowed them to meet the demands of consumers bent on a daily bowl of *wakame* soup regardless of the sea's fickle moods. Yet as the fishermen's economic model changed, so, too, did their relationship to nature. Where they had once managed the wild sea so it would continue giving them seaweed across centuries and even millennia, they now manipulated it in the name of productivity, much like a rice paddy or a wheat field. Okamoto told me that many of Kitadomari's families today specialize entirely in farmed *wakame*, earning enough in the brief harvest season to live on throughout the year.

Seaweed aquaculture can be a fabulously sustainable practice because it requires neither land nor inputs such as feed or fertilizer and produces none of the toxic byproducts that terrestrial farming does. It can also take pressure off wild seaweed beds, the overharvest of which devastates the communities of animals and plants reliant on them for shelter and sustenance. I knew these things, but as I sat in Okamoto's office listening to him recount the recent history of Kitadomari, I could not help worrying about the tendency of us modern human beings to create systems that are far simpler than the wild ones they replace. Surely much must have been lost in that transition. Mouritsen delivers a similar warning, despite his enthusiasm for expanding global seaweed production: "Cultivation of seaweeds is, unfortunately, not without risk for the Earth's ecological systems, as the commercially grown species can crowd out the wild varieties, thereby reducing biodiversity," he writes.

The path toward the harvest and consumption of ever fewer kinds of seaweed is a long one in Japan. The food writer Akira Miyashita chronicled this trajectory his 1974 book *Kaiso* (Seaweed), beginning with the first written references to seaweed in the seventh century. In 720, a collection of governance rules called the Yoro Code included eight varieties of seaweed among the items that adult males could use to fulfill their yearly tribute payments.[26] This tribute seaweed graced the plates of lords, monks, government officials, and priests, to whom it was distributed. Miyashita argues that these upper classes were the primary consumers of seaweed in those days, aside from coastal dwellers themselves, and they seem to have eaten as many different varieties as they could get their hands on. In 938, the *Wamyo ruijusho*, a Japanese-Chinese dictionary, included characters for twenty kinds of seaweed. It was an especially important element of the vegetarian cuisine eaten at Buddhist monasteries during this period. But in the following centuries, as farmed vegetables became more abundant and diverse, the importance of wild seaweeds faded. A cookbook published in 1643 still listed cooking methods for twenty-one varieties, but Miyashita notes that the nationwide trade which began to flourish in this period was largely limited to *konbu, nori, wakame, arame, tengusa, hijiki,* and *funori.* Inland commoners were eating seaweed for the first time, but a less diverse assortment of it than coastal dwellers and the upper classes once had.

By the prewar years, food historian Setsuko Imada writes that fifty kinds of seaweed were eaten regionally, sixteen kinds were eaten in mountainous as well as coastal areas, and five or six were enjoyed throughout the whole country. This laid the foundation

for the seaweed-eating habits of today, which even along the
coasts are dominated by those same five or six varieties: *konbu*
for making *dashi* stock, *wakame* for miso soup and salads, *nori* for
wrapping sushi and rice balls, *hijiki* to simmer as a sweet-salty side
dish, *mozuku* to serve chilled with vinegar, and *tengusa* to make jel-
lied dishes. Of these, *nori* and *konbu* generate the overwhelming
bulk of income for seaweed farmers. Many of the species relished
by tenth-century nobles and monks would be unrecognizable to
Japanese cooks today. This simplification of the diet is mirrored
in coastal communities as a simplification of both livelihoods and
underwater environments.

After we finished our coffee and tea, Okamoto offered to drive me
over to the docks. He parked across from the seawall and strode
confidently through one of the gaps. Despite his grandfatherly
white hair and hand-knit sweater, I realized that as the co-op
president he was likely one of the most powerful members of this
seagoing community. I followed timidly behind him. The far side
of the wall was a hive of activity. On this one dock perhaps ten
families were at work processing their morning haul. Each had set
up a station comprising colored crates, pulleys, and piles of seaweed alongside furiously busy men and women in rain slickers. A
steady stream of small boats pulled up laden with *wakame*, which
was winched up gradually via claptrap bamboo pulley systems.
Kites and crows hovered overhead, no doubt hoping for a scrap
of flesh among all those sea vegetables. Men and women hunched
on upturned crates divided the *wakame* into leaves, stems, and the
prized *mekabu*. The separated parts were then transferred to large

boilers where college boys on temporary spring-break jobs stirred them into steaming vats of water. After a minute or two of blanching the *wakame* was plunged into cold water, pressed between plastic crates to remove excess liquid, and tossed with salt in a machine resembling a miniature cement mixer. Later, the salted, semi-dried *wakame* would be trimmed, packaged, and sold over the course of three or four months. Some of the crop was also dried for longer storage. *Wakame* can be eaten fresh as well, but only for a day or two after harvest, making it a seasonal delicacy enjoyed mainly in fishing villages and surrounding areas.

As we stood on the dock, a grizzled, deeply bronzed old man pulled in on a boat with a *hako megane* box on the prow and a hull full of wild *wakame*. So the wildcrafters really did still exist! When Okamoto told him I was interested in his haul, he smiled conspiratorially and said it was much tastier than the cultivated stuff. He then proceeded to pull out a knife, slice off a massive tangle, and insist that I take it home to try for myself. In fact, he insisted (to the horror of my stomach) that I do a taste test right then and there. Okamoto quickly procured a bag of farmed *wakame* from a worker stationed nearby so that I could make a proper comparison. The most apparent difference was the texture. The cultivated *wakame* was nearly smooth aside from some fine pores and hairs on the blades, while the blades of the wild variety were as wrinkled as an unironed sheet. The wild *wakame* was also a bit closer to al dente pasta than the silky, rather insubstantial farmed variety. I told the fisherman that the wild variety tasted less harsh and perhaps sweeter than the cultivated one, although the difference was nearly imperceptible. Apparently gratified by these impressions, he turned back to his task of unloading the boat.

Leaving the dock, the now thoroughly thawed Okamoto

offered to drive me all the way to the neighboring village of Kita-
nada, where he said a diner run by the fishing co-op there served
fresh local *wakame*. I hesitated for a moment, unsure if my stomach could handle any more seaweed, but ultimately decided to
seize the opportunity, digestive consequences be damned. We
drove inland through the hills, nostalgic *enka* ballads drifting over
the radio and the cloying smell of the sea filling the car. Okamoto emerged on the north side of the peninsula, turned down a
wind-whipped coastal highway, and with a warm farewell dropped
me and my three large bags of *wakame* off at the diner for lunch.
Alone at a plastic-covered table, I no doubt mystified the waitress by ordering everything on the menu with the word *wakame*
in it, which included fish heads simmered with *wakame*, a trough-
sized bowl of *wakame* miso soup, and a side of *wakame* "sashimi."
The latter turned out to be a refreshing mountain of blanched
seaweed served with coarsely grated wasabi and soy sauce. The
pungency that had been so overwhelming in the raw samples was
gone, presumably leached away in a bath of boiling water. This
was slightly disappointing to my taste buds but an immense relief
to my stomach.

Back at the guesthouse that night, my housemates and I followed Okamoto's recommendation and feasted on a simple meal
of fresh *wakame* shabu-shabu. I rinsed the fronds, cut them stipe
and all into three- or four-inch lengths, and arranged them on a
large plate. At the table, we set a clay pot full of boiling water seasoned with a piece of *konbu* over a portable gas burner and took
turns swishing the *wakame* through the bubbling water. Almost
instantly the color changed from amber to a brilliant emerald
green. The transformation was so magical we couldn't help plung-
ing piece after piece into the pot and then plucking them back out

to dip in a dish of citrusy ponzu sauce. This was the happy end to my brief, not so successful search for wild seaweed on Shikoku.

There is one place in Japan where wild seaweed still reigns supreme, and that is the remote and tradition-bound Noto Peninsula of Ishikawa Prefecture. The peninsula juts into the Sea of Japan roughly like a dog's head gazing northeast, its crown battered by the rough waves of the open sea and its mouth a sheltered bay gaping toward Niigata. The varied and rocky coastline supports over two hundred kinds of seaweed, of which the local people eat thirty and sell about ten—a level of culinary diversity far beyond that found anywhere else in Japan. Noto's closest competitor for seaweed foraging is the Ise-Shima region of Mie Prefecture, which encompasses Ise Jingu, one of Japan's most hallowed Shinto shrines. Many types of seaweed are offered up to the gods at this shrine, as they have been for at least a millennium, but the number is still only about half that harvested on Noto. The seaweed scientist Takahiko Ikemori, with whom I had the good fortune to tour the peninsula a little over a year after my visit to Kitadomari, told me that the people of Noto have no interest in offering their seaweed to the gods; they gather it to eat themselves. The culture, Ikemori said, is very similar to that which exists elsewhere in relation to wild mountain vegetables. It is founded on intimate knowledge of place. "People know that if they go to this particular spot, they will find this particular seaweed," he said.

The most avid and skilled seaweed foragers on Noto are its *ama*. These freediving fisherpeople make their living gathering shellfish and seaweed deep below the water's surface, much as their ancestors did for centuries before them. In ancient times ama populated many of Japan's coastal regions, harvesting seaweed not only as food but

Prewar ama.

to burn in order to make a nutrient-rich salt called *moshio*.[27] The salt-burning "shore girls" to whom Kasa no Kanamoto referred in the poem excerpted at the start of this chapter were, in fact, *ama otome*, or "maiden amas" in the original Japanese. Several other poems in the ancient anthology *Man'yoshu* also speak of these enchanting young divers, who seem to have held a mermaid-like mystique for their cultured observers. A few poems refer to the tale of Tekona of Mama, a lovely ama who was courted by two suitors. Too kind to turn either one down, she escaped her dilemma by drowning herself at the inlet of Mama where beautiful seaweed grew.

Female ama have thus drawn the eye of writers across history and today continue to be the frequent subject of newspaper articles and television programs. One might conclude based on this that only women can become ama, but in fact there are three characters for the word: 海人, "ocean person"; 海女, "ocean woman"; and 海士, "ocean man." A 1934 survey counted 17,000 male and 10,000 female ama in Japan. The total figure has since dropped to just over 2,000, with many now in their sixties or even older, according to the Toba Sea-Folk Museum. Noto has the second highest number of ama in Japan, after Mie, with most living in the city of Wajima on the peninsula's outer coast.

Ama once wore only a loincloth and bandana to dive, which perhaps accounts for some of their appeal to those ancient poets. Today they dress in wetsuits and masks, but still forgo oxygen tanks or any scuba equipment, relying instead on powerful lungs and masterful diving techniques to reach the sea floor. They sometimes dive alone but more often in husband-wife or mother-daughter pairs. In this case, one steadies the boat while the other (usually the wife) plunges straight down to a depth of up to sixty feet, secured by rope to a float on the surface and sometimes carrying a rock to speed their descent. In the space of a minute or so they gather *wakame, arame,* abalone, sea cucumbers, sea urchins, and whatever else season and place offer before returning to the surface for air. Abalone is by far their most valuable catch.

On the rainy Monday I spent tooling around the Noto Peninsula with the scientist Ikemori, he took me to an eclectic little seafood restaurant run by an ama named Satsuki Bansho and her family. Ikemori is one of the region's leading seaweed scientists, but his scruffy hair, large, owlish glasses, and habitually jolly demeanor efficiently counterbalance all trace of intimidating *sensei* aura. By the time we arrived at the restaurant, called Tsubaki Jaya, or Camellia Teahouse, I already felt the kind of intuitive ease that comes from sharing a fundamental worldview with one's companion—in this case, an affection for plants (or algae, in his case) and a looming fear for their future relationship with humankind.

Satsuki's restaurant perches midway down a steep hillside at whose base lies a rocky shore where she often dives. The walls are decorated with driftwood, seashells, and model boats, and the menu consists of little wooden tubs full of stones picked from the beach, each with a different menu item painted on it, so that guests have only to select the stone that appeals to them when ordering. I suppose Ikemori had warned Satsuki I was coming, but when we arrived she was nowhere to be found. Instead, her grown daughter greeted us from behind the counter. She introduced herself as Satomi. "I'm thinking of changing it to Satoumi," she joked. *Satoumi* is the sister term to *satoyama*, the half-wild, half-tended village forests like the one I visited at the Afan Woodland in Nagano. *Sato* means village in both cases, but instead of *yama* for mountain, in this case it is joined with *umi* for ocean. Together the two characters refer to coastal areas that have traditionally been protected, nurtured, and on occasion altered so as to serve as sources of food and other essential items for the people who inhabit them. Noto is much renowned for its *satoumi*, which earned recognition from the Food and Agriculture Organization of the United Nations in 2011 when the peninsula was designated a Globally Important Agricultural Heritage System.

After a few minutes, Satsuki emerged awkwardly from the kitchen. She had been diving that morning and was still wearing pink rainboots with her indigo apron and blouse. Ikemori told her I wanted to ask her about seaweed. "What is there to say? I dive for *sazae* [turban shells]. To us, everything else is just *mo*," she retorted, using the generic Japanese term for seaweed and algae. Ikemori, who had known her for years and was well aware her shyness hid a detailed knowledge of local seaweeds, prodded her gently for more information. "Well, I do eat *kajime* in miso soup, but I only collect what washes to shore. And I dive for *wakame*," Satsuki grudgingly admitted. I said I had never eaten *kajime*. "It's very slimy and a little bitter," Satomi explained. "We have to tell customers it's healthy, otherwise they think it's gross. But for us, if it's not slimy, it's not seaweed." This did not sound very appealing to me. "It's hard to

explain," Satsuki said. "You'd better try it yourself." She disappeared into the kitchen.

Outside the picture windows, the rain had lifted and the sun
was slicing through the clouds, illuminating a large camellia bush
further down the hill and glittering off the ocean. I wandered over
to look at two black-and-white photographs hanging on the wall.
They were taken underwater in 1960 and showed three gorgeously
muscled, nearly nude women diving for abalone. "That was how my
grandmother did it. The women in our family have been ama for
many generations," Satomi said. In Noto, it is usually the women
who dive and the men who fish or harvest seaweed from boats.
True to form, both Satsuki and Satomi are divers, while Satsuki's
husband is captain of a fishing boat. Satomi is unusual among her
friends, however; she said that few people in her generation have
an interest in diving.

Satsuki reappeared carrying a red lacquer bowl of steaming miso soup and set it before me. Shreds of firm green seaweed
coated in what looked like clear mucus were floating in the broth.
I slurped up a sip. The *kajime* was as slimy as promised but surprisingly mild. "Sometimes it's more bitter than others," Satomi
said. "When the waves beat it against the shore, they take away the
bitterness." This is one reason her mother gathers what washes up
rather than dives for it. The other reason is that *kajime* is a favorite
food of abalone, so the ama traditionally leave it alone. "When
you dive for abalone, you have to keep your eyes on the abalone,"
Satsuki said. "Sometimes I do gather a little *mozuku* when I'm all
done and it's time to go home, but just for myself. For me, seaweed
is a hobby." I was beginning to feel like the hungry traveler in the
story of stone soup, extracting not carrots and potatoes but seaweed information from my hostess.

She gestured out the window. "I grew up on that island," she said, handing me a pair of binoculars. I could barely make out a tiny bump on the horizon: Hegurajima, the island of the ama. The small, rocky piece of land sits thirty miles from shore in the midst of a magnificent fishing ground rife with abalone, turban shells, *wakame*, and various kinds of fish. The water is so clear you can watch a diver go down forty-five feet, Satsuki said. The land, on the other hand, is entirely unsuited to growing rice, vegetables, or anything else. The ama used to trade their salted shellfish for rice and gather the rest of their diet from the sea. "I was raised on *heshiko* [fish pickled in salt and rice bran] and salted abalone and turban shells," Satsuki said. And seaweed, of course. The island was settled by ama who migrated from the northwestern coast of Kyushu beginning some four hundred and fifty years ago. The settlers sent gifts of abalone to the lord of the Kaga Domain, who ruled over Noto, and in return the lord granted them the island as well as a piece of land in Wajima on which to build their winter residences (until the 1950s, Hegura-jima was only inhabited seasonally). This district came to be called Amamachi, or Ama Town, though the ama themselves call it Ten-chi, meaning simply "the land." It is still populated by the descendants of those seafaring people from Kyushu.

By this time our lunches had arrived on individual trays. Each was crowded with dishes holding a simmered yellowtail head, vinegared whitefish sashimi, gingery pickled daikon, simmered shreds of *kajime*, boiled chard, potato salad, miso soup, rice, pickled cabbage, and simmered bamboo shoots. A far cry from the simple meals of Satsuki's childhood, but in the middle of it all was a dish she had sent out especially for me: a bitingly salty, pungent piece of *heshiko*. It tasted of the sea. Before we left, Ikemori asked her once again to list the kinds of seaweed she collected. "Well, there's *kajime* and *wakame* and *mozuku*, and then of course *iwanori*, *tsurumo*, and *umizomen*," she said, counting them off on her fingers. Funny how the list seemed to have grown.

Ikemori and I spent the rest of the afternoon driving down the coast to central Wajima and back around to my guesthouse on the peninsula's landward side, talking about the past and future of seaweed. From the restaurant we circled around the rocky outcropping we had been looking down on from high above, where Satsuki and Satomi sometimes gathered seaweed, then passed through the village where they live and the little port where Satsuki's husband docks his boat. It was raining lightly as we drove along the picturesque coastal road. Many of the houses were built in the traditional style, with shiny black roof tiles and wooden walls and little gardens full of hollyhocks and flowering onions and potato plants. Those facing directly onto the sea were shielded from the wind by tall bamboo fences called *magaki*, their frayed tops poking toward the sky like rows of upturned brooms.

I asked Ikemori if Noto was historically a poor place. He replied that its residents did all right because the fishing was so good, but winters on the outer shore were harsh, so people used to spend that part of the year working cash jobs in distant cities. He himself had grown up on the landward side of the peninsula, playing along the shore and collecting seaweed with his friends before his family moved away to Kanagawa. The memory stuck with him, and after a stint studying snapping shrimp at university, he eventually shifted his focus to the distribution and ecology of seaweed around the Noto Peninsula (his father, too, had been a scholar of seaweed). He periodically maps the species growing there, diving at upward of a hundred locations to complete each survey. Recently he has been studying the decline of *garamo* (sargassum) and *amamo* (eelgrass) beds in the region, both of which are important habitats for fish and crustaceans. The former are suffering from pollution and the latter from the rising temperature of the sea in summer, likely linked to climate change. His work keeps him out in the field most of the time—a fact I confirmed when I made the mistake of trying to reach him by phone at his office in the Ishikawa Prefecture Fisheries Research Center before my visit. He and his wife are also enthusiastic eaters of wild seaweed.

As we headed west toward Wajima, Ikemori slowed down to point out a patch of shore where concrete had been pasted onto the rocks to encourage the growth of *nori*. He is skeptical of such efforts. "Reproducing nature is a difficult thing," he told me in his usual amiable tone. Inevitably, aquaculture involves putting man-made objects into the ocean. He estimates, however, that Noto's wild seaweed is currently being harvested at only about ten percent of its sustainable potential. In this context, he believes it is more environmentally sustainable to use the wild resource than attempt aquaculture. I asked him why, then, did he think people persisted in trying to farm the sea even here, where seaweed is so naturally abundant? He echoed what Okamoto told me in Kitadomari: "Probably because at some point it becomes economically infeasible to live off the wild resources. There isn't enough predictability."

In Wajima, we stopped by a little factory where an elderly woman named Junko Shinki and a handful of employees turn local seaweed into various value-added products. Over tea and buns stuffed with sweet bean paste, Shinki told me about the seaweeds she grew up eating and the ones she sells now in an attempt to inject life into the local foraging economy. My impression was that she is something of a hero for Ikemori. In the car he described her simply as "a person who loves seaweed." He is desperate to support such people however he can, because he believes that even on Noto, the culture of collecting and eating wild seaweed is fading. "When the older generation of women die, I'm afraid this culture will wither away," he told me. "They are the ones who have the knowledge, but they haven't passed it on to the next generation because lifestyles have changed. When they die, the culture may die with them." He worries this will not only impoverish the local diet but also irreparably harm the health of the ocean, because it is through harvesting the wild seaweed that people come to know and value the ocean. "The relationship is fading," he said. "When the ocean becomes simply something that flows in and out with the tides, simply a scenic location to visit, people stop treating it as valuable." He believes that a conservation ethic is best fostered when local people make moderate use of the ocean's resources and, in doing so, gain a more personal motivation to take care of it. The ocean becomes a part of their kitchens, their meals, their very bodies.

His words made sense to me. I am attached to the overgrown railroad right-of-way near my house because it is where I pick black raspberries and mulberries, to the stream in my local state park because it is where I find watercress, and to the patch of woods ten miles downriver because it is where I compete with squirrels for hickory nuts. I will fight for these places. Oh, I have lofty abstract reasons for wanting to protect wilderness, but I would be lying if I denied that my strongest attachments have grown out of food. I suspect I am not unique, so perhaps Ikemori is right to argue that seaweed is a more powerful motivator of conservation than pretty views.

Wakame shabu-shabu

Shabu-shabu is a hotpot meal in which diners swish thinly sliced pieces of vegetables, meat, or fish through a clay pot of broth kept simmering over a burner at the table. Nearly all Japanese families own one of these single-burner ranges fired by a small canister of gas, which are essential for hotpot eating because they allow ingredients to move from platter to broth to mouth in a matter of seconds. In the US, similar ranges are sold as portable butane stoves for outdoor use and are well worth the investment if you like homestyle Japanese cooking. *Wakame* shabu-shabu can be as simple as a pot of water, a pile of fresh *wakame*, and a sauce or two to dip it in. This more elaborate version is adapted from a pamphlet on the seaweed cooking of the Noto Peninsula published by the Ishikawa New Agriculture Total Support Organization. Serves 4.

INGREDIENTS

Fresh *wakame*
8 fresh shiitake or large white mushrooms
1 large carrot
½ daikon radish
1 package firm (*momen*) tofu
½ lb thinly sliced pork with some fat (optional)
6-inch x 6-inch piece of *konbu*
6 cups water
¼ cup sake
1½ tsp salt

As we drove back up the coastal road toward my guesthouse, the placid sea scrolling by on our left, the full significance of his words began to sink in. What a stupendous loss this peninsula faced.

What if Noto's culture of foraging seaweed really did disappear, or fade to the point that it was no different from that which lingers in other parts of Japan? With it would go an immense body

Store-bought ponzu sauce for serving (a mixture of soy sauce and
lemon juice can be substituted)
Store-bought sesame sauce for serving (optional)
2 single-serving packages of fresh udon noodles

INSTRUCTIONS

1. Wash the *wakame* and cut into lengths measuring several inches long.
Remove the mushroom stems. Use a peeler to shave the carrot and daikon into long, thin strips. Drain the tofu and cut into 8 cubes. Arrange
these ingredients attractively on a large serving plate. Arrange the pork,
if using, on a separate plate.

2. Place the *konbu*, water, sake, and salt in a clay hotpot or large saucepan and begin heating it over a portable range at the table. Set out a
small bowl for each diner, into which they can pour a small amount of
either sauce.

3. When the broth comes to a boil, reduce heat to a low simmer. Diners
should pick up ingredients from the serving dish with their chopsticks
and swish through the broth until just cooked, then dip into their bowl
of sauce and enjoy. When all the ingredients have been eaten, the meal
can be finished by briefly simmering the udon noodles in the flavorful
broth. Alternately, use the broth to make a savory porridge for breakfast
the next morning—just bring to a simmer, add about one bowl of rice per
cup of broth, cook over low heat for 5 minutes, and stir in 2 beaten eggs
immediately before serving.

of always-changing knowledge about what and when and where—
specific knowledge that can only be accumulated piece by tiny
piece, collectively, over huge spans of time. It is not the kind of
knowledge that can be safeguarded solely by scientists and journalists and books. It must be a living knowledge, embedded in culture and cuisine and love for particular places. So it is for seaweed,
and so it is for sansai.

Conclusion

Kina haru ku=kar wa /
ku=kor wa k=arpa yakka /
naykorkamuy / sirkorkamuy
/ apkas=an yakka / epunkine
wa / nep ne yakka /
poronno k=uk wa / cise or ta
k=arpa yakne / aynu patek
e kusu / ku=ki sir somo ne
nankor / hosknopo / huci ape
paroosuke kusu / ku=kar wa
k=ek ne kusu / naykorkamuy
/ sirkorkamuy / epunkine /
en=kore yan

God of the Streams, God of the
  Earth
Protect us as we walk here collect-
  ing wild plants.
For even if we gather many plants
  and take them to our homes,
  they are not for human mouths
  alone.
We gather them so that first we may
  cook them for the Goddess of
  Fire.
And so we ask you, God of the
  Streams, God of the Earth,
  please protect us.

*Prayer said by the Nibutani Ainu on
their first outing to collect sansai each
spring, shared by Naomi Oikawa*

The Ainu are the Indigenous people of Japan's northernmost island, Hokkaido. Today they are a small minority on that island, superficially indistinguishable in many ways from the ethnic Japanese colonizers who flooded in a century and a half ago with their agrarian culture. Yet for many centuries—until much more recently than the Wajin, as the Ainu call their southern neighbors and eventual conquerors—the Ainu were a society of hunters and gatherers who supplemented their diet with a bit of grain, rather than a society of farmers who supplemented their diet with a bit of wild food.[28] The colonizers tried to wipe out this foundational cultural difference through decades of racist assimilation policies, but ultimately failed. Ainu activists resisted cultural erasure. They held onto the vast knowledge of wild plants and animals that long sustained life in Ainu Mosir, the "Land of the Humans," and are now passing it on to their children. Ludicrous as it may seem, this knowledge rarely finds its way into Japanese field guides or cookbooks on wild foods. I, too, do no justice to the depth and breadth of Ainu food culture in the few short pages that follow, but in the interest of at least opening up a path of inquiry for curious readers, I will conclude these essays by touching on this other, also Japanese way of eating from nature.

In late March 2018, I traveled to Hokkaido to meet with two Ainu women working to document and preserve traditional food culture. Tamaki Nagano and Naomi Oikawa are employees of a government-funded project intended to counter the impacts of a dam that will inundate abundant traditional foraging grounds.[29] Their office is in Nibutani, a village in south-central Hokkaido that is said to have the highest concentration of Ainu residents in all of Japan. According to geographer Naohiro Nakamura, the Ainu and their ancestors have lived in the area since 200 BCE, and in the twentieth century it became the center of the movement to revitalize traditional culture.

I spent the entire day before my visit traveling north by train from Tokyo. The further we strayed from the sprawling metropolis the emptier the train became and the wilder the scenery outside. As we passed through the long underwater tunnel connecting Honshu and Hokkaido, the conductor welcomed us to the north country where "delicious food and beautiful nature" awaited, a classic romanticization of the far north. But the next morning as I took a series of trains and busses from the capital of Sapporo to Nibutani, the countryside struck me as desolate. The snow was mostly melted but the fields and forests still lacked even the faintest hint of green, and the periodic dull, gray towns felt like scabs on the land. Nibutani greeted me with a faded orange sign reading "Hometown of the Yukar," a reference to the sagas of Ainu oral literature. Since Oikawa would be away until the afternoon, I spent the morning alone, wandering through the two Ainu cultural museums in town. The beautiful cloaks and wooden trays with bold, curving patterns mesmerized me, and even more so the old photographs of Nibutani Ainu gathered together singing and dancing, praying and smiling knowingly. I sensed more than understood that some essential difference did indeed exist between this northern culture and the southern one I had spent so much time in.

In the afternoon, Oikawa and Nagano and I sat on folding chairs in the cultural center where the two of them work, sipping yellow herbal tea and nibbling on dried *warabi* (bracken, Ainu: *warumpe*) fiddleheads and *nirinso* (flaccid anemone, Ainu: *pukusakina*) leaves pulled from brown paper bags in their office. Both women were middle-aged grandmothers with black hair flowing down their backs, but their personalities could not have been more different. Where Nagano was quick to grin and joke, Oikawa was imposingly serious, the solemn bearer of an endangered culture. She told me that in Nibutani, the salmon that swam upstream from the coast were once the most important food, so central that the local word for them, *shipe*, means "our true food." By the time the fish made the eleven-mile journey to Nibutani they were lean enough to keep for as long as ten years if cleaned and hung by the hearth to dry. There were also deer, as abundant in the meadows as cows are in the pastures today, and brown bears, which the men tracked through the mountains for days at a time with their dogs. The women and children gathered sansai (Ainu: *kina*, *ohawkop*), roots, nuts, and wild fruits. The most important plants for the Nibutani Ainu were *nirinso*, a petite forest-floor plant with soft, toothed leaves and delicate flowers, and garlicky *gyoja ninniku* (alpine leeks, Ainu: *pukusa*), both of which they collected and dried in large quantities to eat through the long winters (the Ainu traditionally recognized two main seasons, summer and winter). The bulbs of a plant with lily-like flowers called *oubayuri* (Japanese cardiocrinum, Ainu: *turep*) were also collected and processed to produce a fine starch used in dumplings served at ceremonies and a coarser byproduct for everyday use. In addition, many other wild plants were gathered as medicine, seasonings, and ingredients for various dishes.

In other words, wild food was simply food, eaten in lean times and good times and ordinary times. This was a refreshing discovery. So much of my research into the foraging culture of the Wajin had circled around the associations between wild foods and either deprivation or privilege. From Reiko Hanaoka I had learned about the wild-herb soup offered to ancient emperors, and in the snowy mountains of Iwate I had watched a pastry chef recreate bouncy bracken-root balls enjoyed by medieval aristocrats. But I had also seared my tongue on horse chestnuts that once nourished hungry villagers, and listened to a farmer's son describe how bracken staved off starvation. Japan's agrarian culture was the underlying force shaping all of these contradictory roles. Wild plants were famine foods because they could be had when rice harvests failed, and they were luxury foods because they were more fleeting and exciting than field crops. But here in Nibutani, I was beginning to sense, wild plants and animals were not defined in relation to agriculture. They were simply themselves. The more I thought about it, the more I came to feel this was the nexus of difference in how the two cultures approached foraging.

Oikawa said that the Ainu of old did not remove the bitter *aku* from their sansai, as modern Ainu do and the Wajin always have. They ate them as they were—though they tended to choose plants that were naturally more palatable. "If you're going to give me meat, then let me eat it with salt alone," an Ainu woman is quoted as saying in a book on Ainu food culture that I picked up in Kyoto. Her words echo the central culinary philosophy that Nagano and Oikawa impressed on me: Flavors are to be experienced as nature provides them, never manipulated or concealed. This may sound similar to the philosophy behind mainstream Japanese cooking, famous as it is for revering good ingredients, but in fact quite a lot of homestyle Japanese cooking is heavily seasoned, and Japanese cooks go to great lengths to remove "unpleasant" and bitter flavors from their sansai.

The balance of foods in Ainu meals was also very different from those of the Wajin. For the latter, rice and other grains formed the core of the diet, accented by vegetables and a little meat or beans. For the Ainu, meat and fish were the core foods, followed by wild vegetables and only then by starches and cultivated vegetables and grains. Oikawa told me that, in the old days, the Ainu ate only one or two meals each day. Usually there was a midday meal of soup called *ohaw*, and perhaps an evening meal consisting of simmered beans and vegetables or a grain porridge called *sayo*. *Ohaw* was the most typical dish, made by stewing deer or bear meat with wild vegetables, salt, and occasionally sardine oil as a seasoning. Sometimes it was served with starchy cakes made from *oubayuri* bulbs. Salt was a precious commodity obtained by trading meat with coastal people. Later, as the cultural influence of the Wajin deepened, *ohaw* came to be seasoned with soy sauce or miso. It was kept constantly simmering over the hearth fire, which was never allowed to go out, not even in summer, because the goddess of fire was the most sacred of all deities. In this sense, Oikawa said, religion was one and the same with food culture. I asked her and Nagano if they felt Ainu culture could persist if traditional foods were lost. Both said it could not. All were intertwined. Oikawa told me about visiting an old woman to collect traditional recipes. The woman said she felt sorry for the younger generations. When Oikawa asked her why, she said it was because they did not know about the foods of the mountains, and without this knowledge, she wondered how they could survive difficult times. "As long as the mountains remain, they will give us food, so we must take good care of them," Oikawa said to me.

The Ainu way of gathering and preparing foods was once nearly lost, however. When Nagano was a child, the only wild plant she ever ate was *gyoja ninniku*. Even this was often shunned by the other Ainu families because it made them smell like garlic when they went to work among the Wajin—a reviled mark of difference. It was only when Nagano's children began to learn the Ainu language that she became involved in traditional dance and other forms of cultural revival, eventually taking a job alongside Oikawa cataloging traditional foods and the uses of wild plants. Similarly, Shigeru Kayano, a Nibutani native and Japan's first Ainu parliamentary representative, wrote that as a child in the 1920s and '30s he sampled bear only a handful of times, never tasted deer meat, and witnessed his father arrested for "illicitly" catching salmon for the family. Later, he did much to document and revive traditional foods, together with other aspects of the culture.

Both Nagano's and Kayano's stories fit within a long history of cultural repression and gradual recovery. Parts of Hokkaido began falling under Japanese control in the 1500s, but it was only during the Meiji period beginning in 1868 that the occupation process was finalized. In the last several decades of the 1800s, Japanese settlers began to arrive in large numbers from the mainland to "develop" the island, much as pioneers did in the American West. Because the Ainu and their lifestyle stood in the way of this transformational project and its monetary benefits, the Japanese government passed laws banning them from practicing their own culture. The repression, both formal and informal, extended to traditional foods. Hunting deer and fishing for salmon in rivers was banned, and by the twentieth century the Ainu way of eating had become quite similar to that of mainland Japanese—which is to say, their relationship to the land had also become more "Japanese." Meanwhile, the settlers were busy transforming the natural environment that provided the foundation of the hunter-gatherer lifestyle. Logging turned forests into warships and matchsticks, tractors made meadows into farm fields, and guns killed huge numbers of deer, their meat bound for canning factories and eventual export.

The transformation of Ainu food culture had actually begun much earlier, as environmental historian Brett Walker describes in *The Conquest of Ainu Lands*. The Matsumae clan established a foothold in southern Ezochi (the Wajin's old word for Hokkaido, the second character of which means "barbarian") in the 1500s, and in 1603 the shogun Tokugawa Ieyasu granted the clan exclusive rights to trade with the Ainu. Within several decades, runoff from Matsumae-run gold mines was destroying salmon runs and commerce was flourishing. The Ainu became increasingly dependent on trade with the Japanese for food. They had long traded independently with the Chinese, Russians, and other inhabitants of the Asian mainland, but now they were exchanging an increasing number of fish products and animal skins for Japanese grain, sake, and other goods. Walker writes that the Japanese intentionally cultivated Ainu dependency on imported grains, in part by prohibiting the local small-scale cultivation of sorghum, millet, and other crops, to ensure the Ainu would keep supplying goods that Japanese traders wanted. This dependence, in turn, pushed the Ainu to hunt more than they needed for subsistence. As early as the mid-1600s, Walker writes, "the hunt, which had once dramatized the spiritual relationship between Ainu chiefdoms and their local environment, and the kamuy [gods] that lived there, took on more commercial connotations. . . . By the 1830s, in fact, Ainu hunted largely for the purpose of killing animals for trade."

Today, the old ways are experiencing a resurgence. The work Nagano and Oikawa are doing to revive traditional foods is only one part of a much broader movement to carry forward the many strands that together form the fabric of a living culture: food, language, dance, prayer, stories. This is not without drawbacks. With the rising knowledge of and interest in traditional foods, people have begun to come from as far away as Sapporo to strip the mountains around Nibutani of sansai each spring, charging uninvited onto private and community-held land. The problem, Nagano said, is that knowledge has been preserved without the spirit surrounding it. In the past, plant-collection sites were rotated between families yearly, each taking only what it needed to survive. This well-organized structure of use has mostly disappeared, making overharvest and unequal access to certain plants a serious problem. Which is to say, if foraging is to be sustainable, it must be accompanied by local systems for regulating access to the land. Preserving non-agrarian food cultures is not simply a question of cataloging knowledge but rather of maintaining the power of communities to protect their own resources—both from mammoth threats like dam construction, nuclear disaster, and climate change, and also from the quieter but perhaps equally destructive self-interest of modern culture.

The first time I visited Nibutani the sansai weren't up yet, and so I returned the following spring, a little later in the season, to share a meal with Nagano and Oikawa. This time I rented a car and came from the opposite direction, through the Hidaka and Ishikari Mountains to the northeast. Whereas the land had struck me as barren and dull the previous year, it now appeared a burgeoning paradise. Enormous *obuki* (giant butterbur, Ainu: *korkoni*) and *oitadori* (giant knotweed, Ainu: *ikokutu*) flourished along the roadsides, delicate *nirinso* and *mitsuba* (wild chervil, Ainu: *micipa*) carpeted the forest floor, and glowing new leaves arched overhead. Here and there wild azalea bushes exploded with fire-engine-red blossoms. I had read that in southern Hokkaido the appearance of these blossoms signals that *oubayuri* are ready to harvest, and true enough, when I arrived once again in the Nibutani cultural center, a pile of freshly pulled *oubayuri* lay draped across a steel counter in the kitchen. Oikawa had harvested them in the mountains a day or two earlier.

Nagano was already at work with another of her colleagues, Manami Kimura, chopping carrots, potatoes, and burdock. She greeted me with a wide smile, looking very much like a storybook grandmother in her plaid apron, long skirt, and leggings. Bowls of *nirinso* and *kogomi* (ostrich-fern, Ainu: *sorma*) fiddleheads sat on the counter and a warm spring breeze floated in from an open window. Nagano tossed the vegetables into a large pot of water to simmer. She was making a vegetarian version of sansai *ohaw*, the classic Ainu soup. A few minutes later, Oikawa bustled in to take charge. As head chef of their sansai documentation project, she had personally tested most of the recipes in the cookbook they wrote based on interviews with local elders. "I make *ohaw* at home just about every day," she said, sprinkling salt into the pot (she was going traditional for my sake—usually she adds miso). "I put in meat, fish, whatever, but I only use sansai for special occasions." This was interesting: What had once been an everyday staple was now reserved for ceremonies and celebrations, one of the many instances in which old foods survive but take on completely new roles.

With the *ohaw* bubbling on the stove, we moved on to the next menu item: *kosayo*, a grain porridge flavored with the potent berries of the *kihada* (Amur cork, Ainu: *sikerpe*) tree. Nagano had already simmered a few of the small, black berries with a handful of plump tiger beans. Now she sifted sugar and yellow millet flour into the pot, stirring the mixture over a low flame until it gradually became thicker and stickier. Meanwhile, Oikawa got to work on the *turep shito*, or *oubayuri* dumplings. She dumped rice flour into a bowl along with starch that she had laboriously extracted from *oubayuri* bulbs the previous spring, mixed them together with one hand, and kneaded in a cup of water (the dumplings were traditionally made with pure *oubayuri* starch or millet flour). When the white dough began to feel like stiff, smooth clay, she deftly tore

Kina ohaw for a crowd

This recipe is adapted from *Shokubunka shiko reshipi* (Recipes from Our Food Culture), a collection of Ainu recipes from the Nibutani area published by the Saru River Development Project, for which Nagano and Oikawa work. A vegetarian version can be made by omitting the pork, as they did the day I visited for lunch. Today miso is often used in place of salt—just remember you'll need quite a lot for this quantity of soup (1 tablespoon per cup of liquid is a general guideline). Serves 14.

INGREDIENTS

2½ oz dried *nirinso* or about 1¼ lbs fresh
30 dried or fresh *kogomi* (2 per serving)
2 lbs thinly sliced pork with some fat
2 TBS vegetable oil
3 carrots
1 daikon radish
2 burdock roots

off chunks and patted them into palm-sized disks. "Granny, boil these for me!" she shouted at Nagano. "I've never boiled *turep shito* before!" Nagano shouted back with a grin, gamely taking on the task anyway.

Lest all of this sound too idyllic, I should mention that it was actually complete chaos. I was traveling this time with my sister and ten-month-old son, who was not taking well to the aftermath of the long journey from western Illinois a few days earlier or the harsh reality of being replaced in his mother's arms by a camera, notebook, and pencil. Nagano and Oikawa, to my immense gratitude, took turns crawling under tables to entertain him and popping morsels of boiled potato into his mouth like the adoring grandmothers they were, while my sister attempted to calm him with spatulas and spoons. The hand-carved wooden trough and

3 potatoes
2 packages silken tofu
Salt
3 quarts water

INSTRUCTIONS

1. If using dried *nirinso* and *kogomi*, begin soaking them two days before
you plan to serve the soup. When you are ready to cook the soup, drain
the soaked sansai and cut into 1½-inch lengths. Cut the potato into
cubes and the daikon into quarter-moon slices. Slice the carrots and
burdock diagonally. Cut the pork into 1½-inch lengths.

2. In a large pot, sauté the pork in the oil until lightly browned. Add the
water and vegetables except fresh sansai, if using. Bring to a boil, lower
heat, and simmer until the vegetables are tender. Add fresh sansai and
cook another minute or two.

3. Season to taste with salt. Just before serving, break up the tofu into
the soup by hand.

pestle that Oikawa had brought along to show me how to pound
fresh *oubayuri* bulbs sat sadly unused on the table, a victim of the
pandemonium. We did finally manage to sit down to our beautiful handmade meal of *ohaw*, *kosayo*, and *turep shito*. The soup was
soothingly simple, the *turep shito* as comfortingly bland as plain
mochi, and the *kosayo* intriguingly unfamiliar, its crunchy little
kihada seeds exploding in my mouth with medicinal bitterness.

My sister and I finished up our lunch and said goodbye,
guiltily thanking Nagano and Oikawa not only for cooking but
also for tolerating our traveling band of chaos. From the cultural
center we headed back into the mountains to find the guesthouse
we had arranged to stay at for the night. As we turned off the main
highway, skeptically following the navigation system in our rental
car, the road narrowed to one lane hemmed in on either side by

dense forest. For a while it wound up and down and around the steep slopes, threatening to disappear at any moment beneath encroaching vegetation. And then, suddenly, it burst into a verdant, open valley. We had been abruptly delivered into a hidden mountain world. The valley was half deserted now, victim no doubt to its inconvenient location, but breathtakingly beautiful in a dilapidated, pastoral sort of way. Just around the bend stood the guesthouse. Behind that was an overgrown field full of *oitadori*, *obuki*, *mitsuba*, and *warabi*, beyond that a line of trees, and beyond that the fading late-afternoon sky. What an extraordinary and at the same time ordinary place that little valley was. There must be thousands of places like it in Japan, millions and millions of them in the world—hidden, bountiful universes in miniature, waiting to welcome us if only we can manage not to destroy them through neglect or ignorance or greed. My work on this book took me to a handful of them, and for that, I am deeply grateful.

Endnotes

1   Although foragng is today a popular pastime in the United States, its history is deeply fraught, as Gina Rae La Cerva describes in *Feasting Wild: In Search of the Last Untamed Food* (Vancouver: Greystone Books, 2020). European colonists arrived not in the untamed wilderness they perceived but instead in what she terms "a domesticated wild." For thousands of years, Indigenous peoples had used methods such as controlled burns to enhance the diversity and abundance of wildfowl and edible plants in the prairies and forests (and farmed some areas as well). But the new arrivals—my own ancestors among them—viewed these landscapes as wastelands ripe for agricultural development. They expelled Native people from their foraging and hunting grounds, citing as justification John Locke's notion that a person can claim ownership by applying his or her labor to "unused" land (traditional management practices were not considered an application of labor). Soon the abundant eastern forests became pasture and scrubland. Further west, large-scale farming combined with an orgy of overhunting devastated wild game populations. In Illinois, where I live, settlers reduced the extent of the prairie from sixty percent of the state to less than one hundredth of one percent in the space of fifty years (Illinois Natural History Survey). In Michigan, they virtually wiped out the vast stands of wild rice (manoomin) that fed the Anishinaabek people by draining swamps and straightening rivers for industry, logging, and agriculture, as Barbara Barton documents in *Manoomin: The Story of Wild Rice in Michigan* (East Lansing, MI: State University Press, 2018). It was only after the wrenching national transformation was near complete that a conservation movement arose to fence off sections of "pristine" wilderness, often after stripping them of the Indigenous people who had shaped these landscapes for millennia. Today, tribes such as the Cheyenne River Sioux are working to restore vanished landscapes and ways of eating in tandem—a stark contrast to the more extractive versions of foraging often practiced by those less rooted in the land.

2   Quoted in Yukio and Mieko Yamada, *Zoku Sansai Nyumon* [Introduction to edible wild plants, continued] (Osaka: Hoikusha, 1976).

3   See Liza Dalby's essay collection *East Wind Melts the Ice: A Memoir Through the Seasons* (Oakland: University of California Press, 2009) for more on these traditional calendars, along with seasonal meditations inspired by each of the seventy-two periods.

4   Japan's three largest metropolitan areas, Tokyo, Osaka, and Nagoya, now contain more than half the national population, with almost thirty percent in Tokyo. The government predicts that this trend will continue, and that by 2050 twenty percent of currently inhabited areas will be uninhabited. Already, the majority of residents are over sixty-five in about a third of villages nationwide. Between 2015 and 2019, 139 of these villages disappeared altogether because of population loss, with 2,744 more at risk. (Statistics from the Ministry of Internal Affairs and Communications.)

5   In her book *Gathering Moss: A Natural and Cultural History of Mosses* (Corvallis, OR: Oregon State University Press, 2003), botanist, writer, and member of the Citizen Potawatomi Nation Robin Wall Kimmerer writes eloquently about the "web of reciprocity" that is central to many Native American cultures: "The patterns of reciprocity by which mosses bind together a forest community offer us a vision of what could be. They take only the little that they need and give back in abundance. Their presence supports the lives of rivers and clouds, trees, birds, algae, and salamanders, while ours puts them at risk. Human-designed systems are a far cry from this ongoing creation of ecosystem health, taking without giving back.... I hold tight to the vision that someday we will find the courage of self-restraint, the humility to live like mosses. On that day, when we rise to give thanks to the forest, we may hear the echo in return, the forest giving thanks to the people."

6   The history of the holiday I give here is based mostly on Junji Morita's 2010 article "Kisetsu wo iwau tabemono (2) shinnen wo iwau nanakusagayu no hensen" [Food for celebrating the seasons in Japan (2) New Year's food: "Nanakusa-kayu"] in *Doshisha Joshi Daigaku seikatsu kagaku*, vol. 44, which quotes numerous ancient documents that mention related

customs. Unfortunately, no similarly detailed account exists in English to my knowledge. Mori also describes a second, less-well-known New Year's tradition involving wild greens. On the first Day of the Rat of each year according to the Chinese Zodiac (which, by coincidence, sometimes fell on January 7), the custom among aristocrats was to take an outing to the meadows to pick either twelve or seven varieties of greens and make them into a healthful soup. However, this custom gradually faded away, absorbed into the similar tradition of *nanakusagayu*.

7 *Satoyama* woodlands provide a refuge for species like *katakuri* (Asian fawn lily) and *gifu-cho* (Gifu butterfly) that flourished in the forests of the last Ice Age 20,000 years ago. For more on the role of *satoyama* in preserving biodiversity, see my article "Japan's Creeping Natural Disaster" (*Japan Times*, August 23, 2009).

8 Quoted in *Tochi to mochi: Shoku no minzoku kozo wo saguru* [Horse chestnuts and rice cakes: The folklore of food] (Tokyo: Iwanami Shoten, 2005). As the author notes, the meaning of the first half of the saying is clear: only a fool would cut down such an important source of food. The second part is more puzzling, but Nomoto reports that villagers told him it stemmed from the fact that the trees take three generations to begin bearing nuts, so only a fool would hope to improve his own food security by planting such a tree.

9 The account is in Miyamoto's chapter "Nihonjin no shushoku" [Staple foods of the Japanese] in the book *Nihon no shokuji bunka* [The food culture of Japan], Naomichi Ishige and Isao Kumakura, eds. (Tokyo: Rural Culture Association Japan, 1999). Miyamoto's narrative of his journey through Japan is available in an English translation by Jeffrey Irish in *The Forgotten Japanese: Encounters with Rural Life and Folklore* (Berkeley: Stone Bridge Press, 2010).

10 Much of the information in this chapter is drawn from the numerous papers they and their colleagues Yoshihiko Iida and Haruna Yotsuka have published on the social and economic roles of *tochi-no-ki*.

11 The farmer was from the village of Harie, made famous by the gorgeous

NHK documentary *Satoyama: Japan's Secret Water Garden*, narrated by David Attenborough. For several years, residents of Harie and Kutsuki have been collaborating in light of their connection via water: the downstream community is indebted to the upstream one for the purity of its most important resource, while the upstream community relies on the downstream one for help in maintaining the sources of that water. Residents of Harie have grown *tochi* seedlings for replanting in Kutsuki, where the young trees cannot be raised because herds of deer tend to devour the seedlings.

12   Arthur Waley, *The Tale of the Genji: A Novel in Six Parts*, vols. 1 and 2 (North Clarendon, VT: Tuttle Publishing, 1970).

13   Multiple versions of the *Nendaiki* were created over the years, nine of which survive today. In 2000, Nishiwaga's board of education commissioned a compilation of the four most important versions translated into modern Japanese. My discussion of the *Nendaiki* is based on a detailed analysis of this compilation written by former mayor Shigeru Takahashi, who was involved in its creation (posted as a series of entries at the now-defunct Kajika Blog, http://kajikablog.jugem.jp/). I confirmed some information with current city-hall employee Tatsuya Takahashi.

14   His philosophy was later immortalized by a set of simple instructions that Harunori gave to his adopted son Norihiro when he handed over control of the domain in 1785 (translation by Mark Ravina):

> The state (*kokka*) is inherited from one's ancestors and passed on to one's descendants; it should not be administered selfishly.
> The people belong to the state: they should not be administered selfishly.
> The lord exists for the sake of the state and the people: the state and the people do not exist for the sake of the lord.

As Ravina reminds us, however, this was no democracy; rather, "Harunori presented the most enlightened face of Japanese enlightened despotism." *Land and Lordship in Early Modern Japan* (Stanford: Stanford University Press, 1999).

15   According to Shozaburo Sato, curator at the Yonezawa City Uesugi
     Museum, these other measures included encouraging residents of the
     domain to eat porridge and other substitutes for rice, selling stockpiled
     rice at low prices, distributing seed wheat to retainers (in Yonezawa,
     middle- and lower-class retainers also farmed), and dispatching aid
     workers to help suffering villagers. Harunori and Norihiro had also been
     working for decades to improve the overall economic health of the domain,
     which likely boosted its resilience.

16   The quote is from *Toxic Archipelago: A History of Industrial Disease in Japan*
     (Seattle: University of Washington Press, 2010), in which Walker searingly
     documents the devastation of the Watarase River basin by a laundry list of
     heavy metals unleashed by intensive copper mining. Walker writes that the
     disaster poisoned almost 250,000 acres of paddy land, caused catastrophic
     flooding and erosion due to the blighting of forests and their clear-cutting
     to fuel smelters, killed massive numbers of fish, poisoned wells, and likely
     pushed birth rates down and death rates up.

17   An employee of the Historical Folk Materials Museum in Nishiwaga said
     she had never heard of any problems related to mine pollution, and a 1986
     paper on the history of mining in the area said pollution was not men-
     tioned in any historical documents (Satoshi Fujiya, "Iwate-ken Nishiwaga
     no chusho kozan ni okeru seisan keitai no henka to sono yoin" [Changes
     in the form of production at small and mid-sized mines in Nishiwaga,
     Iwate Prefecture], Annals of the Tohoku Geographic Association, vol. 38).
     A representative of the Committee to Protect Clean Water in the Waga
     River, which carried out the 1976 tests and has continued to monitor water
     in the area since, said the group's records showed no sign of elevated
     pollution further downstream and did not mention any related health
     problems. However, no data exist from earlier eras when mining practices
     were less developed.

18   Interestingly, a 2014 survey of data from 186 mostly preindustrial soci-
     eties around the world found that when controlling for habitat quality,
     hunter-gatherer societies were significantly less likely to suffer famine
     than agriculturalist societies. This contradicts the widespread belief that

hunter-gatherers experienced frequent famine. J. Colette Berbesque et al., "Hunter-Gatherers Have Less Famine Than Agriculturalists," *Biology Letters* (January 2014).

19 Different kyogen schools perform different versions of classic plays such as this. Kenny's translation is based on the performance script of the Nagoya Nomura school headmaster Matasaburo and the Izumi school script in *Kyogen Shusei* [Collected kyogen plays], accessed at http://kyogen-in-english.com/.

20 A description of the book, along with an overview of the genre as a whole, can be found in Herbert Eugen Plutschow, "Japanese Travel Diaries of the Middle Ages." *Oriens Extremus*, vol. 29, no. 1/2 (1982), pp. 1–136.

21 Laurel Rasplica Rodd, trans., *Shinkokinshu: New Collection of Poems Ancient and Modern* (Leiden: Brill, 2015), #987.

22 The Japanese term for *warabi* starch is *warabi-ko. Ko*, written using the character 粉 and alternately read as *fun* or *pun*, is a suffix indicating a powdered substance, including but not limited to flour or starch. For example, *komugi-ko* is wheat flour, *kin-ko* is gold dust, and *tomorokoshi-ko* is cornmeal.

23 Mamoru Hosoda, *Wolf Children: Ame & Yuki*, Winifred Bird, trans. (New York: Yen On, 2019).

24 Unfortunately, this is true in many parts of Japan, although some communities have tried relocating problem animals or planting nut-bearing trees to make degraded mountains into more appealing habitats. Oriyama estimates that matagi in the municipality of Kitaakita, to which his hamlet belongs, kill 3 to 4 bears per year during their traditional hunts, but the municipal government asks them to exterminate about ten times that figure for "pest control." Although black bears are not listed as endangered in Akita Prefecture as they are in parts of western Japan, conservationists expressed great concern when 817 bears—an estimated sixty percent of the prefectural population— were killed there in 2018.

25 This is a comparison of the amount of organic carbon they respectively generate per square meter each year, provided in Ole Mouritsen's book

Seaweeds: Edible, Available, and Sustainable (Chicago: University of Chicago Press, 2013). He writes that algae (including phytoplankton) produce as much as eighty percent of Earth's organic matter.

26 As Miyashita points out, the quantities listed in the code were draconian. For *nori*, the most highly valued variety, a male between twenty-one and sixty had to supply 66 pounds of laboriously collected seaweed, enough to make 2,000 sheets of dried *nori*. This is assuming 66 pounds referred to wet seaweed; if this was the dry weight, 66 pounds would have been enough to make 10,000 sheets. The quantities for other varieties were even higher. Akira Miyashita, *Kaiso* [Seaweed], in the series *Mono to ningen no bunkashi* [A cultural history of objects and humans] (Tokyo: Hosei University Press, 1974).

27 Miyashita writes that the exact method by which ancient ama extracted salt from seaweed is unknown, as the practice was already obsolete by the Heian period (794–1185). However, seaweed—which has a higher concentration of salt than seawater—was a source of this precious seasoning and preservative in other parts of the world as well. In *Seaweeds*, Ole Mouritsen describes how the ancient Danes extracted it. Saltmakers first dried and burned the seaweed in a sand pit. They next mixed the black residue with water and heated it over a fire of seaweed and wood (so much wood, in fact, that at least one Danish island was denuded of forests for the sake of salt). When crystals began to form on the surface, they skimmed off the dark, ashy salt.

28 The oldest archaeological evidence of human habitation on Hokkaido dates back about 20,000 years. Clear signs of the Jomon culture appear about 8,000 years ago and persist much longer than elsewhere in Japan, until around the seventh century CE. Around that time the fishing-centered Okhotsk culture spread along the northern coast of the island and the Satsumon culture, which combined small-scale farming with hunting and gathering, emerged in the south. By the thirteenth century, both had given way to the Ainu culture, which remained dominant until the nineteenth century, although the Japanese state began making inroads on the island long before that.

29 The Nibutani area is the site of the highly controversial Saru River Development Project, which includes the Nibutani Dam (completed in 1997) and the Biratori Dam (still under construction on a tributary of the Saru River). The Nibutani Dam was initially planned in the 1970s without consideration for the damage it would cause to Ainu culture by inundating agricultural and foraging land, displacing households, damaging the already struggling salmon fishery, and destroying archaeological and religious sites. Michael Ioannides provides a neat summary of these impacts in *Colonization, Statemaking, and Development: A Political Ecology of the Saru River Development Project, Hokkaido, Japan* (presented for the degree of Master of Arts in Applied Anthropology at Oregon State University on December 7, 2017). Two local leaders, Shigeru Kayano and Tadashi Kaizawa, refused to sell their land to the government, however, and when the government expropriated it anyway, they sued. Although the suit was not settled until after the dam was complete and Kaizawa had passed away, the courts eventually delivered a landmark decision deeming the expropriation illegal for not respecting Ainu culture. When it came time to plan the Biratori Dam, the government was forced to conduct an extensive Cultural Impact Assessment—the first of its kind in Japan. However, its findings had no impact on the fate of the project itself, which continues despite lengthy delays; for further details, see Naohiro Nakamura, "An 'Effective' Involvement of Indigenous People in Environmental Impact Assessment: The Cultural Impact Assessment of the Saru River Region, Japan" in *Australian Geographer* (December 2008). The assessment and its aftermath are what Nagano and Oikawa have been involved in. According to Ioannides, the Biratori Dam is predicted to inundate a forested area that at least 37 people still use for hunting, fishing, and gathering; destroy at least 7 archaeological sites; and harm 128 plant species used for food, medicine, or daily goods.

Guide to Plants

List of Plants

Ashitaba

Chishimazasa

Fuki

Gyoja ninniku

Icho, Ginnan

Itadori

Kajime

Kogomi

Koshiabura

Mitsuba

Mozuku

Myoga

Nirinso

Onigurumi

Oubayuri

Sansho

Sugina

Tara-no-ki

Tengusa

Wakame

Warabi

Wasabi

Yama-udo

Yamaguri

Yomogi

Zenmai

About the Guide to Plants

Choosing which plants to include in this brief glossary-like guide was a near-impossible task. The selection includes many, but not all, of the plants mentioned in the chapters, along with a few that are not mentioned. It thus represents a sampling of Japan's most iconic and common edible wild plants, although limited space has led to many arbitrary exclusions. I have generally left out weedy plants that grow and are eaten in many parts of the world, such as plantain, dandelion, and purslane, so as to provide as much information as possible that is otherwise unavailable in English (see the section in Chapter 1 on my lunch with Reiko Hanaoka for more on edible weeds and the Names of Edible Plants in the back of this book for their Japanese, English, and scientific names). Personal experience was also a key filter; because written information about sansai and other wild foods varies so widely from source to source, I wanted to write from experience wherever possible. I therefore focus mostly on plants I have cooked with myself at least a few times. Like familiar faces in a crowd of strangers, these plants drew my attention even when they were perhaps not the most logical of choices. However, I have harvested only some of them, which leads to a word of caution.

As I mentioned in the Introduction, this guide is not intended to serve as a field guide. I give no detailed descriptions of plant form, habitat, or season—all of which are essential for safe identification—and ask that readers refer to reliable botanical guides for that information. The scientific names should help when searching in English sources. I have included synonyms (alternative scientific names that have been officially rejected but may still be in widespread use) in parentheses where I feel they may be useful in looking up the plant in older reference books. I have also listed some of the Japanese nicknames and local names for each plant, but in almost all cases many more exist.

The information in this section is drawn from numerous sources, including the stack of Japanese foraging guides dating from the 1960s onward that has occupied a corner of my desk for the past few years (see the Selected Bibliography for specifics), online sources in both Japanese and English, interviews and casual conversations with many generous plant-loving souls, and finally, my own stock of personal experience. Although I have not footnoted these sources individually, I am indebted to the many foragers, cooks, and scholars who have done the underlying work that made this section possible.

I hope that this Guide to Plants will provide a rudimentary reference for adventurous eaters and cooks of Japanese cuisine, as well as a door to further study for those who would like to try foraging in Japan.

Ashitaba   明日葉

SCIENTIFIC NAME: *Angelica keiskei.*

ALSO CALLED: *Ashitabo, ashitagusa, hachijoso, todaibofu.*

AVAILABILITY: Grows along Japan's temperate east coast from the Kii Peninsula to southern Kanto and on islands lapped by the Kuroshio current, slightly inland from the beach.

DESCRIPTION: *Ashitaba* is said to be so vigorous that if you pick a leaf today it will grow back tomorrow; thus its name, meaning "tomorrow leaf." Like *mitsuba* and *seri*, it belongs to the carrot family (Umbelliferae or Apiaceae) and bears clusters of tiny white flowers on its tall stems. The large, glossy leaves are sturdy, fragrant, and about as bitter as matcha. It is frequently grown and eaten on the island of Hachijojima, a distant outpost of Tokyo where the salt winds during typhoons kill off most other vegetables. Rich in minerals and vitamins, *ashitaba* is thought to have health- and energy-giving properties. According to legend, Qin Shi Huang, who founded the Qin dynasty

Ashitaba.

twenty-two centuries ago, sent an envoy to the eastern seas in search of a "medicinal plant that gives perpetual youth and long life"—quite possibly *ashitaba*. Modern research has in fact uncovered anti-aging properties in the plant, and today it is powdered and sold as a nutritional supplement added to foods such as udon and soba.

TOXICITY/POISONOUS LOOK-ALIKES: *Ashitaba* looks somewhat like *hamaudo* (*Angelica japonica*) and *botanbofu* (*Peucedanum japonicum*), which both grow in the same habitat. Neither is poisonous, but they are not typically eaten.

HARVEST: Pick young leaves before they have fully unfurled.

PREPARATION: Blanch for use in ohitashi or aemono. No special processing necessary.

SUGGESTED RECIPES: *Leaves:* ohitashi (top with toasted *nori*), aemono (*sumiso* or mayonnaise), tempura, nimono, *nameshi*. *Very young leaves:* miso soup or suimono. *Stems:* itamemono, *kinpira*.

Chishimazasa 千島笹

SCIENTIFIC NAME: *Sasa kurilensis.*

ALSO CALLED: *Nemagaridake, jidake, sasadake, himetake* (princess bamboo), *echigozasa.*

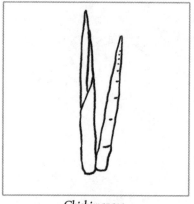

Chishimazasa.

AVAILABILITY: The world's northernmost bamboo species. Grows from central Honshu north, as well as on the Korean Peninsula and Sakhalin Island. It is planted ornamentally elsewhere.

DESCRIPTION: *Chishimazasa* is a slender variety of running bamboo that forms dense thickets in the mountains of central and northern Japan. The shoots—as delicate and refined as their nickname "princess bamboo" suggests— are classic spring fare in northern hot-spring villages. The plant can quickly monopolize the landscape when deer populations explode and selectively graze other plants. Despite this occasional (over)abundance, the popularity of the shoots has led some communities to require harvesters to procure a license. Picking alongside a knowledgeable local is a good idea in any case, since not only are the shoots a favorite snack of black bears, but the head-high thickets themselves pose a risk to inexperienced foragers, who have been known to get lost in them like Midwestern Americans getting lost in corn fields. It is said that eating the seeds, which appear only during the plant's rare flowering cycles, will add three years to one's life—though historically they have been consumed mostly out of desperation during famine and war. *Nemagaridake* means "bent-root bamboo," a reference to the fact that shoots emerge from the ground at an angle. They straighten as they grow, but the base of the stalk always retains a crook.

TOXICITY/POISONOUS LOOK-ALIKES: According to Ted Jordan Meredith's *Bamboo for Gardens*, the shoots of all temperate bamboos are edible, though many are not palatable. Shoots from tropical and semitropical bamboos should always be boiled prior to eating, as some contain high levels of cyanogenic glycoside, an antinutrient that can cause vomiting, dizziness, convulsions, and other symptoms.

HARVEST: Pick young shoots measuring no more than about 4 inches long that are poking up from last year's leaves. Look for thickets where the mature stalks are fat, as these will yield plumper shoots. Grasp the shoot and pull firmly in the direction of growth; you'll hear a distinctive squeaking noise as it breaks off. Overharvest is not generally a concern since thickets become increasingly dense over time, and thinning the young plants helps the stand remain healthy; use reason, however, and leave enough shoots for regeneration.

PREPARATION: Freshness is key; the shoots become astringently bitter as they sit, so always prepare them on the day you harvest. Minutes after picking they can be peeled and eaten raw, together with their sweet juice. Otherwise, submerge in a pot of cold water and heat until foam appears on the water's surface. Drain, slice off the tips, and peel. According to some sources, one reason for peeling after rather than before boiling is that the sheath of leaves encasing each shoot contains compounds that help soften the fibers and whiten the flesh.

SUGGESTED RECIPES: Grill raw, unpeeled shoots over a fire for about 15 minutes, letting each diner peel his or her own portion, then sprinkle with salt like corn at a cookout. Blanched, peeled shoots can be added to miso soup, miso stew (with root vegetables and, optionally, chicken), nimono, *itameni*, *tamagotoji*, tempura, or *takenoko gohan* (rice boiled with bamboo shoots, salt, and a little sake). The leaves of *chishimazasa* and other bamboos are often used to wrap foods, in part because they contain substances that delay spoiling.

Fuki   蕗 (VARIANTS: 苳, 款冬, 菜蕗)

ENGLISH COMMON NAME: Butterbur, Japanese sweet coltsfoot. (Butterbur refers to all species in the genus *Petasites*. Coltsfoot is also a common name for *Tussilago farfara*, a different member of the family Asteraceae.)

SCIENTIFIC NAME: *Petasites japonicus*.

Fuki

AVAILABILITY: Common throughout Japan in both mountainous and flatland regions, from Hokkaido to Okinawa. From Akita northward, a larger subspecies called *akitabuki*, *ezobuki*, or *obuki* (*Petasites japonicus* subsp. *giganteus*) dominates. Also native to China and Korea; naturalized in northern and central Europe, Hawaii, the Pacific Northwest, and Ontario. Easily cultivated in gardens, although prone to spreading aggressively via rhizomes.

DESCRIPTION: *Fuki* flower buds are a beloved sign of spring throughout Japan, relished for their pungent, bitter flavor, while the simmered leafstalks are a classic of country cooking. In *kaiseki* cuisine the buds are sometimes used as a seasonal addition to the light, clear soups served between more elaborate courses. Colonies of the pale-yellow-green buds (*fuki-no-to*) emerge from the earth in earliest spring, sometimes even melting holes in thin snow as they seek the sun. Approximately the size of a brussels sprout, the oval bud is wrapped in pointed, leaf-like bracts. Male flowers are light yellow while females are white, but both are edible. After the buds blossom, round, toothed leaves emerge on thick, rough stalks. Ainu folklore tells of a race of small people called the *koropokkur*, or "people beneath the butterbur leaves," who inhabited the Sakhalin and Kuril islands in ancient times.

TOXICITY/POISONOUS LOOK-ALIKES: *Fuki* contains pyrrolizidine alkaloids, which are harmful to the liver and may cause cancer. The plant should not be eaten raw or in large quantities. The buds resemble those of toxic *fukujuso* (*Adonis ramosa*, *Adonis amurensis*), which also emerge from the earth in early spring. The bracts of the latter lack *fuki*'s white fuzz and contain flowers with large, bright-yellow petals as opposed to spikes of tiny, pale-yellow ones.

HARVEST: Choose compact flower buds that have not yet begun to open and harvest by twisting and snapping at the base. Those in snowy regions are said to have the best fragrance. Because the plants spread by vigorous underground rhizomes, overharvesting is not usually a concern. Later in the season, the fat leafstalks can be harvested with a Japanese *kama* (hand sickle) or knife and all but the most tender young leaves discarded. Look for large plants growing in moist soil, choosing fat, green (not reddish) stalks.

PREPARATION: *Flower buds*: Some of the bitterness in the buds may be removed by either rubbing them with salt and rinsing; blanching briefly; or shredding and soaking in cold water. Be careful not to remove too much of the bitterness, however, as this is their distinguishing characteristic. *Leafstalks and young leaves*: Slice off tops and bottoms and boil in plenty of water for 10 minutes (don't chop them smaller than necessary to fit in the pot, as this will make the tedious task of peeling still more difficult), adding a handful of rice bran if you have it. Drain and submerge in cold water. Peel off the stringy outer skin, working from both the top and bottom of each stalk to make sure you remove all the fibers. Submerge in fresh water for about 12 hours, changing when it becomes brown. Tender young leaves are sometimes cooked with the stalks, and do not require any preparation beyond blanching.

SUGGESTED RECIPES: *Flower buds*: *fuki miso* (finely chopped buds sautéed in oil and mixed with miso to form a paste), tempura (remove outer bracts before frying), miso soup, sautéed and marinated in soy sauce and *dashi*, blanched and marinated in *nihaizu*. *Leafstalks*: itamemono (especially with fish cakes or abura-age), *nimomo*, *tsukudani*. Strong seasoning tempers the medicinal flavor. In Japan the mature leaves are not typically eaten, but in Korea they are used to wrap rice and meat.

Gyoja ninniku   行者葫

ENGLISH COMMON NAME: Alpine leek, victory onion.

SCIENTIFIC NAME: *Allium ochotense.*

ALSO CALLED: *Ainu negi, yamabiru, pukusa* (Ainu language).

AVAILABILITY: Native to eastern Asia and Russia; a similar species, *Allium victorialis*, grows in Alaska and the mountains of Europe and Asia. In Japan, *gyoja ninniku* grows in the mountains of Honshu and lowlands of Hokkaido and on the Sea of Japan coast. Ramp (*Allium tricoccum*), a similar-tasting species, grows widely in the eastern half of North America.

Gyoja ninniku.

DESCRIPTION: *Gyoja ninniku* belongs to the same family as garlic and onions and shares a passing resemblance to those familiar plants. However, the leaves—which are broad and ribbed at the top, narrow and magenta or white near the ground—have a sweet, spicy flavor that is exquisite both raw and cooked. The name means "ascetic's garlic," a reference to the legend that monks ensconced in the mountains for spiritual training used to eat the plants to bolster their energy. A seasonal treat for most mainland Japanese, *gyoja ninniku* was an essential element of traditional Ainu diets. Dubbing the plant *haru ikkeu*, or "backbone of life," they ate it fresh in early spring and harvested large quantities when it flowered to dry and store in woven bags called *saranipu* for flavoring soups through the winter. It makes an outstanding addition to a bowl of miso soup.

TOXICITY/POISONOUS LOOK-ALIKES: Resembles the poisonous lily of the valley (*Convallaria majalis, suzuran*) and false hellebores (*Veratrum* spp.) such as *Veratrum viride, V. oxysepalum* (*baikeiso*), *V. stamineum* (*kobaikeiso*), and, to a lesser degree, autumn crocus (*Colchicum autumnale, inusafuran*). The garlicky scent is one important key to correct identification.

HARVEST: The plants are slow growing and vulnerable to overharvest. Avoid pulling up the bulbs; instead pluck tender individual leaves or slice them off an inch or so above ground level to avoid the dirt stuck to the base. May be picked from early spring until the plants flower.

PREPARATION: No special processing required.

SUGGESTED RECIPES: Tempura, miso soup, *tamagotoji, tamagoyaki, shoyuzuke*. The blanched leaves are sometimes seasoned with *sumiso* or *nihaizu* or added to nimono, but the seasonings in these dishes rather overwhelm the delicate flavor of the leaves. The tender young leaves and stems may be eaten raw with miso or *sumiso*, if you enjoy the pungency of raw garlic. The Ainu steam the stalks in bundles or add to soups and stews.

Icho (TREE) — 銀杏, 公孫樹
Ginnan (SEED) — 銀杏

ENGLISH COMMON NAME: Ginkgo, maidenhair tree.

SCIENTIFIC NAME: *Ginkgo biloba.*

ALSO CALLED: *Okyaku.*

AVAILABILITY: Endangered in the wild, with the known range limited to a single mountain in China, but widely planted as landscape trees and for medicinal use in Japan, the US, and elsewhere.

DESCRIPTION: If you are served the savory custard called *chawanmushi*, you may be lucky enough to find a single smooth, yellow or pea-green orb about the size of an olive embedded in it. This is the seed of the *icho* tree, a species that predates dinosaurs and has a lifespan of over two thousand years (although the edible portion is typically called a "nut" in English, this is a botanical misnomer). *Icho* are not native to Japan but were brought from China some time before the 1500s and planted widely at Buddhist temples, growing into magnificent tall trees that flame brilliant yellow each fall. Frugal city-dwellers can sometimes be spotted collecting the seeds, which also appear on grocery store shelves for a brief period each fall. The Japanese characters for *ginnan* mean "silver apricot," a reference to the appearance of their fleshy but inedible seedcoats.

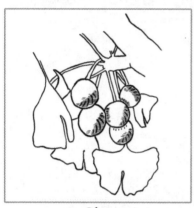

Icho.

TOXICITY/POISONOUS LOOK-ALIKES: Touching the juicy flesh surrounding the seeds causes a skin rash in some people. Eating too many can cause dizziness, spasms, and indigestion due to a substance called ginkgotoxin in the raw seeds. Children in particular should take care not to eat more than a few cooked *ginnan*.

HARVEST: The plant's distinctive fan-shaped leaves make them easy to identify. The seeds drop in late fall, covered in soft, stinking yellow flesh that can cause a rash; rubber gloves are a good idea when harvesting.

Ginnan only form on female trees, so if you've got your eye on one that never seems to bear, it's probably a male (which are preferentially planted in the US to avoid the stinky mess).

PREPARATION: Bury the *ginnan* in soil to rot off their seedcoats, expos-ing the creamy white shells. Alternately, place them in a plastic bag with a little sand and loosen the flesh by rolling them around, then rinse clean. Dry briefly in the sun, being careful not to overdry. At this point the seeds can be stored in the refrigerator for 2 to 3 months; for longer storage, some sources recommend burying 1–2 feet deep in sandy soil with the seedcoats still attached. When ready to eat, remove the shells with a nutcracker, then peel off the brown inner skin. Soaking in warm water for a few minutes or roasting in a frying pan will loosen the skin.

SUGGESTED RECIPES: Roast the peeled *ginnan* and sprinkle with salt for a snack; cook with rice for *takikomi gohan*, adding mushrooms or other vegetables and chicken if you like; boil and suspend in *chawanmushi* (savory custard); thread onto skewers and add to oden.

Itadori 虎杖

ENGLISH COMMON NAME: Japanese knotweed.

SCIENTIFIC NAME: *Reynoutria japonica (Fallopia japonica, Polygonum cuspidatum)*.

ALSO CALLED: *Sukanpo, dongui*.

AVAILABILITY: Ubiquitous from Kyushu to Hokkaido. Invasive in Europe and North America.

DESCRIPTION: A common roadside weed, *itadori* grows throughout Japan on disturbed land. In Hokkaido, great colonies of *oitadori* (giant knotweed, *Fallopia sachaliensis*) measuring 6 feet tall or more line the roads and fields. The characters for the plant mean "tiger wand"—an imaginative allusion to their maroon mottling and tall, tapering stems.

Itadori.

Equally fancifully, Japanese children of old were warned that the hollow stems concealed snakes. Although *itadori* lacks the romance of certain other sansai such as *tara-no-me* and *fuki-no-to*, its sharply sour flavor has a nostalgic appeal all its own.

TOXICITY/POISONOUS LOOK-ALIKES: *Itadori* contains oxalic acid, which can cause diarrhea and even kidney stones if consumed in large quantities; however, spinach, rhubarb, and many other common foods do as well. Blanching removes some of the offending substance, and in any case, the season is short, making excessive consumption unlikely.

HARVEST: Pick the fat, asparagus-like shoots when they are about a foot tall. The plants give a satisfying "pop" when snapped off at the base, a sign that their tough fibers have not yet developed (later, they bend rather than snap). The growing tips of larger plants can be picked as well—look for the point near the top where the stem becomes glossy rather than powdery white and listen for that pop—but since the stalks become thinner the taller they grow, you will have more peeling to do with less reward.

PREPARATION: Strip off the leaves and papery sheaths around the joints. Peel from the bottom up with a knife or your fingernails; there is no need to peel the tender upper section. Blanch in saltwater (2 tablespoons salt to 6 cups water) for about 15 seconds, just until the color lightens—over-boiling spoils the crunchy texture. Plunge into cold water and soak, tasting periodically and stopping when you like the taste (an overnight bath renders them practically flavorless). Western chefs fond of foraged foods don't bother with leaching, treating the plant like rhubarb, but the sour flavor can be overwhelming in the dishes listed below.

SUGGESTED RECIPES: Itamemono, nimono, *sumiso-ae*, sunomono (especially with *sanbaizu* and grated daikon). The leaves can be picked in fall and used raw in tempura.

Kajime 搗布 (KAJIME), 蔓荒布 (TSURU-ARAME), 黒布 (KUROME)

NOTE: On the Noto Peninsula, this term refers to both *tsuru-arame* and *kurome*.

SCIENTIFIC NAME: *Ecklonia stolonifera* (tsuru-arame), *Ecklonia kurome* (kurome).

AVAILABILITY: Both species found in the Sea of Japan; *kurome* also found on Japan's Pacific coast from central Honshu to Kyushu and in the Seto Inland Sea.

DESCRIPTION: Both *tsuru-arame* and *kurome* have large, flat blades that grow from a single stipe, or stem, and resemble yellow-green crepe paper. *Tsuru-arame* grows in rocky areas with strong waves at a depth of about 3 to 60 feet, while *kurome* grows in areas where the waves are slightly gentler. Both are extremely viscous when prepared fresh and can be bitter tasting. Even in Japan, *kajime* is not widely available outside areas such as the Noto Peninsula where it grows and is part of the traditional diet. In ancient times, the word

Kajime.

kajime referred to pulverized *arame*, a separate species in the *Ecklonia* genus of kelp that is still eaten.

TOXICITY/POISONOUS LOOK-ALIKES: Virtually all seaweeds are non-toxic but should nevertheless be competently identified before harvesting. One genus to watch out for is *Desmarestia*, a brown algae that contains sulfuric acid and can cause stomach upset. Make sure to always harvest seaweed from clean water.

HARVEST: Collect washed-up *kajime* along the shore after storms in winter and spring; the action of the waves will have leached away some of the bitterness. Harvest from January through May. The new buds that emerge in late winter are said to be especially tasty.

PREPARATION: Since *kajime* can be quite bitter, especially if it is harvested while growing rather than collected on shore, it requires careful preparation. Shred finely, cook in boiling water for 15 minutes, then drain and soak in three changes of water for a total of about 30 minutes, stirring frequently. Use fresh or spread on mats to dry in the sun for about two days. Dried *kajime* is less viscous than fresh.

SUGGESTED RECIPES: Nimono (alone or with fish or tofu), *kasu jiru*, miso soup, *kajime gohan* (chop *kajime* finely and simmer with shoyu, mirin, and sake before folding into freshly cooked rice). Miso and ginger are good flavor matches.

Kogomi   屈

ENGLISH COMMON NAME: Ostrich fern.

SCIENTIFIC NAME: *Matteuccia struthiopteris* (*Onoclea struthiopteris*).

ALSO CALLED: *Kusasotetsu, kogome.*

AVAILABILITY: Abundant from northern Kyushu to Hokkaido. Also native from the East Coast of the US to Nebraska, as well as throughout Canada and Alaska.

DESCRIPTION: Growing in colonies in forested mountains and damp flatlands, the plump, vibrant green shoots of *kogomi* ferns are slightly less widespread than *warabi* or *zenmai*, the other two fiddleheads commonly eaten in Japan. *Kogomi* are appreciated not so much for their flavor as their lack of it; among a host of sansai that require time-consuming processing or consumption in tiny quantities, these mild plants can be eaten freely. They are particularly beloved in the northern snow country for their beautiful shape and color after the long winter. The name derives from the verb *kogomu*, an alternate reading of *kagamu* meaning to stoop or bend over, because the new fronds lean forward. Their other name, *kusasotetsu*, references their similarity in appearance to cycads, or *sotetsu*. *Akakogomi* (*Diplazium squamigerum*), meaning red *kogomi*, is an entirely different and even more prized species.

Kogomi.

TOXICITY/POISONOUS LOOK-ALIKES: Some varieties of fern are toxic or carcinogenic (and not at all tasty). Their fiddleheads may at first appear similar to edible varieties, so as always make sure you are certain of what you have picked or purchased before eating it. *Kogomi* is among the safest of fiddleheads. However, because a small number of food-poisoning outbreaks in the US and Canada have been linked to eating raw or undercooked *kogomi*, health authorities there recommend boiling for 15 minutes or steaming for 10 to 12 minutes before eating.

HARVEST: *Kogomi* grows in vase-shaped clumps. Snap off several fiddleheads per clump together with a few inches of stem when they are still tightly curled and no more than 3 to 4 inches tall. The window of opportunity is short; miss it and the fronds become overly fibrous.

PREPARATION: Remove the flaky brown scales by washing. No special processing is required. To use in ohitashi or aemono, blanch for about 1 minute in salted water until they take on a whitish cast (note health warning above).

SUGGESTED RECIPES: Blanch and top with shoyu and *katsuo* flakes or lightly crushed sesame seeds; aemono (especially rich sauces containing nuts, seeds, or mayonnaise), itamemono, nimono, sunomono (*sanbaizu*), tempura.

Koshiabura   漉油

SCIENTIFIC NAME: *Chengiopanax sciadophylloides* (*Acanthopanax sciadophylloides*).

AVAILABILITY: Sunny forests from Hokkaido to Kyushu.

Koshiabura.

DESCRIPTION: Called the Queen of Sansai, the translucent new leaves of the *koshiabura* tree share the superb fragrance of their partner on the throne, King *Tara-no-me*. They are far more abundant than the latter, however, since they emerge from each of the countless branches of deciduous trees reaching sixty-five feet tall. The problem, of course, is getting to them. Smaller specimens can sometimes be found in the understory of cedar forests, making a better candidate for picking. The *abura*, or oil, in the plant's name derives from the fact that in the Heian period oil harvested from a related species was used to produce a lacquer-like paint called *kinshitsu* that prevented rust on weapons and mold on paper. *Koshi* may refer to the place in China from which that technology originated.

TOXICITY/POISONOUS LOOK-ALIKES: *Yama-urushi* (*Toxicodendron trichocarpum*) leaves bud at the same time and look somewhat similar to *koshiabura* but redder. They cause a rash in many people.

HARVEST: The new leaves are most prized when they are still gathered in bundles pointed upward like calligraphy brushes. As they unfurl and mature they become more bitter but may be eaten as long as they remain tender and translucent.

PREPARATION: Remove the scale-like leaves at the base if they feel overly tough. Very young, tender leaves and stems need only be briefly blanched. Older leaves can be boiled in saltwater for a few minutes to lessen the bitterness or soaked in water after blanching. For tempura, use raw.

SUGGESTED RECIPES: Tempura renders the bitterness of the leaves unnoticeable, leaving only their lovely fragrance. The leaves are also tasty sautéed in a tablespoon or so of oil till crisp, then seasoned with salt. Use the blanched stems—which are milder than the leaves—in aemono or ohitashi.

Mitsuba 三つ葉

ENGLISH COMMON NAME: Japanese honewort, wild chervil, Japanese parsley.

SCIENTIFIC NAME: *Cryptotaenia japonica* (*Cryptotaenia canadensis* subsp. *japonica*).

ALSO CALLED: *Yamamitsuba, nomitsuba, mitsubazeri.*

AVAILABILITY: Abundant throughout Japan and eastern Asia. The also edible species *C. canadensis* (wild chervil) grows abundantly in the eastern half of the US and Canada.

DESCRIPTION: *Mitsuba* means "three leaves" in Japanese, an apt name for this fragrant plant with toothed, clover-shaped foliage. Widely cultivated on Japanese farms and gardens and sold in grocery stores year-round, *mitsuba* can easily be found growing wild in moist woods and along shady rural roadsides. The wild variety tends to be less tender but more flavorful than the cultivated. The pleasant, crunchy texture and herby taste of the blanched leaves and stalks make them a popular addition to cultivated greens such as spinach and *komatsuna*, as well as a common garnish for soups and egg dishes. The roots and woody, lower portion of the stems (rootstocks) are delectable and sweet but much less frequently eaten than the leaves, perhaps because they can be quite woody depending on their age and growing conditions.

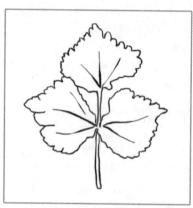

Mitsuba.

TOXICITY/POISONOUS LOOK-ALIKES: The foliage is somewhat similar to that of the poisonous *kitsunenobotan* (*Ranunculus silerifolius*), *karasubishaku* (*Pinellia ternate*, crowdipper), and *umanomitsuba* (*Sanicula chinensis*), although careful observation reveals different leaf shapes for each. *Mitsuba*'s distinctive fragrance also aids in identification.

HARVEST: Pluck the leaves or pull the whole plant up by its roots, which are also edible. Best picked before the sprays of petite, white flowers emerge.

PREPARATION: Use raw or dip very briefly in boiling water; no special processing is required.

SUGGESTED RECIPES: *Leaves*: miso soup, suimono, *chawanmushi, tamago-toji*, ohitashi (often in combination with other greens). *Roots: kinpira.*

Mozuku 海蘊, 水雲, 海雲, 藻付

SCIENTIFIC NAME: *Nemacystus decipiens.*

ALSO CALLED: *Mozoku.*

AVAILABILITY: Grows off the coast of Japan from Hokkaido south as well as in other parts of the world including around the Hawaiian Islands. Most of what is sold in Japan under the name *mozuku* is in fact a completely different species, either *Cladosiphon okamuranus* (Okinawa mozuku, widely cultivated in Okinawa) or *Sphaerotrichia divaricata* (ishi *mozuku* or *kusa mozuku*, which grows on both coasts of North America, including off British Columbia in the west and from New Jersey north in the east).

Mozuku.

DESCRIPTION: *Mozuku* means "attaches to seaweed" in Japanese, a name derived from this brown algae's habit of growing on members of the genus *Sargassum.* The fronds are mild or slightly bitter with a silky, extremely viscous texture and a shape similar to angel hair pasta. *Mozuku* is often eaten in a vinegary sauce and sometimes used in soups or tempura. Of the several pairs of characters used to write the word *mozuku*, one means "water cloud" and another "ocean cloud," both poetic references to the underwater appearance of the long, thin, branching fronds. Coastal people may well have enjoyed this slimy delicacy long before urbanites learned of its pleasures. *Mozuku* was difficult to dry and therefore to transport before the development of modern drying machines, though it was sometimes preserved in salt. Probably for this reason it is not mentioned in ancient poems, typically written by urban elites, or in lists of seaweeds accepted as tribute.

TOXICITY/POISONOUS LOOK-ALIKES: Virtually all seaweeds are non-toxic, but should nevertheless be competently identified before harvesting. One genus to watch out for is *Desmarestia*, a brown algae that contains sulfuric acid and can cause stomach upset. Make sure to always harvest seaweed from clean water.

HARVEST: Depending on the location, *mozuku* can be harvested from February through September. Look for *Nemacystus decipiens* growing in the subtidal zone on certain *Sargassum* species, such as *yatsumatamoku* (*S. patens*). *Ishimozuku* grows on rocks and is harvested between June and August.

PREPARATION: Wash fresh *mozuku* well, cut into bite-size lengths, and drain. Blanching removes bitterness and transforms the color from brown to bright green. It can be preserved by mixing with equal parts salt, but freezing is a better option today. *Okinawa mozuku* is sometimes dried using professional-grade dehydrators.

SUGGESTED RECIPES: Sunomono (*sanbaizu, nihaizu, ponzu, tosazu, sumiso*; garnish with finely grated ginger or wasabi), tempura, miso soup, *zosui*.

Myoga 茗荷

ENGLISH COMMON NAME: Japanese ginger.

SCIENTIFIC NAME: *Zingiber mioga.*

ALSO CALLED: *Mega* (archaic).

AVAILABILITY: Wild range limited to shady, moist areas in Japan, China, and Korea, but occasionally grown as a garden plant in the West.

DESCRIPTION: *Myoga* belongs to the same family as ginger and resembles that plant somewhat in flavor and appearance. Rather than the rhizomes, however, the flower buds are eaten. These emerge at ground level in midsummer and again in fall, eventually sending up a flamboyant spray of soft, yellow petals that wilts in a single day. Some believe *myoga* was introduced from China many centuries ago and planted widely in farmhouse gardens; the "wild" plants one sometimes finds in village woods are likely descendants of garden escapees that spread in favorable conditions. Farmers bury the plants in rice husks in early spring to produce young, tender shoots called *myoga take* for their resemblance to miniature bamboo (*take*); this, however, is not a wild food. According to folklore, eating *myoga* makes one forgetful.

Myoga.

TOXICITY/POISONOUS LOOK-ALIKES: Some English-language sources report that the mature leaves and rhizomes are poisonous. However, while the mature leaves are never eaten in Japan, they were traditionally valued for their germ-killing properties and used to wrap dumplings and rice balls.

HARVEST: The plump, glossy buds are best picked when firmly closed, as their lovely scent fades and their tightly layered texture coarsens after the blossom emerges. The dusky rose color of the buds and their location beneath abundant leaves makes them easy to miss. Slice off at ground level with a small knife.

PREPARATION: *Myoga* may be eaten raw or cooked, requiring no special processing. Shred finely and use sparingly, as the flavor is potent.

SUGGESTED RECIPES: *Raw:* add to sauces for dipping or topping chilled soba or somen noodles, sashimi, *hiyayakko* (chilled tofu), or *yudofu* (boiled tofu); combine with vegetables such as cucumber, eggplant, or okra in salads, sunomono, and ohitashi; make into *shibazuke, nukazuke, misozuke, kasuzuke,* or *amazuzuke* pickles. *Cooked:* tempura, *tamagotoji*, miso soup, and suimono.

Nirinso   二輪草

ENGLISH COMMON NAME: Flaccid anemone.

SCIENTIFIC NAME: *Anemone flaccida.*

ALSO CALLED: *Fukubera, sobana, yamasoba, komochigusa, pukusakina* (Ainu language).

AVAILABILITY: Natural range limited to the forests and forest edges of eastern Asia, but sometimes grown as a garden flower in the West.

DESCRIPTION: *Nirinso* is a delicate woodland plant that prefers dappled shade and moist soil, often growing in large colonies near mountain streams. The dainty white flowers bloom for just a few days in spring, prompting comparisons to ill-fated beauties who die young. Each plant usually has two flowers that bloom in quick succession; this is the source of their name, meaning "two-flower plant" in Japanese. *Nirinso* is an important food of the Ainu, who gather it in large quantities in early spring to dry (or today, freeze) for winter use.

TOXICITY/POISONOUS LOOK-ALIKES: *Nirinso* belongs to the Ranunculaceae (buttercup) family, which has many poisonous members. Be absolutely sure you have correctly identified *nirinso* before picking and eating it. It especially resembles and sometimes grows intermingled with deadly poisonous members of the genus *Aconitum* (*torikabuto*, wolfsbane). It also resembles the poisonous *kikuzaki-ichige* (*Anemone pseudoaltaica*). It is wise to wait until *nirinso* flowers before picking it, as it is easier to distinguish from poisonous look-alikes at this stage. The plants may cause skin or gastrointestinal irritation when raw, but not when dried or cooked.

Nirinso.

HARVEST: Pluck young leaves and flowers in spring, when in bloom.

PREPARATION: *Nirinso* has a light, clean flavor that requires no processing beyond a quick blanching. The flowers and buds may be eaten along with the stalks and leaves. Preserve by drying in the sun or blanching and freezing.

SUGGESTED RECIPES: Ohitashi, sunomono, suimono. Larger, older leaves can be used in tempura. The dried plant is a classic ingredient in the staple soup of the Ainu, *ohaw*.

Onigurumi 鬼胡桃

ENGLISH COMMON NAME: Japanese walnut.

SCIENTIFIC NAME: *Juglans mandshurica* var. *sachalinensis*.

ALSO CALLED: *Ogurumi* (archaic).

AVAILABILITY: Native to Japan (primarily northern areas) and Sakhalin Island. A small, heart-shaped variety of the species called the heart-

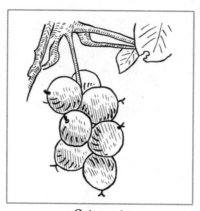

nut (*Juglans mandshurica* var. *cordiformis*, *himegurumi*) was introduced to the US in the 1860s and grown commercially for a period; it is still planted ornamentally and sometimes for nuts in northeastern states too cold for the more common Persian walnut.

DESCRIPTION: As the recent discovery in Fukushima Prefecture of a three-thousand-year-old basket filled with hundreds of *onigurumi* suggests, wild walnuts have played an important role in the Japanese diet since the Jomon period, when they were likely a staple

Onigurumi.

food; one of their first written mentions comes in an acrostic poem published in the early tenth century. Smaller and tougher to crack than English walnuts, the flavor and texture of *onigurumi* are slightly different as well (and different again from the wild black walnuts of the US). Their name, meaning "devil walnuts," may derive from the bumpy, "ugly" texture of the nuts, though it is equally fitting for the extreme hardness of the shells. The trees prefer moist soil and often grow along rivers and creeks in the mountains.

TOXICITY/POISONOUS LOOK-ALIKES: None.

HARVEST: *Onigurumi* are ready to harvest between September and October. You may notice nuts on the ground earlier in summer, but these will generally be empty and not worth collecting. Either gather fallen nuts or beat the critters by knocking the trees with a long stick to shake free just-ripe nuts. Wear gloves or use tongs to keep the husks from staining your fingers black.

PREPARATION: Like all walnuts, *onigurumi* grow inside a thick, green husk. This husk develops black spots just before the nuts fully mature and drop from the tree, eventually turning completely black and wrinkled. It can be removed by hand with some effort or will rot off if the walnuts are left to sit in a bucket of water or buried in soil for several weeks. In either case the inner shells should be scrubbed clean and thoroughly dried in the sun before storing. The next challenge is removing the devilishly hard shells. It is well worth investing in two tools for this task: a nutcracker made especially for *onigurumi*, with a cup on one side and a sharp blade on the other (available at Japanese home centers), and a nut pick. Soaking the nuts overnight in a bowl of boiling water with a handful or two of wood ash thrown in works wonders to soften the shells. This is the method used when making sugar-coated *onigurumi*, a traditional sweet, because it is otherwise nearly impossible to extract the meats whole. Unfortunately, the ash also softens the nutmeats, which will need to be redried or roasted if not used immediately. Alternatively, soak nuts in their shells in cold water overnight, then roast in a frying pan until the seams pop open. Split in two with a knife and pry the meat out. The papery inner skin can more easily be removed if the nuts are briefly boiled in ash-water, though there is rarely a real need to do so.

SUGGESTED RECIPES: Eat raw or roasted; chop finely or pound in a pestle to make *kurumi-ae*, a sauce for cultivated or wild vegetables; add to cookies, cakes, or mochi; make *kurumi-dofu*, a custard-like dish of smoothly pounded nuts mixed with water, sugar, and salt, thickened with starch.

Oubayuri   大姥百合

ENGLISH COMMON NAME: Japanese cardiocrinum.

SCIENTIFIC NAME: *Cardiocrinum cordatum var. glehnii.*

ALSO CALLED: *Turep* (Ainu language).

AVAILABILITY: Grows from central Honshu north through Hokkaido. *Ubayuri*, a smaller variety of the plant, grows as far south as Kyushu.

DESCRIPTION: Although *oubayuri* bears lily-like flowers on its tall stems and means "old lady lily" in Japanese, with *o-* indicating the large north-

Oubayuri.

ern variety, this common plant of the forest floor is not a true lily. The young heart-shaped leaves are reputedly edible but rarely eaten. The bulbs, by contrast, are an important traditional food of the Ainu, who extract from them a flavorless, high-quality starch used to make dense ceremonial dumplings called *turep shito.* After the starch is removed, the pulp that remains is fermented, dried in donut-shaped cakes, and later pounded to make flour. Fortunately for the lazier modern foragers, the fresh bulbs are also delicious either fried or boiled without such laborious preparation. The plant's name relates to its odd life cycle, as well as to the Japanese homophone *ha*, which means both "teeth" and "leaves." The *oubayuri* flowers only once, after six to eight years of leaf growth, and then promptly expires. Thus by the time it reaches its metaphorical womanhood, decked out in gorgeous blossoms, most of its leaves (*ha*) have already fallen off or begun to decay, suggesting a tooth(*ha*)less old woman at death's door.

TOXICITY/POISONOUS LOOK-ALIKES: None.

HARVEST: Dig the scaly bulbs in spring after the young leaves have emerged, selecting the fattest stems possible (four- or five-year-old plants). In Hokkaido, the flowering of wild red azaleas in May is a sign that the bulbs are ready. Try digging around a dried stalk; after flowering, the spent bulbs produce offspring.

PREPARATION: Remove the papery brown outer skin and roots. Separate the bulb into scales (layers) and carefully wash the dirt from each one. Trim off any brown spots with a knife.

SUGGESTED RECIPES: The scales are sometimes added to nimono or *chawanmushi* but take particularly well to fatty, creamy ingredients. Use in tempura or fry unbattered in a generous amount of oil until lightly browned, about 5 minutes per side, and serve with salt or soy sauce. Alternately, boil for about 10 minutes, mash with a fork, and season with oil or butter and salt. The result resembles a cross between mashed potatoes and spaghetti squash. Leftovers can be formed into patties and browned in oil.

Sansho 山椒

ENGLISH COMMON NAME: Japanese pepper, Japanese prickly ash.

SCIENTIFIC NAME: *Zanthoxylum piperitum.*

ALSO CALLED: *Ki-no-me* (young leaves), *hajikami* (archaic).

AVAILABILITY: Native from Kyushu to Hokkaido, as well as in parts of Korea and China. *Zanthoxylum americanum* (prickly ash), which is native to the eastern half of the US and Canada, can also be used as a pepper substitute.

DESCRIPTION: Although *sansho* is called Japanese pepper, it does not belong to the same botanical family as black pepper (*Piper nigrum*) but

Sansho.

rather is a type of prickly ash closely related to and quite similar in flavor to Sichuan pepper, which comes from *Zanthoxylum* species such as *Z. simulans* and *Z. bungeanum*. The fruits are collected in fall when their husks split open; the glossy black seeds are discarded and the husks ground to produce a citrusy, tongue-tingling seasoning essential to Japanese cuisine. Archaeological remains suggest *sansho* has been used in cooking since the Jomon period. It is traditionally paired with grilled eel and bamboo shoots and is also included in *shichi-mi togarashi*, a mixture of chili and ground seasonings such as *sansho*, roasted orange peel, black and white sesame seeds, hemp seeds, ginger, *nori*, poppy seeds, yuzu, *shiso*, and rapeseed. The plants both grow wild in the mountains and are cultivated in greenhouses. The wild variety has stronger *aku* and its leaves discolor quickly.

TOXICITY/POISONOUS LOOK-ALIKES: Inuzansho (*Zanshoxylum schinifolium*; literally "dog *sansho*") looks very similar to *sansho*, though its scent is quite different and its thorns are not opposite. Although *Z. shinifolium* is used in China for Sichuan pepper, Japanese foragers avoid it except for medicinal use.

HARVEST: Fruits form only on female bushes. For powdered *sansho*, pick the pocked fruits in fall when they turn a lovely pinkish brown and split open to reveal a single shiny black seed. Earlier in the season, pick leaves from either male or female bushes and flower buds from male plants. Beware the pair of thorns at the base of each leafstalk.

PREPARATION: Dry the husks well, separate and discard the stems and seeds, and grind to a powder in a spice grinder or pepper mill. When using the leaves for a garnish, crush forcefully between your palms to bring out their fragrance.

SUGGESTED RECIPES: *Powdered husks*: use to season chicken, fish, tofu teriyaki, grilled eel, or noodle broths. *Green fruit*: soak in white liquor (a type of flavorless shochu with less than 36% alcohol content; vodka may be substituted) with rock sugar for several months to produce a flavored drink; combine with *chirimen jakko* (dried whitebait) and seasonings to make *chirimenzansho*, a topping for rice; pickle in salt to serve as a nibble with alcohol or to fold into rice. *Young leaves*: lay decoratively on tofu *dengaku* or pound to a paste with sweetened miso to spread on top; scatter on simmered bamboo shoots or sea-bream heads and bones (*tai no arani*); float in clear soup or *akadashi* (red miso) soup; add to aemono, sushi, or tempura; make a flavored vinegar. *Buds, flowers, and young leaves*: *tsukudani*.

Sugina 杉菜

ENGLISH COMMON NAME: Field horsetail.

SCIENTIFIC NAME: *Equisetum arvense*.

ALSO CALLED: *Tsukushi, tsukuzukushi, tsukushinbo* (reproductive shoots).

AVAILABILITY: Native throughout the temperate and arctic northern hemisphere, including nearly every US state.

DESCRIPTION: The Japanese words *sugina* and *tsukushi* refer to two types of finger-length shoot that look completely different but in fact belong to the same plant, a relative of the ferns (called *sugina* when mature). *Tsukushi*—the reproductive part of the plant, equivalent to its flower—emerge first in early spring. When these slender, pale-tan tubes with caps covered in hexagonal spore cases release their spores and begin

Tsukushi and sugina.

to wither, the infertile *sugina* emerge, each resembling a miniature green bottle-brush. *Tsukushi* and *sugina* are connected by an underground web of rhizomes. Both prefer sun and can be found around farm fields, where they root themselves so tenaciously farmers call them *jigoku-gusa*, or "hellweed." Although *tsukushi* and *sugina* are both edible, *tsukushi* are eaten much more frequently in Japan. They have little flavor or texture; their main value lies in their interesting shape and pretty rosy-tan color.

TOXICITY/POISONOUS LOOK-ALIKES: The infertile shoots of *sugina* (field horsetail) look very similar to those of *inusugina* (*Equisetum palustre*, marsh horsetail), which are inedible and possibly harmful in large quantities.

HARVEST: Pick young *tsukushi* whose spores have not yet emerged and that have little distance between the nodes (like most living things, the stems lose their moisture and fragrance as they age). You will need quite a few of these insubstantial plants to make even a moderate side dish, but fortunately they are abundant and fairly resistant to overharvest. Pick *sugina* when very young and tender, unless you plan to dry it for *furikake*, in which case older plants may be used.

PREPARATION: *Tsukushi*: Gently pluck off the leaves encircling each node on the *tsukushi*'s stem, which have an unpleasant taste. Remove the cap (called a strobilus) as well if you dislike bitter flavors. *Tsukushi* dry out quickly, so use soon after harvesting. If you are using overgrown plants whose caps have opened, blanch and run under water for half an hour or so before continuing with the recipe. Blanch before using in sunomono or aemono. *Sugina*: No special preparation required.

SUGGESTED RECIPES: *Tsukushi*: Itamemono, *kinpira, tsukudani, tamago-toji*, miso soup, *suimono, sunomono (sanbaizu)*, aemono (*karashiae, goma-ae*), *tsukushi* rice (simmer *tsukushi* with mirin, soy sauce, and sake, then fold into rice boiled with a little salt). *Sugina*: tsukudani, nameshi, tempura, *furikake* (dry *sugina* in the sun, powder between your fingers or in a spice grinder, and mix with sesame seeds and salt).

Tara-no-ki 楤の木

ENGLISH COMMON NAME: Japanese angelica tree.

SCIENTIFIC NAME: *Aralia elata (Aralia mandshurica)*.

ALSO CALLED: *Taranbo, tarappe, oni-no-kanabo, hebinoborazu, toritomarazu*.

AVAILABILITY: Grows throughout Japan in sunny forest clearings; also widely cultivated. It has been introduced to the US, including parts of the Midwest, Northeast, and West Coast, and is considered invasive in some places. Very similar in appearance to *Aralia spinosa*, which is native to the US and reportedly eaten as a potherb.

DESCRIPTION: Called the King of Sansai, the tender, fragrant young shoots of the *tara* bush (*tara-no-me*) are a beloved spring treat often enjoyed in tempura. The terminal shoots emerge from the tips of tall, viscously thorny gray branches pointing straight toward the sky like walking sticks left behind by a convention of oversized devils; thus their nickname, *oni-no-kanabo*, or "devil's staff" (similarly, *tara*'s American relative *Aralia spinosa* is called "devil's walking stick"). If you are lucky enough to find some while camping, try wrapping them in foil, roasting over an open fire, and eating them with miso as Japanese mountaineers do.

TOXICITY/POISONOUS LOOK-ALIKES: Both the young shoots and mature plants of *tara-no-ki* resemble *yama-urushi* (*Toxicodendron trichocarpum*), which causes inflammation and severe itchiness if touched. However, *yama-urushi* has smooth rather than thorny branches and reddish rather than green shoots.

Tara-no-me.

HARVEST: Slice off the young shoots with a knife when they are about 3 inches long, taking care to avoid the sharp thorns. Larger shoots lose their fragrance. The plants are highly vulnerable to overharvest; never pick the less tasty secondary shoots or lateral shoots that emerge lower on the branches.

PREPARATION: *Tara-no-me* have an exquisite fragrance and distinctive flavor that is lost with processing or overcooking. Trim off the leaf-like bracts and any hardened areas around the base. Blanch before using in aemono.

SUGGESTED RECIPES: Tempura, *tamagotoji*, nimono, itamemono, miso soup, aemono (especially with walnuts, peanuts, or sesame seeds).

Tengusa   天草

SCIENTIFIC NAME: The word *tengusa* refers to over twenty species in the genus *Gelidium* that are used to make the jelly-like noodles called *tokoroten*. Commonly used species include *Gelidium elegans* (*makusa*), *G. japonicum* (*onikusa*), *Ptilophora subcostata* (*hirakusa*, a member of the family Gelidiaceae), *G. subfastigiatum* (*nanbugusa*), and *G. pacificum* (*obusa*).

ALSO CALLED: *Sekkasai, makusa, tokorotengusa, kantengusa, korumoha* (archaic), *kokorobuto*.

AVAILABILITY: Various *Gelidium* species are distributed throughout Japan's coastal areas. In North America, *G. cartilagineum* is found all along the Pacific Coast and is used as a gelling agent. *G. nudifrons*, used the same way, is common in southern California.

DESCRIPTION: *Tengusa* is a type of red algae used to make the glassy gelled noodles called *tokoroten*, which are served chilled with sweet or savory toppings as a summer treat. The fluffy clumps of fine, highly branched red fronds grow in colonies on underwater rocks, reaching a height of about 8 inches. They have a distinctive oceany aroma that fades during the extensive processing they undergo between sea and plate. *Tokoroten* was historically an important element of Buddhist vegetarian cuisine, and specialty shops in Kyoto date at least to the Muromachi period (1336–1573). The association between the seaweed and the noodles is in fact so strong that the word *tengusa* is believed to derive from the last syllable of the word *tokoroten*.

Tengusa.

Tokoroten is in turn the source of *kanten*, a widely used gelling agent that gives liquids a firm, almost crunchy texture. *Kanten* is said to have been invented in the 1650s or '60s when an innkeeper near Kyoto threw some leftover *tokoroten* out in the snow, discovering that it was much more versatile and easier to use in this freeze-dried form.

TOXICITY/POISONOUS LOOK-ALIKES: Virtually all seaweeds are nontoxic but should nevertheless be competently identified before harvesting. One genus to watch out for is *Desmarestia*, a genus of brown algae that contain sulfuric acid and can cause stomach upset. Make sure to always harvest seaweed from clean water.

HARVEST: *Tengusa* grows on rocks from the low-tide line to deep water. It can be harvested underwater by diving or from a boat using a harrow-like implement or collected along the shore when it washes up. Depending on the location and species, *tengusa* can be harvested throughout much of the year but is often collected in summer.

PREPARATION: Wash thoroughly in fresh water to remove sand and salt, then spread on mats and dry in full sun. Repeat the washing and drying every day for three or four days, until the dark red color fades to white or pale peach. Don't worry if the seaweed gets rained on periodically; this will only lessen the work of washing. *Tengusa* will keep in this form for years. To make *tokoroten*, rehydrate the dried product, cook with water and vinegar, strain, allow to solidify, and cut into noodles using a press called a *tentsuki*.

SUGGESTED RECIPES: *Tokoroten* is usually served with vinegar and soy sauce, syrup made from unrefined sugar, or sesame-soy sauce. Garnish with sesame seeds, shredded *nori*, chili flakes, or grated ginger. In Wajima, on the Noto Peninsula, *tengusa* is simmered with rice flour to make a type of mock sashimi called *suizen* that is eaten with a sauce of ground sesame seeds, miso, and unrefined sugar. The traditional celebratory dish *ebisu* is made by swirling beaten eggs into hot *tokoroten* liquid before it is chilled and cut.

Wakame   若布, 和布, 稚海藻

SCIENTIFIC NAME: *Undaria pinnatifida.*

ALSO CALLED: *Nigime, menoha* (archaic).

AVAILABILITY: Grows in Japan in the Sea of Japan from Hokkaido south and on the Pacific coast from southern Hokkaido to Kyushu. It is found in many other parts of the world as well, including along the

Pacific coast of the United States and Mexico. Outside its native range *wakame* is often considered a harmful invasive species. Winged kelp (*Alaria esculenta*, found on the North Atlantic coast, or *Alaria marginata*, found from California to Alaska) can be substituted for *wakame* but needs to be soaked slightly longer when rehydrating.

DESCRIPTION: Just as cherry blossoms signal spring on land, *wakame* heralds its arrival underwater. Soft and silky with a mild, almost sweet flavor when cooked, this native Asian algae has long numbered among the most important seaweeds in Japanese cuisine. It was used in Buddhist ceremonies since ancient times and distributed to commoners starting in the medieval era. Today many home cooks serve it in miso soup almost daily and often add it to salads, hotpots, rice, and various other dishes. *Wakame* turns from an olive or brownish shade to emerald green when immersed in hot water. Its health benefits include high levels of calcium and omega-3 fatty acids. The plants grow abundantly along Japan's coasts on rocks and other hard surfaces from the low-tide line to the subtidal zone,

Wakame.

thriving at depths of up to 60 feet and preferring winter water temperatures between 35° and 57° Fahrenheit. The long stipes with ragged, wavy blades attached on both sides often form dense underwater forests. *Wakame* was wildcrafted in Japan through the 1950s, but today over 90% of the harvest is farmed.

TOXICITY/POISONOUS LOOK-ALIKES: Virtually all seaweeds are nontoxic, but should nevertheless be competently identified before harvesting. One genus to watch out for is *Desmarestia*, a brown algae that contains sulfuric acid and can cause stomach upset. Make sure to always harvest seaweed from clean water.

HARVEST: *Wakame* dislikes hot weather and should be harvested from late winter through spring, either by diving or from a boat using a long pole tipped with a blade. Alternatively, collect washed up *wakame* along the shore (make sure it is very fresh).

PREPARATION: Blanch raw *wakame* before using; this will brighten the color dramatically and mellow the salty pungency. Freshly harvested *wakame* can be rinsed in seawater and sun-dried, but because the surface salt will absorb moisture in humid weather it must be redried periodically. Alternately, wash raw *wakame* in freshwater before drying. This method is less prone to mold but comes with a sacrifice of some flavor. To preserve color, blanch in boiling water before drying but be aware that the rehydrated product may be overly soft. Another traditional method is to coat the *wakame* in straw- or wood-ash before drying. Be careful to wash off the ash well before using. Rehydrate dried *wakame* in cold water for 10 minutes, which will increase its volume about tenfold, or add it dried to soups. Whatever form of *wakame* you are using, take care not to overcook, as it disintegrates easily. Freezing fresh *wakame* is an easy alternative to the methods listed above.

SUGGESTED RECIPES: *Fresh: shabu-shabu*, sashimi (blanch and serve with shoyu and *wasabi*). Fresh or dried *wakame* or *mekabu* (the wavy spore-bearing blades at the base of the stem): miso soup, salad, sunomono, *wakatakeni* (simmered with *takenoko*). *Mekabu* can be wrapped in foil and cooked under the broiler or in a toaster oven for about 5 minutes. Toast dried *wakame* in a frying pan or microwave with seasonings for a snack, or deep-fry rehydrated *wakame* like potato chips. The popular shredded salad called *hiyashi wakame* is made by blanching fresh *wakame*, salting it overnight, purging the salt, and seasoning with sesame oil and chili, but this dish is typically not prepared at home.

Warabi   蕨

ENGLISH COMMON NAME: Bracken, brackenfern.

SCIENTIFIC NAME: *Pteridium aquilinum*.

ALSO CALLED: *Yamanegusa*.

AVAILABILITY: Grows in most parts of Japan as well as throughout the temperate and tropical world. It is among the most widespread of all plants, viewed as an invasive weed in many areas.

DESCRIPTION: *Warabi*, or bracken, is the most commonly eaten of Japan's three favorite fiddleheads, the other two being *zenmai* and *kogomi*. Even the eleventh-century novel *Tale of Genji* mentions the tender shoots, which have likely been enjoyed since prehistoric times. Although they evoke spring in poems and stories, *warabi* are also a symbol of poverty and starvation. A starch extracted from the roots was historically used as a substitute for rice and other grains during famines. The shoots, which prefer meadows, clearings, and burned or degraded areas to dense forest, emerge singly in mid-spring, sometimes in such great numbers they can be cut down with a hand scythe. Each pencil-width stalk is topped with a cluster of curled fronds, referred to as a *kobushi*, or "fist" in Japanese, which later unfurls into a leathery, triangular frond measuring up to 3 feet high.

Warabi.

TOXICITY/POISONOUS LOOK-ALIKES: Many Western references deem *warabi* toxic and carcinogenic, warning against its consumption. However, boiling with an alkaline substance like baking soda, as the Japanese do, reduces toxicity. Occasional consumption of properly prepared *warabi* is probably safe, though the precautionary principle would dictate against making it a dietary staple. In addition, some other varieties of fern are toxic or carcinogenic (and not at all tasty). Their fiddleheads may at first appear similar to edible varieties, so as always make sure you are certain of what you have picked or purchased before eating it.

HARVEST: Pick before the fiddleheads have unfurled. Snap off where the stem becomes tender, like asparagus.

PREPARATION: Rinse the *warabi*, place them in a rectangular pan, and sprinkle with baking soda (approximately 1 tablespoon per pound of *warabi*). Pour boiling water into the pan to submerge the *warabi*. Soak overnight. In the morning, rinse and soak in two changes of cold water for several hours. This removes the bitterness without turning the *warabi* to mush. A few handfuls of wood ash may be used in place of baking soda, but the proportions are less scientific and the results more prone to failure.

SUGGESTED RECIPES: Ohitashi (especially topped with *katsuobushi* and soy sauce), miso soup, *shira-ae*, sunomono, nimono, marinated in soy sauce as a topping for udon; *shiozuke, kasuzuke,* or *misozuke* pickles.

Wasabi   山葵

ENGLISH COMMON NAME: Japanese horseradish.

SCIENTIFIC NAME: *Eutrema japonicum.*

ALSO CALLED: *Hawasabi, yamawasabi, sawawasabi, honwasabi.*

AVAILABILITY: Mountain streams from Hokkaido to Kyushu, as well as Sakhalin Island and the Korean Peninsula.

DESCRIPTION: *Wasabi* is an indispensable flavor of Japanese cuisine; without it, sashimi would merely be raw fish. Although the plants have been cultivated since the 1600s, they are native to Japan and can be found growing wild in or near clear mountain streams. In fact, they are a symbol of pure water. Few things are quite so pretty as the site of their heart-shaped, near-incandescent young leaves and dainty white flowers sprouting beside a sparkling brook in spring. Although the leaves of the wild plants are tender and tasty, the rhizomes are much smaller than those of their cultivated cousins and hardly worth picking given the risk of depleting the colony over time.

Wasabi.

Yuriwasabi (*Eutrema tenue*, also called *inuwasabi*) is a close relative with smaller leaves and rhizomes that are harvested and prepared the same way as wild *wasabi*. Much of the prepared *wasabi* sold in tubes is actually a blend of Western and Japanese horseradish.

TOXICITY/POISONOUS LOOK-ALIKES: The deadly poisonous *dokuzeri* (*Cicuta virosa*, water hemlock) may be mistaken for *wasabi* simply because both grow in wet ground and have tubular rhizomes. The leaves have an entirely different shape and are easily distinguished with proper study.

HARVEST: The buds, flowers, and leaves may all be eaten, although the season for the first two lasts only a brief month or so in spring. Pinch or bend the stems to harvest rather than pulling in order to avoid uprooting the plants. The rhizomes may be grated like cultivated *wasabi* but take care not to harvest too many.

PREPARATION: Young leaves and flowers are best used raw. Bring out their spicy flavor, which resembles that of mustard greens, by pressing firmly between your palms. Older leaves should be blanched briefly in hot (not boiling) water before using; cooking too long or using overly hot water will make the leaves bitter rather than spicy.

SUGGESTED RECIPES: *Young leaves and blossoms:* Shred and add raw to salad; wrap raw leaves around rice seasoned with salt and sesame seeds; use as a bed for sashimi. *Older leaves:* Blanched in ohitashi, sunomono (*sanbaizu*), or aemono; *shoyuzuke, misozuke,* or *kasuzuke* pickles. *Roots:* Grate and use as you would cultivated *wasabi*; a tiny pinch of salt or sugar or a squeeze of lemon will bring out the flavor.

Yama-udo   山独活

ENGLISH COMMON NAME: Japanese spikenard.

SCIENTIFIC NAME: *Aralia cordata.*

AVAILABILITY: Grows in woods from Hokkaido to Kyushu; the *yama* in the name means "mountain" and indicates the wild variety. A similar plant, American spikenard (*Aralia racemosa*), grows from Kansas east; its roots were traditionally used in root beer.

DESCRIPTION: *Yama-udo* enjoys a place alongside *tara* and *fuki* as one of Japan's iconic sansai, but its strong, bitter flavor earns it as many detractors as fans. For some it is the flavor of spring; for others, a nearly inedible yearly trial. Almost anyone, however, can enjoy a few tender young shoots on a plate of tempura. The domesticated variety is often cultivated in darkness like white asparagus or endive to mellow the flavor and prevent the formation of stringy fibers. The wild plant, which is green with red joints, is said to have a superior fragrance. The Japanese characters for *udo* mean "spontaneous movement," from an old Chinese text claiming *udo* sways of its own accord even on still days. Some areas of Honshu still hold *udo* festivals in which *udo*, *itadori*, *dojo* (a freshwater fish), *tanishi* (river snails), and other wild mountain foods are offered up to the Shinto gods. People who are large but useless are called *udo no taiboku*, or "big udos," a reference either to the fact that the plant grows large in fall but rots away by spring or that the mature plant has no use after its spring shoots are plucked.

Yama-udo.

TOXICITY/POISONOUS LOOK-ALIKES: *Yama-udo* shoots look very much like those of *shishi-udo* (*Angelica pubescens*, "boar *udo*") except the stems of the latter are smooth whereas *yama-udo*'s are hairy. *Shishi-udo* is not poisonous—in fact it is used medicinally—but is not eaten as a vegetable.

HARVEST: The plant dies back in winter and new shoots emerge from the earth in spring. Slice the shoots off at the base or slightly below ground level. They grow quickly, so the window for harvest is short. Do not harvest more than one shoot per plant. Look for shoots with fat, pale bases growing in loose soil and those sprouting from old stumps; these are generally larger and better. The tender growing tips of larger plants may be harvested for tempura until they flower.

PREPARATION: The stems can be dipped in miso and eaten raw immediately after harvesting, before they become bitter and their cut surfaces begin to blacken from exposure to air—although this is a delicacy for true *udo* fans only. Otherwise peel the tough, hairy skin with a knife, drop the pieces into vinegar-water (about ½ cup vinegar to 2 quarts water) to prevent browning, and blanch in vinegar-water for several minutes. This will mellow the bitterness somewhat, but not remove it altogether. For tempura, use as-is.

SUGGESTED RECIPES: Vinegar and oil both temper *udo*'s potent flavor. *Stems*: sumiso-ae (use a high proportion of vinegar to miso and soak in the sauce for 15 minutes before serving), miso soup, sunomono, *misozuke*, *kasuzuke, udoyogoshi* (dressed with walnuts and miso). *Young leaves and upper portion of stems*: itamemono. *Peelings*: kinpira. *Growing tips*: tempura.

Yamaguri   山栗

ENGLISH COMMON NAME: Japanese chestnut.

SCIENTIFIC NAME: *Castanea crenata.*

ALSO CALLED: *Shibaguri.*

AVAILABILITY: Grows wild in mixed forests at low elevations from Kyushu to southern Hokkaido, as well as in South Korea. Introduced in parts of the US including Florida, New Jersey, and New York.

DESCRIPTION: Japan's native chestnuts are smaller than the cultivated ones sold in stores and more intensely flavored, with a tenaciously attached inner skin. Both chestnuts and posts made of chestnut wood have been found in abundance at the five-thousand-year-old Sannai Maruyama archaeological site in Aomori, a large Jomon village, suggesting the plant's importance in prehistoric times. The Japanese began cultivating *kuri* trees in the Heian period (and possibly much earlier), and by the early 1900s over five hundred cultivars existed. However, while the trees are resistant to the blight that has killed most American chestnuts (and in fact were a key source of that blight), they are vulnerable to an insect called the *kuritamabachi*, which wiped out this carefully bred diversity by the mid-twentieth century.

Yamaguri.

TOXICITY/POISONOUS LOOK-ALIKES: *Kuri* look similar at first glance to *tochi* (*Aesculus turbinata*, Japanese horse chestnut), which require extensive processing before eating. However, *kuri* husks are covered in dense spines while *tochi* husks are smooth, and *kuri* nuts have one flat side and a pointed end while *tochi* are round.

HARVEST: The porcupine-prickly husks of *kuri* split open when ripe, easing removal. Still, wear thick gloves. Since wild boars and monkeys also like *kuri*, it may be helpful to bring a long stick and knock ripe nuts from trees rather than simply searching the forest floor.

PREPARATION: Dry chestnuts with their shells still on in the sun for two to three days. Store in the refrigerator to prevent insect infestation and desiccation (cold storage also makes them sweeter). Since the inner skin of Japanese chestnuts is especially hard to peel, they are usually pared with a sharp knife before cooking. Soaking in cold water overnight will make the job a little easier—or pass the work along to diners by boiling in their jackets, slicing in half, and serving with small spoons to scoop out the meat.

SUGGESTED RECIPES: Roasting is traditional, but boiling is more common today. Cook pared chestnuts with rice, salt, and a little sake for *kurigohan*; simmer in syrup to make *kuri no kanroni*, which can be used in a wide range of Japanese desserts or folded into puréed sweet potatoes for the New Year's dish *kuri kinton*.

Yomogi 蓬, 艾

ENGLISH COMMON NAME: Japanese mugwort.

SCIENTIFIC NAME: *Artemisia indica var. maximowiczii* (*Artemisia princeps*).

ALSO CALLED: *Mochigusa, mogusa*.

AVAILABILITY: Common from Kyushu to Hokkaido as well as in China and Korea. *Artemesia vulgaris* (mugwort), a similar plant that is used medicinally and occasionally as a culinary herb, grows in northern temperate zones, including much of the US.

DESCRIPTION: A common weed along roadsides and farm fields throughout the Japanese countryside, *yomogi* has soft, silver-backed

Yomogi.

leaves and an unforgettable scent similar to sage, making identification quite easy. In the cold climates of northern Honshu and Hokkaido, a larger species called *oyomogi* (*Artemisia montana*) is prevalent. Although the tender new leaves are occasionally used for tempura and—at least according to the literature—even more occasionally as a boiled vegetable, the overwhelming preference is to finely chop or purée them for use in *kusa-mochi*, a classic variation on rice cakes. The pounded sticky rice takes on a pretty green color and herby flavor, which makes an interesting contrast to the sweet bean paste inside. The association between *yomogi* and mochi is so strong that one of the plant's nicknames is *mochigusa* or "mochi plant." Dumplings made from rice flour and *yomogi*, called *kusa dango*, are also popular. *Yomogi* is believed to ward off evil, which is why *kusa-mochi* is given as an offering on March 3 (Girl's Day) and *yomogi* leaves bundled together with *shobu* (*Acorus calamus*, sweet flag) are hung from doorways on May 5 (Children's Day).

TOXICITY/POISONOUS LOOK-ALIKES: Some species of *Artemesia* are toxic; *A. vulgaris* was traditionally used to induce abortion. As always, take care to properly identify the plant before eating.

HARVEST: Pick the tender new growth that shoots up in early spring or the growing tips of larger plants later in the season.

PREPARATION: Bring 6 cups of water to a boil with 2 tablespoons salt and 1 teaspoon baking soda. Boil the *yomogi* leaves in this water for 2 minutes, then drain and soak for 20 minutes. This will remove some of the bitterness and help soften the fibers. Purée in a food processor or blender (add a little water in the latter case); alternatively, chop and pound with the back of a knife. The purée may be frozen at this point for later use in mochi. For ohitashi and aemono, tender new stems work best, since even the young new leaves can be too fibrous to chew. Boil and soak as described above.

SUGGESTED RECIPES: *Young leaves*: kusa-mochi, kusa dango, tempura. *Young stems*: ohitashi, aemono.

Zenmai   薇 (VARIANT: 紫萁)

ENGLISH COMMON NAME: Asian royal fern.

SCIENTIFIC NAME: *Osmunda japonica*.

AVAILABILITY: Grows in woods and clearings from Kyushu to Hokkaido, thriving especially in damp areas. A close relative, *yamadori-zenmai* (*Osmundastrum cinnamomeum*, cinnamon fern) grows from central Honshu to Hokkaido and is also native to the eastern half of the US and Canada. Despite its poor reputation among some Western foragers, *yamadori-zenmai* makes an acceptable substitute in the recipes below—although most prefer true true *zenmai* if they can find it.

DESCRIPTION: *Zenmai* fiddleheads are among the iconic sansai of Japan. Rather than being eaten as a delicate spring treat, however, they are dried to produce a year-round staple evocative of long snowy winters and hearty farmers' food. Hiroshi Kataoka described the spring harvest by northern farmers, for whom the plant was an important source of

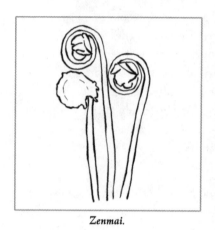

Zenmai.

cash, in his 1968 book *Sansaiki* (Edible wild plant stories). When the rice seedlings had been started but the plowing of paddies not yet begun, families would decamp to simple log huts in the woods to pick *zenmai*. Early each morning they donned straw sandals with cross-shaped metal claws on the bottom for scaling the still-icy hillsides and vests called *zenmai-gimon*, whose left hem they knotted into a makeshift bag. They stuffed the *zenmai* into this bag, which soon became coated with a thick, glossy black coating of *aku*. At the end of the day they carried the *zenmai* back to camp and boiled them, curling up to sleep in the cramped corner of the hut reserved for humans. The next morning, they spread the boiled shoots on straw mats to dry while the picking continued. In about three days, the shoots were dry as bone; these were called *akaboshi*, or "red-dried" *zenmai*. A second variety called *aoboshi* or "green-dried" *zenmai* was made by smoking the boiled shoots on a shelf hung over the family hearth (*irori*). *Aoboshi zenmai* are nearly impossible to find today.

TOXICITY/POISONOUS LOOK-ALIKES: Some varieties of fern are toxic or carcinogenic (and not at all tasty). Their fiddleheads may at first appear similar to edible varieties, so as always make sure you are certain of what you have picked or purchased before eating it and prepare as instructed.

HARVEST: Unlike warabi, *zenmai* grow in clumps. Spore-bearing fronds emerge first, followed by non-spore-bearing ones. Only the young non-spore-bearing fronds are harvested. They are easily distinguished: Spore-bearing fronds are generally taller, with fiddleheads swollen like clams, while non-spore-bearing fiddleheads are flatter and very wooly (the word *zenmai* is said to come from their resemblance to coins, or *zeni*). Snap off a few fronds per clump near the ground or cut with a knife; always leave enough behind to preserve the plant's health.

PREPARATION: *Zenmai* are almost always dried before eating. Remove and discard the curled tops and strip off any cottony fluff on the stems. Boil for 15 seconds and drain; do not rinse in cool water. Cut or snap off the tough bottoms as you would for asparagus. Spread on a straw mat or tray covered with newspaper and place in the sun. When the stalks begin to wilt, gather in a ball and knead with a circular motion to soften the fibers. Spread apart slightly and return to the sun. Repeat this process every few hours, pulling the mats inside at night, until the *zenmai* are completely dry and have changed from reddish brown to dark brown or black. Store in a dry, dark place. When ready to cook, place in a pot of warm water. Heat until bubbles form on the sides and bottom of the pot, remove from the heat, and knead briefly. Submerge the *zenmai* under an *otoshibuta* or plate and leave until cool. Change the water and repeat the entire process. At this point they should be fully reconstituted. They will keep in a bowl of cold water in the fridge for several days. Bundling neatly with rubber bands makes it easier to pull them out later for cooking.

SUGGESTED RECIPES: Reconstituted *zenmai* are usually simmered, alone or with other vegetables, in a light broth of *dashi*, shoyu, and mirin. Serve this nimono as is or drain and dress with *shira-ae*. Alternately, use heavier seasoning and add strips of *abura-age* (deep-fried tofu sheets) or sauté in oil before simmering with pieces of *migaki nishin* (dried herring filet).

Japanese terms used in the guide

AEMONO: Japanese-style salad made of cooked or raw ingredients in a thick dressing..

AMAZUZUKE: Vegetables or other ingredients pickled in sweetened vinegar..

CHAWANMUSHI: Savory egg custard steamed in individual serving cups..

DENGAKU: Skewered tofu or vegetables grilled with a miso topping.

FURIKAKE: A topping for rice made from dried seaweed, sesame seeds, bonito flakes, or other dried or powdered ingredients.

GOMA-AE: Chilled ingredients in a dressing made with ground sesame seeds and sugar, sometimes with *dashi*, vinegar, or other ingredients added

ITAMEMONO: Sautéed or stir-fried food.

KARASHIAE: Chilled ingredients in a dressing that includes hot Japanese mustard.

KASUJIRU: Soup flavored with sake lees.

KATSUOBUSHI: Smoked and dried skipjack tuna, typically shaved into flakes and used to flavor stock or top various dishes.

KASUZUKE: Vegetables or other ingredients pickled in sake or mirin lees.

KINPIRA: Shredded carrots, burdock, or other vegetables sautéed in sesame oil and seasoned with soy sauce, sugar, and chile.

KURUMIAE: Chilled ingredients in a ground walnut dressing.

MISOZUKE: Vegetables or other ingredients pickled in miso

MOCHI: Steamed sticky rice pounded to a smooth mass and formed into cakes, sometimes with the addition of other ingredients.

NAMESHI: Freshly cooked rice mixed with chopped greens.

NIHAIZU: A dressing made of soy sauce and vinegar.

NIMONO: Foods simmered in a seasoned broth.

NUKAZUKE: Vegetables or other ingredients pickled in a fermented mixture of salt and rice bran.

OHAW: A hearty Ainu soup made with vegetables and meat or fish, often including dried sansai.

OHITASHI: Blanched vegetables steeped in seasoned broth.

PONZU: A thin sauce made from citrus juice, usually blended with soy sauce.

SANBAIZU: A dressing made of soy sauce, vinegar, and mirin.

SASHIMI: Sliced raw seafood; sometimes refers to other ingredients such as seaweed served in the manner of sashimi.

SHABU-SHABU: A hotpot dish in which thinly sliced ingredients are swished briefly through a pot of hot broth at the table.

SHIBAZUKE: Sour purple pickles made from eggplant and red *shiso* leaves, often with ginger, *myoga*, cucumber, or other vegetables added.

SHIOZUKE: Vegetables or other ingredients fermented in salt.

SHIRA-AE: Chilled ingredients in a dressing of seasoned mashed tofu.

SHOYUZUKE: Vegetables or other ingredients pickled in soy sauce.

SUIMONO: Clear soup, usually flavored with soy sauce.

SUMISO: A dressing or sauce made from vinegar and miso, usually with the addition of sugar.

SUNOMONO: Vinegared foods

TAKIKOMI GOHAN: Rice cooked with chopped vegetables or meat and seasonings.

TAMAGOTOJI: Vegetables or meat simmered in seasoned broth with beaten eggs added at the end.

TAMAGOYAKI: Rolled Japanese-style omelet—called *dashimaki* when broth is added to the beaten eggs.

TOSAZU: A sauce made from vinegar, soy sauce, mirin or sugar, and *katsuobushi* broth.

TSUKUDANI: A heavily seasoned dish of vegetables or other ingredients simmered in sweetened soy sauce.

ZOSUI: A porridge made from cooked rice simmered with vegetables, meat, or other ingredients—also called *ojiya*.

Recipes

List of Recipes

About the Recipes

This section provides an introduction to traditional Japanese methods for cooking sansai (which, by and large, are the same methods used to cook cultivated vegetables). Although some recipes feature classic ingredient pairings, in general they should be viewed as guidelines to be freely adjusted according to taste and availability of wild foods. If you live in Japan, you'll be able to find most of the sansai that these recipes call for at markets or online vendors in season. In other countries, Japanese grocery stores and well-stocked international produce markets will likely carry a few things, such as *myoga*, *mitsuba*, canned *ginnan* seeds, and possibly fiddleheads, as well as pantry staples such as miso and *katsuobushi*, but many of the sansai will be hard to find. Refer to the Guide to Plants for similar wild plants that grow in North America, and experiment with what you can forage near your own home.

The serving sizes for these recipes are small, for several reasons. First, if you are foraging ingredients yourself, you may only be able to find a small quantity, and I want you to be able to put even that small quantity to good use. Second, quite a few sansai have pungent, bitter, or medicinal flavors that are best consumed in moderation. Finally, these recipes are intended to be served as part of a larger Japanese meal, which traditionally includes rice, soup, pickles, and several other side dishes. Since such small servings can look forlorn on a Western-style dinner plate, you may want to start scouring thrift stores and flea markets for your own collection of tiny, beautiful serving dishes, which will make eating these foods an even greater pleasure.

Sarada / Western-style salads

Green salads are not native to Japanese cuisine, but they feature routinely in homestyle meals and are one of the easiest ways to serve sansai. This does not typically mean mixing raw wild greens into a bowl of lettuce. Instead, more substantial sansai such as fiddleheads, bamboo shoots, *udo*, or *tara-no-me* are blanched, chilled, and arranged over a bed of lettuce together with cultivated vegetables such as tomato and cucumber. These salads require no instructions other than to use common sense and imagination, but either of the following two dressings will lend a bit of Japanese flavor. Tahini can be substituted for Japanese sesame paste (*neri goma*) in the second recipe, although its flavor is slightly stronger and its texture slightly less creamy.

Simple gingery dressing

Shogadare

Serves 4

INGREDIENTS

1 small garlic clove
½-inch piece of ginger
2 TBS rice vinegar
2 TBS vegetable oil
2 tsp soy sauce
1½ tsp maple syrup

INSTRUCTIONS

1. Grate or finely chop the garlic and ginger, preferably using a Japanese *oroshigane* grater, which will reduce them to a near pulp that dissolves nicely into the dressing. You should have about a half teaspoon of each.

2. Combine all ingredients in a small bowl or jar and mix well.

Triple sesame dressing
Gomadare

Serves 4

INGREDIENTS

1 TBS Japanese sesame paste (*neri goma*) or tahini
1 TBS warm water
¾ tsp honey
1 TBS vegetable oil
1 TBS ground toasted sesame seeds (*suri goma*)*
½ tsp sesame oil
2 tsp rice vinegar
¾ tsp soy sauce
Large pinch salt

INSTRUCTIONS

Stir together the sesame paste, honey, and warm water in a small bowl or jar. Add the remaining ingredients and mix well.

NOTE: Although *suri goma* can be bought in plastic packets, sesame seeds are best freshly toasted and ground. Toast in a small frying pan over medium heat, stirring constantly, until just golden. Crush lightly in an earthenware *suribachi* mortar or stone mortar (don't turn them into paste).

Shirumono / Soups

The traditional soups that accompany nearly every Japanese meal are usually simple broths enhanced with a restrained scattering of choice ingredients. This makes them a perfect vehicle for showing off your most precious wild finds—even if you only brought home two fiddleheads or a single *tara-no-me* bud. *Suimono* are light, clear soups often served at fancy meals with two or three ingredients arranged at the bottom of the bowl like a miniature still life. Try a single slice of *myoga* with a handful of tiny clams, a *mitsuba* leaf with a few cubes of tofu and feathery shreds of beaten egg, or a *sansho* leaf floating above the slender tip of a bamboo shoot and a few pieces of *wakame.* Miso soup is heartier family fare that can stand up to just about any sansai you have on hand, as well as various wild mushrooms and seaweeds. Because miso varies in saltiness and flavor as much as individual taste buds vary in preference, you will need to adjust the quantities in the following recipes to taste. I've also provided instructions for making the *dashi,* or stock, that these soups are based on.

Basic soup stock

Ichiban dashi

Dashi—a light broth usually extracted from *konbu* (kelp), *katsuoboshi* (smoky dried bonito flakes), *niboshi* (dried sardines), or a combination of those ingredients—is the indispensable foundation for Japanese soups and many other classic recipes. A wide selection of instant *dashi* products is available at Japanese grocery stores in either powder or tea-bag form, and these work perfectly well in strongly seasoned dishes and those calling for only a tablespoon or two of broth. For delicate dishes like sui-mono and *chawanmushi* where *dashi* provides the main flavor, homemade *dashi* is best. This method produces about two cups of beautifully clear, sweet broth. With these proportions, the flavor is fairly intense; feel free to adjust to taste or to the recipe you'll be using it in.

INGREDIENTS

2 ½ cups cold water
½ oz piece of *konbu* (about 20–40 inches square, depending on thickness)
1/3 oz *hana katsuo* (thinly shaved bonito flakes; about 1 cup loosely packed)

INSTRUCTIONS

1. Place the water and *konbu* in a medium saucepan and let sit for 15 minutes.

2. Bring to a simmer over medium-low heat. As soon as bubbles appear around the edge of the pot, remove the *konbu* (it can be used again in other recipes).

3. Bring to a full boil, remove from heat, and immediately add the *katsuobushi*. Wait for 1 minute, then strain through a fine strainer or a colander lined with a paper towel, coffee filter, or piece of cloth. Gather into a bundle and gently press against the side of the colander to extract remaining liquid (squeezing too hard will cloud the broth). Discard the *katsuobushi* or feed it to your cat.

Vegetarian soup stock
Konbu dashi

Many grades and varieties of *konbu* are available. Since it is the sole source of flavor in this recipe, choose a good-quality product with white powder on the surface. Do not wash the powder off, as it provides *konbu*'s delicious umami, but do brush off any sand or dirt. The quantity called for here yields a strong broth that can stand up to heavily seasoned recipes; for a more delicate broth, reduce to ½ oz or less. The *konbu* can be briefly simmered instead of soaked overnight, but soaking guarantees the broth will not be bitter or viscous, two risks of boiling. This recipe yields about 2 cups of *dashi* (the *konbu* absorbs quite a bit of water).

INGREDIENTS

¾ oz piece of *konbu* (about 30–50 square inches)
3 cups water

INSTRUCTIONS

Place the *konbu* in a mason jar or pitcher and cover with the water. Refrigerate and soak overnight. Remove the *konbu* (it can be used in other recipes).

Instant alpine leek miso soup
Kantan gyoja ninniku no miso shiru

Gyoja ninniku leaves and stems work well in this homemade version of instant miso soup because they cook very quickly. Mix the ingredients in your bowl just before eating or put them in a half-pint glass jar to take to work or school, perhaps with cubes of tofu or strips of deep-fried tofu (*abura-age*) added. Just be sure your colleagues aren't garlic haters—the smell of the leaves is quite strong. Ramps may be substituted.

Serves 1

INGREDIENTS

1 *gyoja ninniku* leaf, sliced into ¼-inch strips
2–3 tsp miso
¼ tsp *dashi* granules
1 cup boiling water

INSTRUCTIONS

1. Place the *gyoja ninniku*, miso, and *dashi* in a serving bowl or jar.

2. Pour boiling water over everything, stir to dissolve the miso, and let sit for a minute or two until the *gyoja ninniku* leaves are wilted.

Clear soup with field horsetail shoots

Tsukushi no suimono

The pleasure of suimono derives as much from appearance as from flavor, and the same is true of *tsukushi*. Tickle your guests' curiosity by floating these peculiar shoots in bowls of clear broth with a few slivers of onion. The quality of the *dashi* determines the success of this dish, so make it just before using and follow the instructions carefully. This recipe yields small servings for pairing with rice and several side dishes.

Serves 4

INGREDIENTS

12–16 *tsukushi* shoots
2 cups homemade *dashi*
½ medium onion, sliced
Salt to taste
Soy sauce to taste

INSTRUCTIONS

1. Prepare the *tsukushi* shoots as described in the Guide to Plants (see page 206). Blanch for 2–3 minutes in boiling water. Drain, submerge in cold water, then drain again.

2. Bring the *dashi* to a simmer with the onions and simmer gently until tender. Season to taste with salt and soy sauce, starting with a scant ¼ tsp each (the dish should not be overly salty).

3. Divide the *tsukushi* shoots between four bowls. Pour the piping hot soup over them and serve immediately.

Yuri Oriyama's mackerel and bamboo shoot soup

Oriyama Yuri no saba to chishimazasa no miso shiru

Yuri Oriyama makes this soup every spring using strong, coarsely tex-tured Akita miso and *chishimazasa* shoots picked on the mountain where her husband, Hideyuki, hunts bears. Other kinds of bamboo shoots and miso can be substituted, but don't expect the same results from canned shoots or sweet, mild white miso.

Serves 4

INGREDIENTS

6 *chishimazasa* shoots
2½ cups *konbu dashi* (see page 234)
1 6-oz can mackerel (*saba*) in water
1½–2 TBS red miso or other strongly flavored miso

INSTRUCTIONS

1. Parboil and peel the *chishimazasa* as described in the Guide to Plants (see page 181). Cut the lower portion of the shoots into thin circles (about ⅛-inch thick). Cut the tender tips into longer lengths. Drain the mackerel, remove large bones, and break into chunks.

2. Bring the *konbu dashi* to a simmer and add the shoots.

3. When the shoots are tender (several minutes), add the canned mackerel and heat through. Be careful not to let the soup boil or stir it too much, as this will cause the fish to disintegrate.

4. Remove from heat and dissolve the miso in the broth, adjusting to taste. The soup is traditionally on the salty side.

Ohitashi / Simple seasoned vegetables

Hitasu means to soak or bathe in Japanese, and this classic side dish features blanched vegetables soaked in a bath of *dashi* seasoned with soy sauce and sometimes mirin or sake. Greens both domesticated and wild are a favorite ingredient for ohitashi, but nearly any vegetable can be used, including mushrooms, fiddle-heads, and buds such as *tara-no-me* (Japanese angelica) or even bitter *fuki-no-to* (butterbur). Ohitashi is often topped with *katsuobushi* (bonito flakes) just before serving.

Simple seasoned flaccid anemone

Nirinso no ohitashi

Nirinso works well in this dish because it is nearly as mild as spinach and therefore does not overpower the flavor of the broth. For stronger greens, you may want to increase the amount of soy sauce.

Serves 3–4

INGREDIENTS

About ¼ lb *nirinso* leaves and flowers
¼ cup *dashi*
1 pinch salt
1 tsp soy sauce

INSTRUCTIONS

1. Briefly blanch the *nirinso*, drain, submerge in a bowl of cold water, and drain again. Gently squeeze to remove excess liquid.

2. In a small bowl, combine the *dashi*, salt, and soy sauce. Submerge the *nirinso* in the seasoned *dashi* and let sit for at least half an hour to absorb the flavors.

Sunomono / Vinegared dishes

Sunomono are tart little explosions of flavor made from raw or cooked vegetables or seafood tossed in vinegary dressing. Although they take the place of salad in traditional Japanese meals, raw greens are not typically used. All wild greens as well as most other sansai should be blanched, chilled, and thoroughly patted dry before dressing. The classic sunomono dressings include *nihaizu*, made from vinegar and soy sauce; *sanbaizu*, made from vinegar, soy sauce, and sugar or mirin; and *amazu*, made from vinegar and sugar. All of these may be mellowed with *dashi* or water and seasoned with *yuzu*, ginger, or any number of other additions.

Japanese horseradish leaves in seasoned vinegar

Hawasabi no sanbaizu

Serves 3

INGREDIENTS

1 TBS rice vinegar
1 TBS mirin
½ TBS soy sauce
10 stalks wild *wasabi* with leaves attached

INSTRUCTIONS

1. Mix the rice vinegar, mirin, and soy sauce in a small bowl.

2. Blanch the *wasabi* for 30 seconds. Slip the stems into barely simmering water first for a few seconds and the leaves last to avoid overcooking. Transfer to a bowl of cold water, drain, and squeeze well to remove excess water and bruise the leaves, bringing out their spicy flavor. Chop into 1-inch lengths.

3. Mix the *wasabi* leaves with the dressing and marinate for at least 15 minutes. Serve small portions, as the leaves have a strong flavor.

Aemono / Japanese-style salads

Aemono play a similar role to sunomono in the Japanese meal, but usually have a thicker dressing that includes miso, ground sesame seeds, mashed tofu, or mayonnaise. As with sunomono, a wide range of sansai, seaweed, wild mushrooms, and even wild fruit can be used in aemono, provided they are precooked, patted dry, and chilled before tossing with the dressing at the last minute before serving.

Daylily leaves and wakame in vinegar-miso sauce

Kanzo to wakame no sumiso-ae

Although *sumiso* means vinegar-miso, this dressing usually includes sugar as well. It is often used to dress pungent or bitter sansai such as *udo*, since the vinegar helps neutralize those flavors. That is not necessary for sweet, mild daylily (*kanzo*) leaves, but the flavors nevertheless go together very well. Use a knife to harvest daylily leaves in spring when they are a few inches tall; be careful not to confuse them with true lilies, some species of which are poisonous. Feel free to adjust the proportions to taste; each family tends to have its own variation on this dressing.

Serves 4

INGREDIENTS

1 TBS dried *wakame* or ⅓ cup fresh
½ cup fresh young *kanzo* leaves
1½ TBS mild miso
1 TBS rice vinegar
1 TBS honey

INSTRUCTIONS

1. Rehydrate the dried *wakame* in a bowl of cold water for about 10 minutes. Drain and squeeze out excess water.

2. Blanch the *kanzo* in boiling water for about 30 seconds, then drain and submerge in a bowl of cold water. Drain again and pat dry.

2. Mix the miso, vinegar, and honey in a small bowl.

3. Just before serving, toss the *wakame* and *kanzo* with the dressing.

Koshiabura with sesame-mayonnaise

Koshiabura no goma-mayo-ae

This rich, mild sauce highlights the delicate fragrance of *koshiabura*. The petiols (leafstalks) of *koshiabura* are tender and not at all bitter, making them a good choice for aemono. The leaves may be used as well; if they taste unpleasant after blanching, soak in cold water until they become palatable. Squeeze or pat dry before adding to the sauce.

Serves 2–3

INGREDIENTS

1 TBS mayonnaise (Japanese brand if possible)
1 TBS ground toasted sesame seeds (*suri-goma*) or sesame paste (*neri-goma*; tahini may be substituted)
½ tsp sesame oil
½ cup *koshiabura* leafstalks (reserve leaves for another recipe)

INSTRUCTIONS

1. Stir together the mayonnaise, ground sesame seeds or sesame paste, and sesame oil.

2. Blanch the *koshiabura* stems briefly in plenty of boiling water. Drain, submerge in a bowl of cold water, drain again, and pat dry with a towel.

3. Just before serving, toss the *koshiabura* stems with the sauce.

NOTE: Although *suri goma* can be bought in plastic packets, sesame seeds are best freshly toasted and ground. Toast in a small frying pan over medium heat, stirring constantly, until just golden. Crush lightly in an earthenware *suribachi* mortar or stone mortar (don't turn them into paste).

Ostrich-fern fiddleheads with ground walnuts

Kogomi no kurumi-ae

Blanched *kogomi* are often served with sesame dressing, but in northern Japan, *onigurumi* (wild Japanese walnuts) sometimes take the place of sesame seeds. Cultivated English walnuts or wild black walnuts make a fine substitute.

Serves 2

INGREDIENTS

10 *kogomi* fiddleheads
2 TBS finely chopped or ground *onigurumi*
1½ tsp *usukuchi* (light) soy sauce

INSTRUCTIONS

1. Clean the *kogomi* and blanch in salted water for about 1 minute. Drain, cool in a bowl of cold water, drain again, and pat dry. If stalks are attached, separate from the curled top portion and slice into 1-inch lengths.

2. Toss the *kogomi* with the *onigurumi*. Add soy sauce and toss again.

NOTE: See the Guide to Plants (page 191) for food-safety concerns related to lightly cooked *kogomi*. The *kogomi* may be boiled for longer but the texture will be very different.

Nimono / Simmered dishes

Nimono, or simmered dishes, make up a vast category of Japanese food served at family tables and fancy restaurants alike. In contrast to Western stews, they are typically cooked for no more than thirty or forty minutes, with any tough or strongly flavored ingredients precooked to ensure they will be tender and palatable. Simmering liquids vary from heavy baths of soy sauce and mirin to delicate broths scented with ginger or yuzu. Sansai are a favorite addition to nimono, though meaty plant parts like shoots, roots, and bulbs generally work better than leafy greens.

Quick-simmered bracken fiddleheads with deep-fried tofu

Warabi to aburage no nibitashi

Since its mild flavor takes well to the sweet-savory seasonings of nimono, *warabi* is a common addition to simmered dishes containing an assortment of wild and cultivated vegetables. It is also delicious simmered on its own or with thin slices of *aburage* (deep-fried tofu sheets) as in this recipe. *Nibitashi* is a subset of nimono in which the vegetables are simmered only briefly in a lightly seasoned broth; this helps prevent the *warabi* from becoming overly soft.

Serves 4

INGREDIENTS

About ½ lb *warabi*
3 pieces *aburage* (don't substitute regular tofu)
1½ cups *dashi*
2 TBS soy sauce
2 TBS mirin
1 TBS sake
1 tsp sugar

INSTRUCTIONS

1. Process the *warabi* as described in the Guide to Plants (see page 214; you will need to start the night before you plan to serve the dish). Cut into pieces several inches long. Slice the *aburage* into strips.

2. Combine the remaining ingredients in a small pot and bring to a simmer.

3. Add the *warabi* and *aburage*. Return to a simmer, cook 1 minute, and remove from heat. Let sit until cool. The longer it rests the more flavor the *warabi* will absorb.

Sweet and salty butterbur stems

Kyarabuki

Fuki has a strong, medicinal flavor that benefits from heavy seasoning. The stems are often cooked this way and served in small portions alongside rice throughout the week. When preparing the stems for this recipe, it is not necessary to soak them in water after peeling, since the soy sauce will turn them brown anyway.

Serves 8

INGREDIENTS

1 lb *fuki* stems
¼ cup soy sauce
¼ cup mirin
¼ cup sake
1 TBS sugar
2 TBS white sesame seeds, toasted until golden

INSTRUCTIONS

1. Prepare the *fuki* stems as described in the Guide to Plants (see page 183). Cut into 2-inch lengths and place in a wide saucepan with the soy sauce, mirin, sake, and sugar.

2. Bring to a boil and cook over medium-high heat until the sauce begins to thicken and coat the *fuki*, about 15 minutes. Swirl the pan frequently to prevent scorching.

3. Remove from heat and cool. The simmered stems will keep for about one week in the refrigerator. Sprinkle with sesame seeds before serving.

Itamemono / Sautéed dishes

Sautéed or stir-fried dishes do not enjoy the historical pedigree in Japan that simmered, grilled, and chilled-and-dressed foods do, but they are nevertheless popular for quick, casual meals. Favorite variations include Chinese-style stirfries and *kinpira*, a mixture of shredded root vegetables such as burdock and carrots sautéed in sesame oil and then briefly simmered in soy sauce and sugar. *Kinpira* is a good choice for *mitsuba* roots, *udo* peels, *ashitaba* stems, and other roots such as those of wild burdock, lotus, and dandelion.

Sautéed myoga

Myoga no itamemono

Although *myoga* is often used raw, it makes a surprisingly tasty side dish when sautéed briefly with a few drops of soy sauce. Sprinkle with toasted sesame seeds if you like and serve with rice. Since the flavor is strong, one *myoga* per person is more than enough.

Serves 3–4

INGREDIENTS

3 *myoga* buds
1 tsp vegetable oil
Soy sauce
White sesame seeds, toasted until golden (optional)

INSTRUCTIONS

1. Wash the *myoga* and slice off the bases. Shred lengthwise.

2. Heat the oil over medium-high heat in a small pan. Add the *myoga* and sauté for 2 to 3 minutes until limp.

3. Season to taste with soy sauce and sauté a few more seconds, until the *myoga* begins to brown. Serve sprinkled with the sesame seeds, if desired.

Soy-sauce-braised ashitaba stems

Ashitaba no kuki no kinpira

Ashitaba stems are tender and cook quickly. Blanching them first removes a bit of the bitterness, but if you like the flavor feel free to skip that step. This recipe omits the usual sugar. The stems are also tasty sautéed in sesame oil and seasoned with salt.

Serves 2–3

INGREDIENTS

¼ lb *ashitaba* stems
1 tsp sesame oil
½ tsp sake
1½ tsp soy sauce
Pinch dried chili flakes or rings (optional)

INSTRUCTIONS

1. Cut the *ashitaba* stems into bite-sized lengths. If they are very fat, slice in half lengthwise. Blanch in plenty of boiling water for 1 minute. Drain, submerge in a bowl of cold water, and drain again. Shake dry, then pat with a towel.

2. Heat the oil in a frying pan over medium heat. Add the *ashitaba* and toss to coat. Add the sake, soy sauce, and chilis and cook, stirring until the liquid has evaporated, about 2 minutes.

Tamago ryori / Egg dishes

According to the Food and Agriculture Organization of the United Nations, the Japanese eat more eggs per capita than any other nationality. Favorite dishes include fluffy rolled omelets, rice-stuffed omelets, savory egg custards, and even raw eggs as a topping for steaming hot rice or a dip for sukiyaki. Eggs taste best with sansai that are not so bitter as to overwhelm their subtle flavor, such as *mitsuba*, *nirinso*, *gyoja ninniku*, fiddleheads, wild mushrooms, and *wakame*.

Wild chervil with soft-set eggs

Mitsuba no tamagotoji

A cousin of the classic *oyakodon*—"parent and child rice bowl" made with chicken, sliced onions, *mitsuba*, and eggs—this comforting home-style dish is surprisingly delicious with *mitsuba* alone. Tofu makes a nice vegetarian alternative to chicken if you want a more substantial dish; simply break up a cake of soft tofu into the pan before adding the eggs.

Serves 2

INGREDIENTS

15 stalks *mitsuba* with leaves attached
2 large eggs
⅓ cup *dashi*

2 tsp soy sauce
2 tsp mirin
2 tsp sake

INSTRUCTIONS

1. Chop the *mitsuba* into 1-inch lengths. Lightly beat the eggs.

2. Bring the *dashi*, soy sauce, mirin, and sake to a simmer in a small frying pan.

3. Add the *mitsuba* and cook until just wilted, about 20 seconds. Pour the eggs over the *mitsuba*, cover, and cook for about 1 minute until barely set.

Rolled omelet with wild vegetables

Sansai no tamagoyaki

Sweet-and-salty omelets rolled into thick, fluffy logs are a staple of the Japanese breakfast table and bento box. Although learning to make them takes a bit of practice, they are a welcoming home for many wild vegetables. Spring greens, wild mushrooms, seaweed, fiddleheads, and aromatic plants such as *gyoja ninniku* or *mitsuba* all work well. Whatever you choose, make sure it is precooked, squeezed and patted dry to remove excess liquid, and chopped into small pieces before adding.

Serves 3

INGREDIENTS

3 large eggs
2 TBS *dashi* (instant is fine)

3 pinches salt
¾ tsp sugar
4 TBS precooked, chopped wild vegetable
Vegetable oil

INSTRUCTIONS

1. Beat the eggs well in a small bowl. Add the *dashi*, salt, and sugar and beat again. Strain through a mesh strainer.

2. Heat a medium (about 8 inches) frying pan or rectangular Japanese *tamagoyaki* pan over medium heat. Either a nonstick or well-seasoned cast iron pan will work. Pour in a teaspoon or so of oil and use a wadded-up paper towel to mop up the excess. Save the paper towel to re-oil the pan later.

3. When the pan is thoroughly heated, pour in ⅓ of the egg mixture and tilt the pan so it evenly covers the bottom. When the surface is semi-set, fold in the right and left edges by about ½ inch (if you are using a round pan). Then, starting at the far end, use a spatula or pair of chopsticks to roll up the omelet toward you in about three folds. Let it sit for a few seconds while you re-oil the pan with the paper towel, then push the rolled omelet to the back of the pan.

4. Pour another ⅓ of the egg mixture into the pan, lifting the cooked omelet so it flows underneath. Scatter 2 TBS of the vegetables over the surface. When the surface is semi-set, fold it toward you again, this time incorporating the mass of previously cooked egg. Re-oil the pan and move the omelet to the back again.

5. Pour in the remaining egg mixture, scatter the remaining 2 TBS of vegetables over it, and repeat the process above. You should end up with a more or less tidy, cylinder-shaped omelet. Spread a tea towel or cloth napkin on a plate, tip the omelet onto it, and wrap it up in the towel. This will help absorb excess moisture as the omelet cools

and give it a firmer shape. Wait till it cools, remove the towel, and slice into rounds. Serve with grated daikon radish and soy sauce if desired.

Savory egg custard with ginkgo seeds

Ginnan no chawanmushi

Ginnan seeds are a classic ingredient in this elegant, silky smooth custard that can be served either hot or cold. Other starchy roots, bulbs, and nuts work well, too, such as chestnuts, lily bulbs (*yuri-ne*), and *oubayuri* bulbs, as do mild greens such as *mitsuba* or *nirinso*. Choose three seasonal ingredients you think will go well together, precooking any you suspect may not fully cook during the brief steaming time.

Serves 4

INGREDIENTS

12 *ginnan* seeds
4 small clusters of *shimoji* mushrooms (other varieties may be substituted)
2 cups fresh homemade *dashi*
Scant ½ tsp salt
2 tsp sake
2 tsp light soy sauce
4 medium eggs
4–8 bite-sized pieces of boiled skinless chicken or lightly steamed carrots

INSTRUCTIONS

1. Prepare the *ginnan* according to instructions in the Guide to Plants
(see page 187); boil them for about 5 minutes and cool. Clean the mushrooms and break or cut into bite-sized sections. Divide the mushrooms
among four 1-cup-capacity heatproof ceramic or glass custard cups
or teacups. Line the upper section of a steamer with a damp, folded
napkin or tea towel to prevent cups from jostling, pour several inches
of water into the bottom section, and begin heating. Tie a napkin or
tea towel around the lid of the pot to absorb steam and prevent it from
condensing and dripping into the custard.

2. Combine the *dashi*, salt, mirin, and soy sauce. Beat the eggs well and
strain through a mesh strainer. You should have between ⅔ and 1 cup.
Gently stir in the seasoned *dashi* (avoid creating foam, which will lead
to bubbles in the cooked custard).

3. Ladle about ⅔ of the egg mixture into the custard cups, dividing
evenly. Set the cups in the steamer, cover with the wrapped lid, and
steam over medium heat for 10 minutes. Remove the lid and test the
custards, being careful not to burn yourself with the steam. The egg
should be set but still jiggle when shaken, and clear liquid should
appear when you insert a toothpick. If they are not set, steam for a few
more minutes.

4. Divide the chicken or carrots and *ginnan* nuts between the custard
cups and ladle the remaining egg mixture on top. Replace the lid and
steam until set, about 5 minutes (test as described above, being careful
not to overcook the custard). Serve hot or chilled.

Agemono / Fried foods

Deep-fried foods are common in Japan, though typically they are served in smaller quantities than in the United States, often alongside rice, miso soup, and several non-fried side dishes. Tempura is a particularly popular method of preparing all sorts of sansai, from leaves to flower buds to roots. An even simpler method is *suage*, which involves patting bite-sized ingredients dry and frying them in an inch or two of hot oil, with no batter of any kind. As with tempura, the oil should be heated to about 350° F and cooking should take no more than a minute or so. Serve *suage* sprinkled with salt.

Wild tempura with Reiko Hanaoka's chickweed salt

Sansai tempura to Hanaoka Reiko no hakobe-jio

Japanese housewives and chefs produce magically light, crisp tempura using batter made from nothing more than egg, water, and ordinary flour. No matter how carefully I follow the admonishments to use ice-cold ingredients, not overmix, and fry at a low temperature, mine inevitably comes out doughy and oily. I've found crispy deliciousness much easier to attain with the admittedly inauthentic mixture of cornstarch and flour given here. It works especially well for producing crisply battered leaves.

For vegetables, nearly any wild green will do, as well as fiddleheads, dandelion flowers, *tara-no-me*, *koshiabura*, *udo*, *oubayuri*, or almost anything else that strikes your fancy. For more ideas and cooking tips, see Chapter 1. Forgoing the usual sweet-and-savory dipping sauce in favor of salt keeps the focus on the flavor of the sansai. Better yet, make a batch of Reiko Hanaoka's bright green *hakobe* salt to sprinkle over your *hakobe* (and other) tempura.

Serves 4–6

INGREDIENTS

Assorted wild greens and/or other sansai
Vegetable oil for frying
1 egg
About ¾ cup ice water
½ cup cornstarch
½ cup plus 2 TBS all-purpose or cake flour

INSTRUCTIONS

1. Fill a wok or other wide, deep pan with several inches of oil (enough for the vegetables to float). Begin heating over low heat. Wash the greens only if they are dirty and shake off excess water. Separate into individual leaves, sprigs, or clusters. Trim other sansai such as *warabi* and *tara-no-me*, removing any tough portions and cutting long or thick stems into manageable lengths. Separate *oubayuri* and lily bulbs (*yuri-ne*) into individual scales. It is not necessary to precook or otherwise process most sansai before using in tempura. Sift a little flour over the meatier vegetables but not the leaves.

2. When the oil has reached about 350° F and you are ready to start frying, make the batter (making it right before you use it improves crispiness). Break the egg into a measuring cup and beat well. Add ice water to make 1 cup and pour into a bowl. Sift the cornstarch and ½

cup of the flour over the liquid and stir together quickly with a fork or pair of chopsticks. Leave some lumps, as you would for pancake batter. It should be thick enough to coat the vegetables; if not, add an extra tablespoon or two of flour.

3. Adjust the temperature of the oil so that a drop of batter sinks to the bottom then rises fairly quickly to the surface. Dip your sansai into the batter one at a time and fry in the oil until crisp and pale gold. Keep the coating of batter thin and don't overcrowd the oil. Start with the leaves because the oil will be slightly cooler at the beginning and less liable to burn them. Coating only one side of each leaf with a thin cloak of batter is another key to crispiness. As you remove the cooked sansai, hold them over the pot for a few seconds to let the excess oil drain off, then transfer to a plate lined with paper towels. Serve piping hot, sprinkled with green salt.

For the green salt:

INGREDIENTS

Hakobe
Water
Salt (5 TBS per cup of extracted liquid)

INSTRUCTIONS

1. In spring, pick two or three large bowlfuls of tender *hakobe* stems and leaves. Giant or water chickweed (*Myosoton aquaticum*) works especially well because it is large and juicy.

2. Wash and drain the *hakobe*. Extract juice using a juicer or blender. If you use a blender, add water as needed and strain through a colander lined with cloth or a paper towel, squeezing to extract all the liquid. Measure the liquid (two cups of chopped, packed greens blended with one cup of water will yield about 1 cup of strained liquid).

3. Stir in as much salt as the liquid will absorb, about 5 TBS per cup of liquid.

4. Pour the mixture into a heavy-bottomed frying pan or wide pot and cook over low heat, stirring often, until all of the liquid evaporates. For 1 cup of liquid, this takes about half an hour. If the heat is too high, the pretty green color will be lost. Take care not to burn the mixture as the last of the liquid evaporates. You may need to move the pan on and off the burner to control the temperature. Store in an airtight container.

Tsukemono / Pickles

Tsukemono are one of the great pleasures of Japanese cuisine, as anyone who has sampled the rainbow-hued goods at one of Kyoto's pickle emporiums knows. Pickling bases range from salt, fermented rice bran, and sake lees to soy sauce, miso, and vinegar, while no vegetable appears to be off-limits for pickling. Even greens—both wild and domesticated—are pickled. Although pickling was once a method of preserving sansai to eat throughout the winter, today the purpose is usually culinary entertainment. The following three recipes represent only a tiny sampling of what is possible.

Quick sweet-and-sour myoga pickles

Myoga no amazuke

Myoga's strong flavor stands up well to many pickling bases, but the bright tang of vinegar and sugar is perhaps the best match. The sake in this recipe mellows the vinegar but may be omitted if you like more zing to your pickles. Although blanching temporarily dulls the beautiful color of the *myoga*, it returns as if by magic once they are submerged in the flavored vinegar. The liquid, too, takes on a rosy pink hue that looks very pretty in a glass jar.

INGREDIENTS

4 *myoga*
2 TBS rice vinegar
2 TBS sake
2 TBS sugar
Pinch of salt

INSTRUCTIONS

1. Wash the *myoga*, trim off the bottoms, and slice in half lengthwise. Blanch in boiling water for 30 seconds. Drain, cool under running water, and place in a small glass jar or container with a lid.

2. Combine the remaining ingredients in a small saucepan and bring to a simmer. Stir until the sugar and salt have dissolved.

3. Remove from heat and pour over the *myoga*. These pickles are ready after several hours, and will keep in the refrigerator indefinitely. Slice lengthwise before serving.

Miso-pickled Japanese spikenard

Yama-udo no misozuke

Anything from meat, fish, hard-boiled eggs, and cheese to cultivated and wild vegetables can be pickled in miso. Some cooks use pure miso as their pickling base, while others thin it with mirin or sake or sweeten it with sugar. Red miso is classic, but any variety can be used. Substitute domesticated *udo* if you can't find it growing wild.

INGREDIENTS

2 *yama-udo* shoots
2 TBS miso

INSTRUCTIONS

1. Cut off the leafy upper portion of the shoots (you can use them in tempura or sauté with miso and mirin). Peel the stalks and taste a thin slice. If it is overly bitter, soak in vinegar water or blanch in vinegar water and then soak in plain water. Check every few hours until it tastes mild enough to eat, changing the water as necessary.

2. Drain the *yama-udo* and pat dry with a towel. Slice into bite-sized lengths. Halve or quarter the thicker lower portions lengthwise.

3. Place the *udo* and miso in a container with a lid or a zipper storage bag and massage to coat.

4. Let sit overnight. Wipe or rinse off the miso before serving.

Soy-pickled alpine leeks

Gyoja ninniku no shoyuzuke

This tasty, extremely simple recipe is a good way to preserve a bounty of *gyoja ninniku* or ramps. Use it to top soba or udon noodles, adding a spoonful of the flavorful soy sauce to the broth, or serve with rice. The same method works with *wasabi* leaves (blanch them very briefly in hot, not boiling, water before using).

INGREDIENTS

Gyoja ninniku stems and leaves
Soy sauce

INSTRUCTIONS

1. Wash the *gyoja ninniku* and shake the leaves dry, then carefully pat with a towel to remove any remaining moisture. Cut into bite-sized lengths or leave whole.

2. Pack into a sterilized glass jar.

3. Pour soy sauce over to cover, pressing a piece of plastic wrap onto the surface of the liquid if the leaves refuse to stay submerged. May be eaten after one week, but the flavor of the soy sauce and leaves will continue to improve with time. Keeps for up to a year in the fridge.

Gohan mono / Rice dishes

Gohan, or rice, is the heart of the classic Japanese meal, and almost all of the recipes in this book would typically be eaten with a steaming bowl of it. But a handful of traditional rice dishes also incorporate sansai more directly—namely porridge with wild greens, steamed rice with wild greens, and *onigiri* (rice balls) stuffed with sautéed, simmered, or pickled sansai. I have not provided a recipe for the last of these, but I encourage you to improvise with whatever sansai leftovers you have on hand.

Rice with ashitaba

Ashitaba no nameshi

Nameshi literally means "leaf rice," and as the name suggests, this simple, ancient dish features chopped raw or blanched greens folded into freshly cooked rice, historically in order to stretch that precious commodity. *Ashitaba* has an herby, slightly bitter flavor that mellows when mixed with the cooked rice. Feel free to experiment with other wild greens, but avoid those with a very bitter flavor. *Dengaku* (grilled miso-topped tofu) is a popular menu pairing.

Serves 4

INGREDIENTS

1 cup uncooked short-grain white rice
1¼ cups water
About 2 cups raw *ashitaba* leaves, washed
¼ tsp salt
1 TBS white sesame seeds, toasted until golden

INSTRUCTIONS

1. Wash and drain the rice and place in a medium pot with the water. Bring to a simmer and reduce heat to low. Cover and cook for 10 to 15

minutes until the water is absorbed. Remove from heat and let steam with the lid on for another 5 to 10 minutes.

2. Blanch the *ashitaba* in plenty of boiling water for about 20 seconds until wilted but still bright green. Drain and submerge in a bowl of cold water. Drain again and squeeze out excess water.

3. Chop the *ashitaba* finely and massage with salt.

4. Gently fold the *ashitaba* and sesame seeds into the freshly cooked rice, taking care not to smash the grains of rice. Make any leftovers into *onigiri* (rice balls).

Rice porridge with seven wild greens

Nanakusagayu

In Japan, families eat *nanakusagayu* on January 7 to refresh their digestive systems after gorging on the rich foods of the New Year's holiday and to bring good health throughout the year. The simple porridge is traditionally made with *seri, nazuna, gogyo, hakobera, hotokenoza, suzuna,* and *suzushiro* (Japanese parsley, shepherd's purse, cudweed, chickweed, Japanese nipplewort, turnip, and daikon radish), but do not feel limited by this list or by the number seven. Any tender, young spring or winter green can be used—try watercress, dandelion, chicory, plantain, or whatever else grows in your neighborhood. Include a baby turnip or daikon radish, with its greens, to add some variety to the texture. If your greens are very bitter, reduce the quantity; Japanese recipes typically use half the amount of greens recommended here. You may substitute short-grain brown rice by increasing the water to 5½ cups and simmering for about two hours, removing the lid for the last half hour if the porridge seems too watery. The texture will be slightly less glutinous than if you use white rice.

Serves 4

INGREDIENTS

½ cup short grain white rice
4 cups water
¼ lb tender wild spring greens, including one small turnip or daikon
    radish (see note above)
Salt

INSTRUCTIONS

1. Combine the rice and water in a medium saucepan. Let soak for 30 minutes.

2. Bring the rice to a boil. Lower heat and cover, leaving lid ajar to prevent overflows. Simmer gently, stirring occasionally, for 40 minutes or until the rice has broken down into a thick porridge.

3. While the rice is cooking, wash the greens thoroughly and remove any tough stems. Separate the turnip or radish from its greens and slice into thin, bite-sized pieces. Bring a medium pot of water to a boil and blanch the turnip or radish pieces until just tender. Remove with a slotted spoon and drain. Using the same water, blanch the greens until wilted but still bright green. Drain, rinse under cold water, and squeeze firmly to remove excess water. Chop into small pieces.

4. When the porridge is done cooking, stir in salt to taste. Start with about ⅓ teaspoon; it should not be overly salty. Stir in the chopped greens and turnip or radish. Serve hot.

Acknowledgments

This book would not exist without the generosity of the many people who shared their knowledge, experience, and support at every stage of its creation. I am especially grateful to those of you who opened your homes and places of business to me, fed me at your tables, and took me on walks in the woods: Sadako Ban, Reiko Hanaoka, C. W. Nicol, Kentaro Fukuchi, Kazuhiro Koriki, Myong Hee Kim, Robert Kowalczyk, Misato Shimizu, Akemi Komatsu, Tsuyuko Yamashita, Kaoru Odashima, Shinobu and Kumiko Takahashi, Akira and Ikuko Takahashi, Yoshinobu Komatsu, Shoji Onoue, Yasufumi Ueda, Hideyuki and Yuri Oriyama, Takumi Sugibuchi, Akira Okamoto, Satsuki and Satomi Bansho, Junko Shinki, Tamaki Nagano, Naomi Oikawa, and Manami Kimura.

Thank you, too, to all those who shared your knowledge about sansai and other topics, including Munehiko Iwaya, Norifusa Yoshida, Shingo Taniguchi, Yuichiro Fujioka, Koki Teshirogi, Yoshihiko Iida, Nathan Hopson, Kenji Namikawa, Keiko Nakayama, Tamura Yoneo, Takaaki Chiba, Tatsuya Takahashi, Don Kenny, Shozaburo Sato, Masatoshi Watanabe, Chiyako Miura, Keito Kobayashi, Hironori Isomoto, Takahiko Ikemori, Minoru Suzuki, Yoshikata Ishihara, Kenji Sekine, Shiro Kayano, Mike Day, and Chris Gavin.

To the introducers, thank you for opening the door to many otherwise-closed worlds: Tatsuhiro Ohkubo, Haruna Yatsuka, Chikako Takahashi, Naoyuki Takahashi, Andrew Kershaw, Naoki Naito, Maki Sekine, Jen Teeter, Taka Okazaki, Kya Kim, and Mariko Yamauchi.

To my fellow writers and translators, thank you for reading drafts, critiquing poetry, translations, and most of all for keeping me sane throughout the long process of reporting, writing, and editing: Jane Braxton Little, Simran Sethi, Adela Laczynski, Lynne E. Riggs, Daniel Joseph, Susanna Lang, and Hannah Kirshner.

Paul Poynter, thank you for the beautiful illustrations, which capture the spirit of the people, places, and plants in this book so well; Sumire, I am grateful for your suggestions on which sansai to focus on and to the entire family for your friendship and hospitality. Akiko Shimizu, I appreciate your meticulous care in checking the accuracy of the Guide to Plants, and Ayaka Kitano, thank you for checking the list of culinary terms. To Peter Goodman, thank you for having faith in this odd book and seeing it through to publication with such patience, trust, and skill, and to Michael Palmer, for doing so much to help it find its readers. Any remaining errors are my sole responsibility.

To my family, thank you for always believing in me, even when I didn't share your confidence. Elektra, you are an angel for spending three weeks eating weeds and hanging out with a jetlagged baby so that I could complete my research. John, thank you for all the weekends you spent watching the boys so I could work on this project, and for helping me keep it all in perspective. I couldn't have done it without you.

Winifred Bird

Names of Edible Plants

JAPANESE COMMON NAME	ENGLISH COMMON NAME	SCIENTIFIC NAME
akamatsu	red pine	Pinus densiflora
arame	—	Eisenia bicyclis
ashitaba	—	Angelica keiskei
azami	thistle	Cirsium spp.
chishimazasa	—	Sasa kurilensis
dokudami	fishwort	Houttuynia cordata
fuki	butterbur	Petasites japonicus
funori	—	Gloiopeltis spp.
gishigishi	dock	Rumex spp.
gogyo	cudweed	Pseudognaphalium affine
gyoja ninniku	alpine leek	Allium ochotense
hakobe/hakobera	chickweed	Stellaria spp.
hijiki	—	Sargassum fusiforme
hotokenoza	Japanese nipplewort	Lapsanastrum apogonoides
icho	ginkgo	Ginkgo biloba
itadori	Japanese knotweed	Reynotria japonica
iwanori	—	Pyropia spp.
kajime	—	Ecklonia stolonifera, E. kurome
kakidoshi	ground ivy	Glechoma hederacea
kanzo	daylily	Hemerocallis spp.
katakuri	Asian fawn lily	Erythronium japonicum
kihada	Amur cork	Phellodendron amurense
kogomi	ostrich fern	Matteuccia struthiopteris
konbu	kombu	Saccharina spp.
koshiabura	—	Chengiopanax sciadophylloides
kureson	watercress	Nasturium officinale

kusa-fuji	tufted vetch	*Vicia cracca*
kuzu	kudzu	*Pueraria montana var. lobata*
mitsuba	wild chervil	*Cryptotaenia japonica*
mizu	nettle	*Elatostema involucratum*
mosodake	moso bamboo	*Phyllostachys edulis*
mozuku	—	*Nemacystus decipiens*
myoga	Japanese ginger	*Zingiber mioga*
nazuna	shepherd's purse	*Capsella bursa-pastoris*
nirinso	flaccid anemone	*Anemone flaccida*
nobiru	wild onion	*Allium macrostemon*
obako	Asiatic plantain	*Plantago asiatica*
onigurumi	Japanese walnut	*Juglans mandshurica var. sachalinensis*
oubayuri	Japanese cardiocrinum	*Cardiocrinum cordatum var. Glehnii*
renge	Chinese milkvetch	*Astragalus sinicus*
sansho	Japanese pepper	*Zanthoxylum piperitum*
seri	Japanese parsley	*Oenanthe javanica*
shiode	wild asparagus	*Smilax riparia*
tanpopo	dandelion	*Taraxacum platycarpum*
taranoki	Japanese angelica tree	*Aralia elata*
tengusa	—	*Gelidium spp.*
tochi	Japanese horse chestnut	*Aesculus turbinata*
tsukushi	field horsetail	*Equisetum arvense*
tsurumo	sea lace	*Chorda filum*
umizomen	—	*Nemalion vermiculare*
wakame	—	*Undaria pinnatifida*
warabi	bracken	*Pteridium aquilinum*
wasabi	Japanese horseradish	*Eutrema japonicum*
yamaguri	Japanese chestnut	*Castanea crenata*
yama-udo	Japanese spikenard	*Aralia cordata*
yomogi	Japanese mugwort	*Artemisia indica var. maximowiczii*
yukinoshita	creeping rockfoil	*Saxifraga stolonifera*
zenmai	Asian royal fern	*Osmunda japonica*

Selected Bibliography

Below I have listed some of the books and articles that informed the writing of this book; additional sources are included in the Endnotes after the Essays. During my research I also referred to the many excellent websites about edible wild plants that exist online in both English and Japanese and learned from the collective knowledge of vibrant online foraging communities such as the Will Forage for Food and Edible Wild Plants groups on Facebook. Websites listed at the end will be helpful to readers searching for reliable information about specific plants and seaweeds.

ENGLISH SOURCES

Bartholet, Jeffrey. "He's Big, He's Bad, He's ... Japanese?" *Outside Magazine* (May 1999).

Deng, S., et al. "Tree Species Classification of Broadleaved Forests in Nagano, Central Japan, Using Airborne Laser Data and Multispectral Images." *The International Archives of the Photogrammetry, Remote Sensing, and Spatial Information Sciences*, vol. XLII-3/W3 (2017).

Elpel, Thomas J. *Botany in a Day: The Patterns Method of Plant Identification: An Herbal Field Guide to Plant Families of North America.* 6th ed. Pony, MT: HOPS Press, 2013.

Farrelly, David. *The Book of Bamboo: A Comprehensive Guide to This Remarkable Plant, Its Uses, and Its History.* San Francisco: Sierra Club Books, 1984.

Frazer, James, *The Golden Bough: A Study in Comparative Religion.* New York: MacMillan, 1894.

Habu, Junko, et al. "Shell Midden Archaeology in Japan: Aquatic Food Acquisition and Long-term Change in the Jomon Culture." *Quaternary International*

239 (2019), pp. 19–27.

Hopson, Nathan. *Ennobling Japan's Savage Northeast: Tohoku as Japanese Postwar Thought, 1945–2011.* Cambridge: Harvard University Press, 2017.

Isagi, Yuji, et al. "Predominance of a Single Clone of the Most Widely Distributed Bamboo Species *Phyllostachys edulis* in East Asia." *Journal of Plant Research* 129 (2016), pp. 21–27.

Ishihara, Yoshikata, "Ama Divers are Incredible!" Ocean Newsletter Selected Papers, no. 23 (2019), pp. 12–13.

Knight, John. *Waiting for Wolves in Japan: An Anthropological Study of People-Wildlife Relations.* Honolulu: University of Hawaii Press, 2006.

Kreischer, Lisette, and Marcel Schuttelaar. *Ocean Greens: Explore the World of Edible Seaweed and Sea Vegetables: A Way of Eating for Your Health and the Planet's.* Translated by Marleen Reimer and Victor Verbeek. New York: The Experiment, 2016.

La Cerva, Gina Rae. *Feasting Wild: In Search of the Last Untamed Food.* Vancouver: Greystone Books, 2020.

Meredith, Ted Jordan. *Bamboo for Gardens.* Portland, OR: Timber Press, 2001.

Mouritsen, Ole. *Seaweeds: Edible, Available, and Sustainable.* Translated and adapted by Mariela Johansen. Chicago: University of Chicago Press, 2013.

O'Connor, Kaori. *Seaweed: A Global History.* London: Reaktion Books, 2017.

Ohnuki-Tierney, Emiko. *Rice as Self: Japanese Identities through Time.* Princeton: Princeton University Press, 1994.

Pflugfelder, Gregory M., and Brett L. Walker, eds. *JAPANimals: History and Culture in Japan's Animal Life.* Ann Arbor: University of Michigan Center for Japanese Studies, 2005.

Smith, R. T., and J. A. Taylor, eds. *Bracken: Ecology, Land Use, and Control Technology.* Carnforth, Lancs.: Parthenon Publishing Group, 1986.

Thayer, Samuel. *Nature's Garden: A Guide to Identifying, Harvesting, and Preparing Edible Wild Plants.* Bruce, WI: Forager's Harvest Press, 2010.

————. *The Forager's Harvest: A Guide to Identifying, Harvesting, and Preparing Edible Wild Plants.* Bruce, WI: Forager's Harvest Press, 2006.

Totman, Conrad. *A History of Japan.* 2nd ed. Hoboken, NJ: Wiley-Blackwell, 2005.

Tsuji, Shizuo. *Japanese Cooking: A Simple Art.* Revised ed. Tokyo: Kodansha International, 2006.

Turner, Nancy J., and Adam F. Szczawinski. *Common Poisonous Plants and Mushrooms of North America.* Portland: Timber Press, 1991.

Walker, Brett L. *The Conquest of Ainu Lands: Ecology and Culture in Japanese Expansion, 1590–1800.* Oakland: University of California Press, 2006.

JAPANESE SOURCES

Ainu Bunka Hozen Taisaku-shitsu, ed. *Shokubunka shiko reshipi* [Recipes from our food culture] (draft). Biratori, Hokkaido: Biratoricho Ainu Shisaku Sui-shin-ka, 2016.

Ban, Sadako. *Kane no oto* [The sound of the bell]. Self-published, 1999.

Fujioka, Yuichiro; Haruna Yatsuka; and Yoshihiko Iida. "Commodification of Tochi Rice Cakes in Kutsuki, Shiga Prefecture, Central Japan." *Human Geography* 67, no. 4 (Jan. 2015), pp. 40–55.

Haginaka, Mie; Asako Hatai; Hisakazu Fujimura; Toshihiro Kohara; and Miyuki Muraki. *Kikisho Ainu no shokuji* [Foods of the Ainu, an oral history]. 2nd ed. Tokyo: Rural Culture Association Japan, 2011.

Henmi, Kinzaburo. *Taberareru yaso* [Edible wild plants]. Osaka: Hoikusha, 1967.

Imada, Setsuko. *Kaiso no shokubunka* [The food culture of seaweed]. Tokyo: Seizando-Shoten Publishing, 2003.

Imai, Kunikatsu, and Makiko Imai. *Yoku wakaru sansai daizukan* [Easy to understand illustrated guide to edible wild plants]. Tokyo: Nagaoka Shoten, 2007.

Ishige, Naomichi, and Isao Kumakura, eds. *Nihon no shokuji bunka* [The food culture of Japan]. Vol. 2 of *Koza shoku no bunka* [Lectures on food culture].

Tokyo: Rural Culture Association Japan, 1999.

Ishikawa Nogyo Sogo Shien Kiko. *Nokaminshuku sapotto bukku: Noto no kaiso hen* [Support book for farm guesthouses: Seaweeds of Noto]. Kanazawa: Ishikawa Nogyo Sogo Shien Kiko, 2017.

Kataoka, Hiroshi. *Sansaiki* [Edible wild plant stories]. Tokyo: Jitsugyo no Nihonsha, 1968.

——. *Zoku sansaiki* [Edible wild plant stories, continued]. Tokyo: Jitsugyo no Nihonsha, 1968.

Kobayashi, Mikio. "Kudamono no bunkashi (8) kaki" [A cultural history of fruit (8): persimmons]. *Bulletin of Keisen Institute of Horticulture* 6, pp. 119–25.

Matsumoto, Mitsushi. *Kokusai Washoku: Makurobiotikku no kihon wo manabu* [Plant-based Japanese cooking: Learning the basics of macrobiotic cooking]. Tokyo: Shibata Shoten, 2005.

Miyashita, Akira. *Kaiso* [Seaweed]. In the series *Mono to ningen no bunkashi* [A cultural history of objects and humans]. Tokyo: Hosei University Press, 1974.

Muroi, Hiroshi, and Hata Okamura. *Take to sasa: sono seitai to riyo* [Bamboo and bamboo grass: Ecology and uses]. Osaka: Hoikusha, 1971.

Nagayama, Hisao. *Wa no shoku zenshi* [A complete history of Japanese food]. Tokyo: Kawade Shobo Shinsha, 2017.

Narita, Yasuhiro. "Ken saidai tochi no ki hakken: juminra hogo yobo" [Prefecture's largest horse chestnut tree discovered: Citizens call for protection]. *Asahi Shimbun* (October 6, 2015).

Nihon Tokuyo Rinsan Fukokai. *Sansai wo tsukatte tsukuru chugoku ryori to dento ryori* [Chinese and traditional Japanese recipes using sansai]. Tokyo: Nihon Tokuyo Rinsan Fukokai, 2011.

Nishiwaga Eco Museum. *Nishiwaga no sansai* [Edible wild plants of Nishiwaga]. 2nd ed. Nishiwaga, Iwate: Nishiwaga Eco Museum, 2012.

——. *Nishiwaga no sansai ryori* [The edible wild plant cuisine of Nishiwaga]. Nishiwaga, Iwate: Nishiwaga Eco Museum, 2016.

Nomoto, Kan'ichi. *Tochi to mochi: Shoku no minzoku kozo wo saguru* [Horse chestnuts and rice cakes: The folklore of food]. Tokyo: Iwanami Shoten, 2005.

Sansai to ki no mi no zukan [Illustrated guide to wild fruits, nuts, and edible plants]. Tokyo: Popular Publishing, 2003.

Soda, Ryoji, "Wajimashi Amamachi no ryomin shudan—sono tokushitsu to jizokusei no haikei" (The fishing community of Amamachi, Wajima: Characteristics and sustainability). *Jinbun Chiri* 48, no. 2 (1996).Okuyama, Hisashi.

Taniguchi, Fujiko. *Yamanba Noto wo kurau: Yama wo shiritsukushita 83 sai* [The mountain woman eats Noto: 83 years of deep mountain knowledge]. Kanazawa: Hashimoto Kokubundo, 2014.

Taniguchi, Shingo, and Ryozo Wada, *Tochi no ki no shizenshi to tochi no mi no shokubunka* [A natural history of the Japanese horse chestnut tree and the food culture of horse chestnuts]. Tokyo: Nihon Shinrin Chosakai, 2007.

Tatsumoto, Tokiji. *Kita no kuni no shokumotsushi* [Food stories from the north country]. Tokyo: Asahi Shimbun Company, 1984.

Teshirogi, Koki; Yuichiro Fujioka; and Yoshihiko Iida. "Natural and Social Environments in a Large Old-Growth Japanese Horse-Chestnut Forest in Shiga Prefecture, Central Japan." *Geographical Review of Japan* Series A 88-5 431–50 (2015).

———. "Regional Characteristics of Commodification of Japanese Horse Chestnut Food Products at Roadside Stations in Japan." *Quarterly Journal of Geography* 68, no. 2 (2016).

Ueda, Koichiro. *Take* [Bamboo]. Tokyo: Mainichi Shimbunsha, 1968.

Watanabe, Masatoshi. "Mosochiku no torai shosetsu" [Various theories on the introduction of moso bamboo]. *Take* 97, pp. 14–17.

Yamada, Yukio. *Sansai nyumon: Saishu to ryori* [Introduction to edible wild plants: Gathering and cooking]. Osaka: Hoikusha, 1975.

Yamada, Yukio, and Mieko Yamada. *Zoku sansai nyumon* [Introduction to edible wild plants, continued]. Osaka: Hoikusha, 1976.

Yamaguchi, Akihiko. *Sansai gaidobukku: Miwakekata, torikata, gurume no ryoriho* [Edible wild plant guidebook: Identification, harvest, and gourmet cooking]. Tokyo: Nagaoka Shoten, 2009.

Yanagihara, Toshio. *Sansai saijiki* [An almanac of edible wild plants]. Tokyo: Chuko Bunko, 1981.

Yatsuka, Haruna, and Yuichiro Fujioka. "Creating Tochi (*Aesculus turbinata*) Nuts Use Networks to Enable Production of Tochi Rice Cakes in Kutsuki, Shiga Prefecture, Central Japan." *Biostory*, vol. 24 (November 2015).

USEFUL ONLINE SOURCES

Ainu to Shizen Dijitaru Zukan. http://www.ainu-museum.or.jp/siror/. A searchable illustrated glossary of plants and animals important to Ainu culture, with Ainu and scientific names (in Japanese).

Encyclopedia of Life. http://eol.org. A reliable source of information about all forms of life on Earth, including seaweeds.

Katemono. http://katemono.jp. A user-friendly site featuring the plants in *Katemono*, the nineteenth-century famine-plant guide, searchable by habitat type, appearance, name, or cooking method (in Japanese).

PLANTS Database of the USDA. http://plants.usda.gov. Useful distribution maps of native and introduced plant species in the United States and Canada.

Sansai Zukan. http://sansaibook.com. Basic information about harvesting and preparing common edible wild plants (in Japanese).

World Flora Online. http://www.worldfloraonline.org. A reliable, up-to-date source of information on global plant species.

Index